CW01495032

Samuel Beckett in Confinement

Historicizing Modernism

Series Editors

Matthew Feldman, Professorial Fellow, Norwegian Study Centre, University of York; and Erik Tonning, Professor of British Literature and Culture, University of Bergen, Norway
Assistant Editor: David Tucker, Associate Lecturer, Goldsmiths College, University of London, UK

Editorial Board

Professor Chris Ackerley, Department of English, University of Otago, New Zealand; Professor Ron Bush, St. John's College, University of Oxford, UK; Dr Finn Fordham, Department of English, Royal Holloway, UK; Professor Steven Matthews, Department of English, University of Reading, UK; Dr Mark Nixon, Department of English, University of Reading, UK; Professor Shane Weller, Reader in Comparative Literature, University of Kent, UK; and Professor Janet Wilson, University of Northampton, UK.

Historicizing Modernism challenges traditional literary interpretations by taking an empirical approach to modernist writing: a direct response to new documentary sources made available over the last decade.
Informed by archival research, and working beyond the usual European/ American avant-garde 1900–45 parameters, this series reassesses established readings of modernist writers by developing fresh views of intellectual contexts and working methods.

Series Titles

Arun Kolatkar and Literary Modernism in India, Laetitia Zecchini
British Literature and Classical Music, David Deutsch
Broadcasting in the Modernist Era, Matthew Feldman, Henry Mead and Erik Tonning

Samuel Beckett in Confinement

The Politics of Closed Space

James Little

BLOOMSBURY ACADEMIC
LONDON • NEW YORK • OXFORD • NEW DELHI • SYDNEY

BLOOMSBURY ACADEMIC
Bloomsbury Publishing Plc
50 Bedford Square, London, WC1B 3DP, UK
1385 Broadway, New York, NY 10018, USA
29 Earlsfort Terrace, Dublin 2, Ireland

BLOOMSBURY, BLOOMSBURY ACADEMIC and the Diana logo
are trademarks of Bloomsbury Publishing Plc

First published in Great Britain 2020
This paperback edition published in 2021

Copyright © James Little, 2020

James Little has asserted his right under the Copyright, Designs and Patents Act, 1988,
to be identified as Author of this work.

For legal purposes the Acknowledgements on p. xii–xiii constitute an extension
of this copyright page.

Cover design by Eleanor Rose and Jade Barnett

All rights reserved. No part of this publication may be reproduced or transmitted
in any form or by any means, electronic or mechanical, including photocopying,
recording, or any information storage or retrieval system, without prior
permission in writing from the publishers.

Bloomsbury Publishing Plc does not have any control over, or responsibility for,
any third-party websites referred to or in this book. All internet addresses given
in this book were correct at the time of going to press. The author and publisher
regret any inconvenience caused if addresses have changed or sites have
ceased to exist, but can accept no responsibility for any such changes.

A catalogue record for this book is available from the British Library.

A catalog record for this book is available from the Library of Congress.

ISBN: HB: 978-1-3501-1232-2
       PB: 978-1-3502-4322-4
     ePDF: 978-1-3501-1233-9
    eBook: 978-1-3501-1234-6

Series: Historicizing Modernism

Typeset by Integra Software Services Pvt. Ltd.

To find out more about our authors and books visit www.bloomsbury.com
and sign up for our newsletters.

 EUROPEAN UNION
European Structural and Investment Funds
Operational Programme Research,
Development and Education

 MINISTRY OF EDUCATION,
YOUTH AND SPORTS

*This work was supported by the European Regional Development Fund project
'Creativity and Adaptability as Conditions of the Success of Europe in an
Interrelated World' (reg. no.: CZ.02.1.01/0.0/0.0/16_019/0000734).*

Contents

List of Figures

Editorial Preface to *Historicizing Modernism*

This book series is devoted to the analysis of late nineteenth- to twentieth-century literary modernism within its historical contexts. *Historicizing Modernism* therefore stresses empirical accuracy and the value of primary sources (such as letters, diaries, notes, drafts, marginalia or other archival materials) in developing monographs and edited collections on modernist literature. This may take a number of forms, such as manuscript study and genetic criticism, documenting interrelated historical contexts and ideas and exploring biographical information. To date, no book series has fully laid claim to this interdisciplinary, source-based territory for modern literature. While the series addresses itself to a range of key authors, it also highlights the importance of non-canonical writers with a view to establishing broader intellectual genealogies of modernism. Furthermore, while the series is weighted towards the English-speaking world, studies of non-Anglophone modernists whose writings are open to fresh historical exploration are also included.

A key aim of the series is to reach beyond the familiar rhetoric of intellectual and artistic 'autonomy' employed by many modernists and their critical commentators. Such rhetorical moves can and should themselves be historically situated and reintegrated into the complex continuum of individual literary practices. It is our intent that the series' emphasis upon the contested self-definitions of modernist writers, thinkers and critics may, in turn, prompt various reconsiderations of the boundaries delimiting the concept of 'modernism' itself. Indeed, the concept of 'historicizing' is itself debated across its volumes, and the series by no means discourages more theoretically informed approaches. On the contrary, the editors hope that the historical specificity encouraged by *Historicizing Modernism* may inspire a range of fundamental critiques along the way.

Matthew Feldman
Erik Tonning

Acknowledgements

My work on this book was supported by the Progres Programme at the Department of Anglophone Literatures and Cultures, Charles University. I gratefully acknowledge this support.

Writing a book about space requires space to write; Justin Quinn and David Robbins have been most generous in this regard. For their kind assistance with administrative matters, I wish to thank Ondřej Pilný, Petra Poncarová, Jiřina Popelíková and Martin Procházka. As well as this help from colleagues at Charles University, the supportive working environments at Masaryk University (where I teach) and the University of Antwerp (where I am part of the Beckett Digital Manuscript Project) have been key to my work on this book. I wish to thank Katie Perkins for proofreading the book and the Indexing team at Integra for compiling the index.

I am very grateful to Edward Beckett for permission to use my own versions of Samuel Beckett's sketches and to Chris Morash and Shaun Richards for permission to adapt a sketch from their book *Mapping Irish Theatre*. Excerpts from Samuel Beckett's unpublished manuscripts are reproduced by kind permission of the Estate of Samuel Beckett c/o Rosica Colin Limited, London. All unpublished manuscripts © the Estate of Samuel Beckett.

Sections of this book have previously appeared in *Litteraria Pragensia*, 25 (50) and the *Journal of Beckett Studies*, 27 (2). I am grateful to the editors for their permission to republish.

My principal debt of gratitude is to Nicholas Grene and Chris Morash for their supervision of the PhD thesis out of which this book arose. My thesis examiners Dirk Van Hulle and Sam Slote posed stimulating questions which helped develop my research further. For their valuable responses to drafts, I am grateful to Chris Ackerley, Helen Bailey, Anthony Cordingley, Will Davies, Burç Îdem Dinçel, Nicholas Grene, John Ptacek, Shaun Richards and the anonymous readers at Bloomsbury. The series editors of *Historicizing Modernism*, Matthew Feldman and Erik Tonning, together with editorial assistant David Tucker, have been very supportive throughout the publication process and I am delighted to be part of their series. It has likewise been a pleasure working with David Avital and Lucy Brown at Bloomsbury and Shanmathi Priya at Integra to bring the book to press.

I wish to thank the staff of the Houghton Library, the Harry Ransom Humanities Research Center, the John J. Burns Library, the Library of Trinity College Dublin, the National Library of Ireland, the Library of English and Romance Studies at Charles University, the Václav Havel Library, the Library of the University of Nantes and the University of Reading, Special Collections for their helpful professionalism. Matthew Feldman kindly shared the appendix of his PhD thesis, containing Beckett's transcriptions of his Psychology Notes. A special thank-you to Wesley Thompson for his warm hospitality during my visit to Austin and to Anne Thompson for her assistance with archival materials at the HRC.

It gives me great pleasure to thank my parents (Joe and Mary) and siblings (Conor and Úna) for their consistent support of my research. I would also like to thank my family in the Karkonosze for making me feel so at home there.

I am grateful to Magda Hejna for her love and always brilliant advice. It is to her I dedicate this work.

Notes on the Text

Transcription conventions

~~Deletions~~ are indicated using strikethrough. Illegible words of three or fewer letters are indicated using x's enclosed in square brackets, with each x representing one letter of the word: [x], [xx], [xxx]. [? Uncertain readings] are enclosed in square brackets and preceded by a question mark.

Dates

Dates in parentheses after a work denote date of first publication unless otherwise indicated. French titles in parentheses denote first publication in that language.

Translations

Translations are my own unless otherwise indicated.

Abbreviations

Published works by Beckett

BDMP I   *Stirrings Still / Soubresauts and Comment dire / what is the word*, digital genetic edn (The Beckett Digital Manuscript Project, module 1), ed. Dirk Van Hulle and Vincent Neyt, Brussels: University Press Antwerp, 2011, http://www.beckettarchive.org.

BDMP II   *L'Innommable / The Unnamable*, digital genetic edn (The Beckett Digital Manuscript Project, module 2), ed. Dirk Van Hulle, Shane Weller and Vincent Neyt, Brussels: University Press Antwerp, 2013, http://www.beckettarchive.org.

BDMP III   *Krapp's Last Tape / La Dernière Bande*, digital genetic edn (The Beckett Digital Manuscript Project, module 3), ed. Dirk Van Hulle and Vincent Neyt, Brussels: University Press Antwerp, 2015, http://www.beckettarchive.org.

BDMP IV   *Molloy*, digital genetic edn (The Beckett Digital Manuscript Project, module 4), ed. Édouard Magessa O'Reilly, Dirk Van Hulle, Pim Verhulst and Vincent Neyt, Brussels: University Press Antwerp, 2016, http://www.beckettarchive.org.

BDMP V   *Malone meurt / Malone Dies*, digital genetic edn (The Beckett Digital Manuscript Project, module 5), ed. Dirk Van Hulle, Pim Verhulst and Vincent Neyt, Brussels: University Press Antwerp, 2017, http://www.beckettarchive.org.

BDMP VI   *En attendant Godot / Waiting for Godot*, digital genetic edn (The Beckett Digital Manuscript Project, module 6), ed. Dirk Van Hulle, Pim Verhulst and Vincent Neyt, Brussels: University Press Antwerp, 2017, http://www.beckettarchive.org.

BDMP VII   *Fin de partie / Endgame*, digital genetic edn (The Beckett Digital Manuscript Project, module 7), ed. Dirk Van Hulle, Shane Weller and Vincent Neyt, Brussels: University Press Antwerp, 2018, http://www.beckettarchive.org.

CDW   *The Complete Dramatic Works*, London: Faber and Faber, 2006.

CPSB   *The Collected Poems of Samuel Beckett*, critical edn, ed. Seán Lawlor and John Pilling, London: Faber and Faber, 2012.

CSP   *The Complete Short Prose, 1929–1989*, ed. S. E. Gontarski, New York: Grove Press, 1995.

D   *Dream of Fair to Middling Women*, ed. Eoin O'Brien and Edith Fournier, Monkstown: Black Cat Press, 1992.

Dis   *Disjecta: Miscellaneous Writings and a Dramatic Fragment*, ed. Ruby Cohn, London: John Calder, 2001.

DN   *Beckett's Dream Notebook*, ed. John Pilling, Reading: Beckett International Foundation, 1999.

EB   *Echo's Bones*, ed. Mark Nixon, London: Faber and Faber, 2014.

LSB I *The Letters of Samuel Beckett*, 4 vols, I: *1929–1940*, ed. Martha Dow Fehsenfeld, Lois More Overbeck, George Craig and Dan Gunn, Cambridge: Cambridge University Press, 2009.

LSB II *The Letters of Samuel Beckett*, 4 vols, II: *1941–1956*, ed. George Craig, Martha Dow Fehsenfeld, Dan Gunn and Lois More Overbeck, Cambridge: Cambridge University Press, 2011.

LSB III *The Letters of Samuel Beckett*, 4 vols, III: *1957–1965*, ed. George Craig, Martha Dow Fehsenfeld, Dan Gunn and Lois More Overbeck, Cambridge: Cambridge University Press, 2014.

LSB IV *The Letters of Samuel Beckett*, 4 vols, IV: *1966–1989*, ed. George Craig, Martha Dow Fehsenfeld, Dan Gunn and Lois More Overbeck, Cambridge: Cambridge University Press, 2016.

MC   *Mercier and Camier*, ed. Seán Kennedy, London: Faber and Faber, 2010.

MD   *Malone Dies*, ed. Peter Boxall, London: Faber and Faber, 2010.

Mo   *Molloy*, ed. Shane Weller, London: Faber and Faber, 2009.

MPTK   *More Pricks than Kicks*, ed. Cassandra Nelson, London: Faber and Faber, 2010.

Mu   *Murphy*, ed. J. C. C. Mays, London: Faber and Faber, 2009.

NABS   Beckett, Samuel and Alan Schneider, *No Author Better Served: The Correspondence of Samuel Beckett and Alan Schneider*, ed. Maurice Harmon, Cambridge, MA: Harvard University Press, 1998.

NHO   *Nohow On*, London: John Calder, 1989.

PTD   *Proust and Three Dialogues with Georges Duthuit*, London: John Calder, 1976.

TFN   *Texts for Nothing and Other Shorter Prose, 1950–1976*, ed. Mark Nixon, London: Faber and Faber, 2010.

TN I   *The Theatrical Notebooks of Samuel Beckett*, gen. ed. James Knowlson, 4 vols, I: *Waiting for Godot*, ed. Dougald McMillan and James Knowlson, London: Faber and Faber, 1993.

TN II   *The Theatrical Notebooks of Samuel Beckett*, gen. ed. James Knowlson, 4 vols, II: *Endgame*, ed. S. E. Gontarski, London: Faber and Faber, 1992.

TN IV   *The Theatrical Notebooks of Samuel Beckett*, gen. ed. James Knowlson, 4 vols, IV: *The Shorter Plays*, ed. S. E. Gontarski, London: Faber and Faber, 1999.

U   *The Unnamable*, ed. Steven Connor, London: Faber and Faber, 2010.

W   *Watt*, ed. C. J. Ackerley, London: Faber and Faber, 2009.

Archives

BDL   *The Beckett Digital Library*, ed. Dirk Van Hulle, Mark Nixon and Vincent Neyt, Brussels: University Press Antwerp, 2016, http://www.beckettarchive.org.

BnF   Bibliothèque nationale de France, Paris.

CU   Rare Book and Manuscript Library, Columbia University, New York.

HL   Houghton Library, Harvard College Library.

HRC   Harry Ransom Humanities Research Center, The University of Texas at Austin.

HRC CL   Samuel Beckett papers in the HRC's Carlton Lake collection.

HRC SB   Samuel Beckett papers in the HRC's Samuel Beckett collection.

HTC	Harvard Theatre Collection, Houghton Library, Cambridge, MA.
JBL SB	Samuel Beckett Collection, MS.1991.001, John J. Burns Library, Boston College.
ML	Morgan Library and Museum, New York.
OSU	Ohio State University Library.
SU	Special Collections Research Center, Syracuse University Libraries.
TCD	The Library of Trinity College Dublin.
UoR	University of Reading, Special Collections
UoR JEK	James and Elizabeth Knowlson Collection, University of Reading.
VHL	Václav Havel Library, Prague.

Abbreviations for individual manuscripts

| 'FD' | 'Fancy ~~Dead~~ Dying' Notebook, TCD MS 11223. |

Reference works

| OED | *Oxford English Dictionary*. |
| PR | *Le Petit Robert*, iPad application, version 3.1, Paris: Dictionnaires Le Robert / Sejer, 2016. |

All biblical references are to the King James Bible.

Proper names in correspondence and diary entries

AS	Alan Schneider
BB	Barbara Bray
RC	Rick Cluchey
SB	Samuel Beckett
TM	Thomas MacGreevy[1]

---

[1] McGreevy changed his name to MacGreevy in 1943. I use the latter spelling throughout.

Journals

JOBS   *The Journal of Beckett Studies*
SBT/A   *Samuel Beckett Today/Aujourd'hui*

Introduction

Beckett's Spatial Politics

In 2002, Peter Boxall called for 'a political reading of Beckett's aesthetic' (2002: 159). Taking to task a critical tradition which has failed to come up with a language to describe either the way in which Beckett undoes the link between his work and the world or 'the residual cultural specificity of his writing' which remains after this undoing (2002: 162), Boxall imagines a political reading that would take into account the limit at which Beckett's prose narrators find that 'the residual referential relationship between the story and the world' has become 'unlessenable':

> The political reading of Beckett's work envisaged here would approach this limit boundary, as it stretches throughout the oeuvre, in order to understand the politics both of Beckett's relentless resistance to it as a constraint on the freedom of his imagination, and his equally relentless attempt to find a way of writing this limit, of accepting and integrating it into the economy of his writing. (2002: 168)[1]

In 2017, the publication of Emilie Morin's *Beckett's Political Imagination* made a crucial contribution to our understanding of Beckett's relationship to his cultural contexts – Irish, French, British and beyond. Morin outlines Beckett's extensive involvement with international political networks in an attempt 'to reinscribe Beckett and his work into their political milieux' (2017: 2). One of the principal ways this is achieved is through an examination of Beckett's signature of petitions. Morin details Beckett's support for a wide range of causes: nine black teenage boys accused of raping two white women in Alabama in 1931 (2017: 86); his French publisher Jérôme Lindon when Lindon was found guilty in 1960 of publishing a book constituting 'public provocation to military disobedience' during the

---

[1] Boxall here develops Maurice Blanchot's concept of a 'space of literature' which is 'vast, unlimited and empty', shown to us by a literary work which is 'limited, inadequate, and partial' (Boxall 2002: 164). For Blanchot, art 'indicates the menacing proximity of a vague and vacant outside, a neutral existence, nil and limitless' (1989: 242–3). Yet it only does so by having its origin 'in the other of all worlds' ['dans l'autre de tout monde'] (1989: 75; 1955: 72), making it 'exceptionally difficult to read such detachment as having any sort of critical capacity' (Boxall 2002: 163).

Algerian War (2017: 218–19); a 1963 call for a cultural boycott of apartheid theatres in South Africa (2017: 83); a French writer 'convicted for assisting Che Guevara in an attempted *coup d'état*, and serving a prison sentence in Bolivia' in 1969 (2017: 16–17); as well as a number of petitions for those persecuted in the Soviet Union (2017: 241–2). What emerges is a picture of Beckett as 'specific intellectual' ['l'intellectuel "spécifique"'] (Foucault 2001b: 109, qtd and trans. in Morin 2017: 18), who tended not to make pronouncements on politics in the abstract but was instead engaged with various particular political causes, often for personal reasons.

In revealing these engagements, Morin's book changes the empirical landscape in which the debate concerning Beckett's politics can now take place. In spite of this, important questions remain concerning Beckett's political aesthetics. In a June 2018 review, Fintan O'Toole notes that *Beckett's Political Imagination*

> is so convincing in its meticulous recreation of Beckett's political worlds that it raises an entirely new question: Why, given all of this immersion in oppression, propaganda, totalitarianism, colonialism, and racism, is Beckett's artistic work not more explicitly engaged? Why does someone who knew so much and cared so deeply about history and politics create a body of work in which they are approached so obliquely? (2018)

This book contends that a study of Beckett's use of confined space can answer the questions as to why and how Beckett created his deeply political oeuvre. 'Explicit', 'oblique' – these terms will return at key stages in my argument. But the most important term in this book is 'confinement', and my focus will be on how Beckett repeatedly finds new ways of putting a body in a confined space across his six-decade writing career.

Why does a study of confinement allow for a reconsideration of Beckett's politics? There are two primary reasons: firstly, different forms of closed space are found at key points throughout the Beckett canon, from the 'images of confinement' which appear in his earliest prose and critical writing (see Chapter 1) to the spaces of confinement which he uses thereafter. This alone would be grounds enough for a study of how confinement, a central topic in post-Enlightenment thought, serves Beckett as a crucial imaginative resource, with institutions of coercive confinement appearing as important locales in eight of his works of prose fiction (see Chapters 2–4). The second reason is even more important: Beckett not only created closed space in his writing, he also worked with it as a theatre practitioner, a fact which informs the 'material imagination' of all his subsequent writing (Connor 2014).[2] Yet in spite of trying three times to write a play for a prisoner (see Chapters 5 and 9), Beckett never represented a carceral scenario onstage. In moving away from the explicitly political spatial settings of asylums and prisons, Beckett created a deeply political aesthetic form, in which what is unseen beyond the closed space helps define the limits of an 'unlessenable' world. As Tim Lawrence notes in *Beckett's Critical Aesthetics*: 'The unknown is crucial to many of the ways in which Beckett's writing figures the limit' (2018: 3). This book argues that the attention Beckett draws to what is unseen beyond his closed spaces provides a new way of understanding the 'residual cultural specificity' which is key to the politics of his writing. In other words, Beckett's move from depictions of institutions of confinement to the closed spaces of his later work does not constitute an evasion of political concerns but is instead central to Beckett's politics of aesthetics.

The production of closed space

O'Toole closes his review by examining 'the strange architecture of confinement' of Beckett's cylinder piece *The Lost Ones*, whose opening line '[a]bode where lost bodies roam each searching for its lost one' (*CSP*: 202) O'Toole glosses with the conclusion: 'Much as we like to think otherwise, politics is always such an abode' (2018). As my central research hypothesis is that Beckett's use of confined space is central to the political dynamics of his work, I start from the theoretical position that these confined abodes are always political.

The claim that the production of space is inherently political is not new. In the wake of the so-called 'spatial turn' in the humanities, described by David Harvey in 2005 as involving 'an immense debate on the role of space in social, literary and cultural theory' (2019: 129), Henri Lefebvre's idea that '([s]*ocial) space is a (social) product*' (1991: 26; emphasis in original) has become an established part of critical discourse (see Hetherington 2003; Morash and Richards 2016: 7–8; Soja 1990; Soja 1996; Tompkins 2012: 4).[3] What Lefebvre means is that space is not just an empty container in which social relations are forged but plays an active part in the shaping of these relations. Yet his is not a form of material determinism. Lefebvre's key conceptual framework is his 'spatial triad', which involves

---

[2] Steven Connor describes Beckett's 'material imagination' as being 'always on the alert against its own tendency to levitate or refine itself out of existence' (2014: 8).

[3] '*L'espace (social) est un produit (social)*' (Lefebvre 2000: 35; emphasis in original).

1. Spatial practice, or 'perceived space' ['l'espace perçu'], in which people experience their everyday lives.
2. Representations of space, or '*conceived* space' ['l'espace *conçu*'], in which map-makers and architects plot the spaces we live in.
3. Representational space, or '[l]ived space' ['l'espace vécu'], which embodies 'complex symbolisms, sometimes coded, sometimes not, linked to the clandestine or underground side of social life, and also to art (which may come eventually to be defined less as a code of space than as a code of representational spaces)' ['espaces de représentation'] (1991: 38, 361, 362, 33; 2000: 48, 418, 43; emphasis in originals).

It is this third mode which structures my argument, with my central fifth chapter focused on Beckett's move into the 'representational space' of the theatre. Nevertheless, Lefebvre's model cannot work without taking into consideration all three modes simultaneously, and we will see evidence of 'perceived space' in Beckett's close attention to spatial embodiment and 'conceived space' in his multiple notebook diagrams. As Chris Morash and Shaun Richards argue, though Lefebvre's own comments on the theatre are fleeting, the dynamic nature of his model of space makes it 'profoundly theatrical' since the production of space is seen as happening in the 'present continuous, just as happens in the theatre' (2016: 8).[4] Yet in spite of the fact that Beckett made his name in the spatial art of theatre, there has been little analysis of how the politics of his work are tied up with those of the spaces he creates. While Myriam Jeantroux has identified 'a *huis clos* structure in Beckett's theatre, a structure on which rests all the organization of the scenic space', we have yet to understand the politics of Beckett's move from writing *about* closed space to creating an art *of* confinement.[5]

As part of his effort to shift focus from spatial '*products*' to spatial '*production*', Lefebvre argues that space should be studied 'genetically', examining not just the relations between things as they occur in space but also how such relations come to be constructed in the social sphere (1991: 26, 171; emphasis in original). In literary studies, the field of genetic criticism provides a useful set

---

[4] 'Theatrical space certainly implies a *representation of space* – scenic space – corresponding to a particular *conception* of space (that of the classical drama, say – or the Elizabethan, or the Italian). The *representational space*, mediated yet directly experienced, which infuses the work and the moment, is established as such through the dramatic action itself.' Lefebvre also mentions the importance of 'perceived space' in the production of theatrical space (Lefebvre 1991: 188; emphasis in original).

[5] '[U]ne structure du huis clos dans le théâtre de Beckett, une structure sur laquelle repose toute l'organisation de l'espace scénique' (Jeantroux 2004: 6). Jean-Paul Sartre's play *Huis clos* is most often translated as *No Exit* or *In Camera*.

of methodologies for such a study of Beckett's closed spaces. Genetic criticism focuses on the author's pre-publication documents (the so-called '*avant-texte*') in order to shed light on the 'temporal dimension' of the creative process (de Biasi 2004: 37). In doing so, genetic critics go beyond the structuralist conception of the text as a 'synchronic structure': 'Genetic criticism opens up this research focus to include the diachronic axis, drawing attention to the fact that literary texts are also structured by time' (Van Hulle 2008: 43). Since Beckett created texts which 'go on' after publication in translation and performance, I will also be focusing on the 'epigenetic transformations' of the *après-texte* (Beckett's written records of changes to the text in translation and performance) as well as the *avant-texte* in order to outline his politics of closed space (Van Hulle 2013: 230). My analysis will therefore draw on compositional manuscripts, reading notes, production notebooks and other material from his 'grey canon' to analyse Beckett's production of closed space as writer and director.[6]

Iain Bailey makes the point that genetic criticism, 'which grounds its knowledge about what external material made its way into the author's oeuvre wholly on [...] "written traces", also relies on a tacit understanding that the documentation represents only a portion of the author's activity' (2010: 92).[7] This raises the question as to how far the concept of the 'text' – and with it the 'genetic dossier' – should be extended.[8] Though genetic criticism 'grows out of a structuralist and poststructuralist notion of "text"', it generally retains a stricter idea of the text than some of its theoretical stablemates (Ferrer and Groden 2004: 2). When analysing a literary work, it makes sense to use a relatively narrow definition of the text as 'the sequence of words and pauses recorded in a document', rather than expanding its boundaries, and consequently those of the genetic dossier, to the extent that both become unmanageably large (Shillingsburg 1999: 174). This has direct implications for the study of texts in performance, which cannot be divorced from the study of the spaces in which these performances take place. Anne Ubersfeld has pointed out that 'a refusal to accept the text–performance

---

[6] S. E. Gontarski coined the term 'grey canon' to denote Beckett's 'letters, notebooks, manuscripts' and other written material which falls outside the published 'white canon' (2006: 143).

[7] Bailey here cites Grésillon, who states: 'toute investigation génétique se fonde sur l'existence de traces écrites' ['all genetic investigation is based on the existence of written traces'] (1994: 215; Bailey 2010: 92).

[8] I use Almuth Grésillon's definition of the genetic dossier as a 'set of all the preserved written genetic witnesses of a work or of a project of writing, classed according to successive stages of their chronology. Synonym: "*avant-texte*"'. ['ensemble de tous les témoins génétiques écrits conservés d'une œuvre ou d'un projet d'écriture, et classés en fonction de leur chronologie des étapes successives. Synonyme: "avant-texte"'] Grésillon suggests this term as an alternative to '*avant-texte*' to allow for the genetic analysis of written evidence of the creative process for which a textual model is not suitable (Grésillon 1994: 242, 109).

distinction will lead to all kinds of confusion since the same tools are not used for the analysis of both' (Ubersfeld 1999: 5). Because of the spatial nature of performance, and because of the importance of non-textual elements in Beckett's production of closed space more broadly, I will use the tools of spatial theory and historicism in parallel with those of genetic criticism.

Beckett's heterotopias

So how does Beckett's move into the theatre come to inform his politics of confinement? One way of understanding this shift is in terms of Michel Foucault's concept of the 'heterotopia'. First, let us examine the points of contact between Beckett's writing of closed space and the work of the most influential twentieth-century theorist of coercive confinement.

In the early months of 1948, as Beckett was writing *Malone meurt* while living on the Rue des favorites in Paris, Foucault was studying in the nearby École Normale Supérieure, where Beckett had worked as a *lecteur* from 1928 to 1930. Anthony Uhlmann has argued that, as well as sharing a common intellectual tradition with poststructuralist philosophers such as Foucault, Beckett's way of 'thinking differently' was analogous to theirs (1999: 4–5). In certain ways this is true. Like Foucault, Beckett's deep engagement with spaces of confinement overlapped with an interest in folly and unreason. In the section of his *History of Madness* dealing with the eighteenth century, Foucault argues that *'reason becomes alienated in the very movement through which it takes possession of unreason'* (2006: 346; emphasis in original).[9] In a discussion with Michael Haerdter in 1967, Beckett likewise saw a strain of unreason underpinning the age of reason:

> The eighteenth century has been called the century of reason, *le siècle de la raison.* I've never understood that: they're all mad, *ils sont tous fous, ils déraisonnent!* They give reason a responsibility which it simply can't bear, it's too weak. (qtd in McMillan and Fehsenfeld 1988: 231)

Such alienation from the world of reason is commonplace among Beckett's protagonists and depictions of the asylum in eighteenth-century literature are

[9] '[L]a raison s'aliène dans le mouvement même où elle prend possession de la déraison' (Foucault 1977: 366; emphasis in original). Foucault's text was first published as *Folie et déraison: histoire de la folie à l'âge classique* (1961) and then in a revised version as *Histoire de la folie à l'âge classique* (1972).

key to his portrayals of the asylum in *Murphy* and *Watt*. But when it comes to their writing of institutional confinement, there are important differences between Beckett and Foucault. While Foucault set out to undo the silencing of madness that stemmed from the Enlightenment, Beckett's writing holds out no such hope.[10] As early as his first monograph *Proust* (1931), Beckett claims that to 'speak and act for others' constitutes 'a lie' (*PTD*: 64). This inability to testify on another's behalf is a crucial part of Beckett's politics; it leads directly to his avoidance of the depiction of particular institutions of confinement.

As in Foucault's model of the 'carceral archipelago' ['l'archipel carcéral'], the institutions described in Beckett's prose are very often carceral, not therapeutic (Foucault 1995: 297; 1994: 304). However, within Beckett's carceral institutions, there is an absence of what Foucault terms a 'political tactics' (1995: 23). In *Discipline and Punish*, Foucault sees the task of modern carceral institutions as one of rendering inmates 'docile and useful' (1995: 231). There are instances in which Beckett's characters are put under such pressure. When the narrator of 'The End' offers to do some work in exchange for being allowed to remain institutionalized, staff member Mr Weir dismisses the idea out of hand: 'Useful, he said, joking apart you would be willing to make yourself useful? [...] If they believed you were really willing to make yourself useful they would keep you, I'm sure.' Here, there does seem to be some kind of a reward for being 'useful', though this has not been enough to change the behaviour of the narrator: 'The number of times I had said I was going to make myself useful, I wasn't going to start that again' (*CSP*: 80). Such a character does not fit the picture as a victim of the soft coercion of modern disciplinary punishment. Rather, he is so dismissive of the forces of social order that he simply turns his back on them, as when he walks away from the Marxist orator haranguing him in the street (see Chapter 4). Ultimately, though institutional space is central to the construction of Beckett's prose work, the forces which oppress his narrators extend beyond their forms of confinement in ways which differ from Foucault's model of disciplinary discourse based on a given set of carceral institutions.

Rather than his writing on the discursive formations of institutional space, it is Foucault's brief but foundational work in the field of spatial theory which can help conceptualize Beckett's shift from writing *about* confinement to working

---

[10] In his preface to the 1961 edition, Foucault sets out to make visible 'the realm in which the man of madness and the man of reason, moving apart, are not yet disjunct; and in an incipient and very crude language, antedating that of science, begin the dialogue of their breach' ['le domaine où l'homme de folie et l'homme de raison, se séparant, ne sont pas encore séparés, et dans un langage très originaire, très fruste, bien plus matinal que celui de la science, entament le dialogue de leur rupture'] (1988: x; 1976: 8). For a critique of this project, see Derrida (2005: 36–76).

in closed space. In 1966–7, Foucault composed three separate works dealing with the heterotopia: while in his preface to *The Order of Things* (*Les mots et les choses*, 1966), he treats the heterotopia as a discursive formation in which incommensurable orders exist (1966: 9), two other pieces give an analysis of heterotopias as 'extra-discursive locations' (Genocchio 1996: 37): a radio address called 'Les hétérotopies' (1966), which was then edited for presentation at a conference as 'Of Other Spaces' ('Des espaces autres', 1967; published 1984). In 'Of Other Spaces', Foucault defines heterotopias as 'counter-sites' ['contre-emplacements'], in which 'other real sites that can be found within the culture, are simultaneously represented, contested, and inverted' (1986: 24; 2001a: 1574). Unlike the imagined space of utopia, heterotopic spaces actually exist within society: they are 'those real places outside all places [...] gardens, cemeteries, asylums, brothels, prisons, Club Med villages and many more.'[11] What these spaces have in common is their ability to reshape our relationship to other social spaces through processes such as ritual, leisure, the containment of social deviation or performance. As Jeremy Crampton puts it, this transformative aspect of heterotopias results not in their creation of 'disorder' but in the possibility of 'other orders' (2013: 386).

As well as institutions of confinement – which he terms 'heterotopias of deviation' (1986: 25) – Foucault also lists the theatre as an important heterotopic space: 'The heterotopia is capable of juxtaposing in a single real place several spaces, several sites that are in themselves incompatible. Thus it is that the theater brings onto the rectangle of the stage, one after the other, ["fait succéder sur le rectangle de la scène"] a whole series of places that are foreign to one another' (1986: 25; 2001a: 1577). Foucault seems to have in mind here the heterotopic space of the rectangular proscenium stage, which remained Beckett's performance space of choice throughout his career. As well as bringing different spaces together on the same stage, the proscenium stage is heterotopic in that it depends on what is imagined offstage to act as a guarantor for what we see onstage (see Chapter 5).

Foucault is not the only postwar philosopher to stick with a conception of performance as being inherently dualist, in spite of the fact that such dualism was under attack from contemporary theatre practitioners at the very time he was writing about the heterotopia. For Jacques Rancière, it is the division between stage and auditorium that is constitutive of the politics of performance: 'Politics

---

[11] '[C]es lieux réels hors de tous les lieux. Par exemple, il y a les jardins, les cimetières, il y a les asiles, il y a les maisons closes, il y a les prisons, il y a les villages du Club Méditerrané, et bien d'autres' (2009: 25).

plays itself out in the theatrical paradigm as the relationship between the stage and the audience' ['comme rapport de la scène et de la salle'] (2011a: 17; 2000: 22). Key to Rancière's analysis is Plato's condemnation in the third book of the *Republic* of the mimetician, who draws Socrates' ire by transgressing the principle of the division of labour, becoming in his theatrical work a 'double being' who occupies a 'shared political space' not meant for artisans (Rancière 2011a: 42; see Plato, *Republic* 394d–395b7). Plato's democratic distribution of the sensible depends upon each citizen 'doing one's own work' and not dividing oneself between occupations (Plato, *Republic* 433a8, 433b3). In Rancière's analysis: 'The mimetic act of splitting in two, which is at work in theatrical space, consecrates this duality and makes it visible' (2011a: 43).[12] Drawing on Rancière's work, Benjamin Wihstutz argues that the 'inevitable dual differentiation of space' – between performance event and audience as well as between each performance and daily life – 'can be described as the topology of theatre' (2013: 4), informing the political decisions made by artists when shaping their spaces of performance.

Though he never got around to doing so himself, Foucault called for a systematic investigation of the 'other spaces' he called heterotopias, giving this enquiry the provisional title 'heterotopology' (1986: 24). Rancière's related concept of a 'heterology', which denotes a disturbance of 'the meaningful fabric of the sensible', can help us better understand the politics of Beckett's refashioning of proscenium performance space (2011a: 63). For Rancière, a heterology – in which he includes the disciplines of art and politics – is explicitly political, not because of its content but because it reshapes 'the territory of the visible, the thinkable, and the possible' ['le territoire du visible, du pensable et du possible'] (2011a: 41; 2000: 65). In *Proletarian Nights* (*La nuit des prolétaires*, 1981), Rancière gives an account of heterological thinking in his analysis of how nineteenth-century French workers challenged the ways in which their work and leisure spaces were divided (2012). The concept of utopia is important here: Rancière sees it as both 'a no-place' 'which breaks down the categories that define what is considered to be obvious' and 'the configuration of a proper place' where the possibilities for one's behaviour are strictly prescribed (2011a: 40). In their letters, poetry, plans and manifestos, these workers carved out opportunities for intellectual debate which were not meant to be theirs, thus refashioning the spaces of utopia being envisaged at the time by socialist engineers. As Rancière notes:

---

[12] 'Le dédoublement mimétique à l'œuvre dans l'espace théâtral consacre et visualise cette dualité' (Rancière 2000: 68).

The workers, for their part, did not set practice in contrast with utopia; they conferred upon the latter the characteristic of being 'unreal', of being a montage of words and images appropriate for reconfiguring the territory of the visible, the thinkable, and the possible. The 'fictions' of art and politics are therefore heterotopias rather than utopias. (2011a: 41)

Andrew Gibson identifies *Proletarian Nights* as Rancière's 'most poignant' analysis of the rarity of social equality (2006: 271). For Gibson, Rancière is more interested in tracing occasional instances of 'politics in its specificity' (Rancière 1999: 139, qtd in Gibson 2006: 269) than he is in creating a 'philosophical system' (Gibson 2006: 270). As the passage above suggests – with art and politics tied to heterotopic spaces which exist in the social sphere – Rancière's redistribution of the sensible 'depends closely on the coordinates of a given space' ['un espace donné'] (Zabunyan 2014: 8). Beckett too was aware of the importance of spatial specificity in his aesthetics, defining theatre work in the following terms: 'We are dealing with a given space and with people in that space' (qtd in Gontarski 1992: xiii). In his refashioning of the proscenium stage, Beckett uses confined space to reorder the limits of the sensible.

Beckett's politics of aesthetics

In its focus on the spaces of Beckett's work, this book is part of the critical movement which has sought to make explicit the importance of historical context in political interpretations of Beckett's writing. In doing so, I agree with James McNaughton that 'Beckett's work has a valuable, pertinent, and radical political intelligence that deserves our attention' (2018: 24). McNaughton rightly critiques Beckett critics who 'understand politics too tightly as allusion, rather than formal engagement' (2018: 19). Indeed, in using the spatial form of confinement, Beckett redefines what it means to interpret political allusions in closed space.[13]

Many of Beckett's own comments on the relationship between his work and the world concentrate on the importance of form in the creative process. In 1961, he famously told Tom Driver that the task of the contemporary artist was to create a form that 'admits the chaos and does not try to say that the chaos

---

[13] However, it is going too far to say that Beckett's topography is 'strictly filtered through the no-place of political imagination' – traces of places remain crucial to such interpretations (McNaughton 2018: 23).

is really something else [...]. To find a form that accommodates the mess, that is the task of the artist now' (2005: 243). In response to Charles Juliet's questions on the ethics of his work, Beckett again stressed the importance of form, this time as a means of dealing with the problem of ethical value: 'Paradoxically, it is through form that the artist can find some kind of a way out. By giving form to formlessness' (Juliet 2009: 24). By analysing the closed spaces of Beckett's work, from the asylums and prisons of his early prose to the bins, boxes, urns and rotundas of the later writing, I aim to show you specific ways in which the spatial form of confinement allowed Beckett to expand the field in which political interpretation takes place.

Before examining the carceral spaces which play such an important role in Beckett's prewar prose, it is first necessary to investigate the images of confinement that he borrowed from other writers and artists as he formed his own poetics in the early part of his career.

1

Images of Confinement

Proust, Dream of Fair to Middling Women

There is no evidence that Beckett read Plato's *Republic*, instead picking up most of his knowledge of Ancient Greek philosophy from secondary sources. But while on his formative tour of German art galleries in 1936–7, he did see a dramatization of the legend in which Gyges becomes invisible by using a magic ring, discussed by Glaucon in the *Republic* (359c6–360c5).[1] Responding to Friedrich Hebbel's *Gyges und sein Ring* (1856) in a diary entry of 12 January 1937, Beckett stated his belief in 'the universal antithesis between the individual & collective' (qtd in Nixon 2011: 53).[2] This idea of a fundamental separation between self and world was a key concept for Beckett, expressed in deeply spatialized language in his early writing. In his review-cum-aesthetic manifesto 'Recent Irish Poetry' (1934), Beckett uses the image of a physical gap to outline the distance between the world and the artist aware of 'the new thing that has happened, or the old thing that has happened again', namely the breakdown of the relation between subject and object:

> The artist who is aware of this may state the space that intervenes between him and the world of objects; he may state it as no-man's-land, Hellespont or vacuum, according as he happens to be feeling resentful, nostalgic or merely depressed. (*Dis*: 70)

Beckett would spend most of his writing career trying to articulate this gap. Whether outlining the 'antithesis' between individual and collective or the 'no-man's-land' of artistic alienation, images of confinement were central to his early aesthetics.

---

[1] Glaucon assigns the ring to an ancestor of Gyges but Socrates assigns it to Gyges himself (Plato, *Republic* 612b4).

[2] I would like to thank Mark Nixon for his assistance with my research into Beckett's German Diaries.

Uhlmann has compared Beckett's use of philosophical concepts to the way in which he used painters' images in his work: 'Images can pass between literary and philosophical discourse, no doubt being transformed in the process of translation, but also carrying with them something in common, a translatable component which inheres in the image which is put into circulation' (2006: 3). Beckett drew on images of closed space when formulating key aesthetic positions on literature, philosophy, painting and music, all of which served as testing grounds in which he explored the 'universal antithesis' between the perceiving subject and the perceived world. It is with this multi-generic formation in mind that I have chosen in my chapter title the term 'image', which incorporates metaphor while also emphasizing the spatio-visual aspects of Beckett's early aesthetic development. Uhlmann's conceptual source Michèle Le Dœuff demonstrates how philosophers use images to veil parts of their systems of thought that take them to the edge of logic: 'the image, far from being a more or less pedagogical "illustration" of an abstract thesis contained elsewhere in the system, is always the mark of a tension, a signification incompatible with the rest of the work' (Le Dœuff 2002: 93). In his use of closed space, confinement would become much more than just an image in Beckett's work. But images of confinement were key to the way he created tension between what is presented and what lies beyond.

John Pilling has remarked that Beckett's early poetry is marked by 'inwardness', with Beckett regularly using a first-person voice that deliberately excludes the reader with its range of references (2004: 5). As the speaker of the poem 'Casket of Pralinen for a Daughter of a Dissipated Mandarin' (1931) would put it, somewhat understatedly, Beckett's early writing 'was perhaps inclined to be just a shade too self-conscious' (*CPSB*: 33). The early fictional figures are as damned-up as their over-educated author, who stated that he had 'enough "butin verbal" ["verbal booty"] to strangle anything I'm likely to want to say' (SB to TM, 8 November 1931, *LSB* I: 93, 95). Alongside the hermeneutic enclosure created by Beckett's erudite references, there is a strong focus on alienation from the outside world which is frequently described using images of confinement in his early fiction. From the 'caged resentment' of the protagonist of his debut short story 'Assumption' (1929) onwards, Beckett's characters are repeatedly portrayed as being trapped within themselves (*CSP*: 4). This self-confinement of Beckett's early protagonists is part of a focus on alienation which he developed not only through his writing but also through his reading, his listening to music and his viewing of artworks in the 1930s.

Beckett's veil

A key metaphor in Beckett's writing during this period is that of a veil which cuts the subject off from reality. In a much-quoted letter of 1937, Beckett wrote in German to publisher Axel Kaun:

> It is indeed getting more and more difficult, even pointless, for me to write in formal English. And more and more my language appears to me like a veil which one has to tear apart in order to get to those things (or the nothingness) lying behind it. (SB to Kaun, 9 July 1937, *LSB* I: 518)

Beckett's image of language as a veil is indebted to the philosophy of Arthur Schopenhauer, whose own highly figurative style has made him extremely popular among literary writers. Beckett was attracted to read the philosopher while composing his monograph on Proust in 1930 and returned to his writing later in his career, finding that Schopenhauer could be read 'like a poet, with an entire indifference to the apriori forms of verification' (SB to TM, 21 September 1937, *LSB* I: 550). Schopenhauer was a rich source of philosophical images for Beckett.[3] In *The World as Will and Representation*, Schopenhauer uses the Buddhist concept of the 'veil of *māyā*' to describe the self's alienation from the outside world. This veil obstructs the self from seeing the thing-in-itself by clothing it in the '*principium individuationis*' of appearance, through which time, space and causality divide a unitary reality into individuated representation (Schopenhauer 2010: 280). In an August 1936 entry in his 'Clare Street' Notebook, Beckett echoes this, writing of a 'veil of hope' which can be momentarily torn apart so that 'the liberated eyes can see *their* world, as it is, as it must be. Alas, it does not last long, the revelation quickly passes, the eyes can only bear such pitiless light for a short while, the membrane of hope grows again and one returns to the world of phenomena' (qtd and trans. in Nixon 2011: 170; emphasis in original). In Schopenhauer's philosophy, the body is the one object in the world of ideas that can also be experienced subjectively, giving us a means of accessing the blind, desiring will by escaping the categories of thought. For Beckett, language – specifically formal English – performs a similarly obstructive function as Schopenhauer's principle of individuation with regard to the something, or nothing, that lurks behind it.

---

[3] Among the images Beckett draws from Schopenhauer are those of life as a pendulum between pain and boredom, life as a *pensum* and the intellect as a magic lantern (Pothast 2008: 119, 122; Van Hulle 2010: 256).

If the formal register of his mother tongue functioned as a deceptive veil, then it is perhaps no surprise that in Beckett's texts, the incapacity of words to express reality leads often to gaps in the form of silence. This is a pervasive concern in his work: from the opening line of 'Assumption' – '[h]e could have shouted and could not' – to the main protagonist of *Murphy* – whose 'silence' is 'one of [his] highest attributes' – to his last dramatic fragment, the unpublished 'Endhörspiel' (written *c.* 1987–8), comprising a brief dialogue between Silence and Voice (*CSP*: 3; *Mu*: 103).[4] Beckett's attempts in the 1930s to articulate what the narrator of *Dream of Fair to Middling Women* (written 1931–2; published 1992) calls an 'aesthetic of inaudibilities' frequently reference the use of silence in the music of Ludwig van Beethoven (*D*: 141). For instance, he complained about the shortcomings of an edition of Paul Éluard's poetry translated into English in which he had been involved: 'no attempt seems to have been made to translate the pauses. Like Beethoven played strictly to time' (SB to TM, 17 July 1936, *LSB* I: 359). The narrator of 'Ding-Dong' (1934) tells us that *Dream*'s central protagonist Belacqua Shuah 'lived a Beethoven pause, he said, whatever he meant by that' (*MPTK*: 32). In *Dream*, a spatial analysis of Beethoven's music follows Belacqua's fantasy of writing a book which would be experienced 'between the phrases, in the silence, communicated by the intervals, not the terms, of the statement' (*D*: 137):

> I think of his earlier compositions where into the body of the musical statement he incorporates a punctuation of dehiscence, flottements, the coherence gone to pieces, the continuity bitched to hell because the units of continuity have abdicated their unity, they have gone multiple, they fall apart, the notes fly about, a blizzard of electrons; and then vespertine compositions eaten away with terrible silences, [...] pitted with dire stroms of silence, in which has been engulfed the hysteria that he used to let speak up, pipe up, for itself. (*D*: 138–9)

Beckett's use of silence has its hermeneutic equivalent in the physical gaps that appear in his work, both at a textual level and in the minimalist stage spaces he created.

In his 1937 letter to Kaun, Beckett again uses spatial imagery when writing about Beethoven. He asks:

> Is there any reason why that terrifyingly arbitrary materiality of the word surface should not be dissolved, as for example the sound surface of Beethoven's Seventh

---

4   Two undated versions of the very short 'Endhörspiel', which differ slightly from one another, were posted by Beckett to Barbara Bray, one in an envelope postmarked 22 January 1987 (possibly misdated), the other in an envelope postmarked 21 March 1988 (TCD MS 10948/1/700–1). I would like to thank Sam Slote for drawing my attention to this piece. See also SB to Hans-Jochen Schale, 8 April 1988 (*LSB* IV: 704).

Symphony is devoured by huge black pauses, so that for pages on end we cannot perceive it as other than a dizzying path of sounds connecting unfathomable chasms of silence? (*LSB* I: 518–19)

Beckett wanted his own work to perform a similar function with regard to language. Language then could become a screen which would create an impression of there being 'something or nothing' beyond it. Here, the veil is something to be broken through, rather than removed:

> To drill one hole after another into it until that which lurks behind, be it something or nothing, starts seeping through – I cannot imagine a higher goal for today's writer. (*LSB* I: 518)

This idea of a veil covering the 'something or nothing' beyond it would become crucial in Beckett's theatre work, which allowed him to test out in different spatial formulations the ways in which confinement can produce new relations between the work and the world.

Proust's 'imprisoned microcosm'

As well as thinking of the 'sound surface' of music as a material screen which composers like Beethoven could puncture, allowing for an articulation of seeming nothingness through the framing of silence within a particular aural context, Beckett also wrote about music itself as a means of breaking through what he terms in *Proust* the 'screen' of habit, which 'spare[s] its victim the spectacle of reality' (*PTD*: 21). This again echoes Schopenhauer's veil while also drawing on the exalted place of music in the German philosopher's aesthetics. For Schopenhauer, music 'stands completely apart from all the others [other art forms]' and beyond the individuating principle of appearance governed by time, space and causality. As it is 'wholly independent of the appearing world', music is able to get behind this veil and access 'the inner essence, the in-itself of all appearance, the will itself' (Schopenhauer 2010: 283, 285, 289). Beckett's definition of music in *Proust* as 'the Idea itself' (*PTD*: 92), which momentarily transcends the suffering endured by the physical body but still exists within time, is a modified version of the aesthetics of Schopenhauer, who states 'unlike the other arts, music is in no way a copy of the Ideas; instead, it is a *copy of the will itself*, whose objecthood the Ideas are as well' (Schopenhauer 2010: 285; emphasis in original). Aside from this misreading – or intentional modification – of Schopenhauer's philosophy, what is interesting about *Proust* is that it quite baldly lays out an essentialist version of being. Given that his work is so dominated by incompletion and fragmentation, it might seem strange to come across Beckett writing about getting at 'the essence of ourselves' through involuntary memory (*PTD*: 31). However, in much of Beckett's aesthetic writing, there is a tension between the system described and the practice evident in his work.

In spite of opening *Proust* with a declaration of intent to follow the French author's refusal to fashion his 'creatures' according to 'spatial scales' and focus instead on the 'double-headed monster of damnation and salvation – Time', Beckett continually returns to metaphors of spatial restriction throughout the text (*PTD*: 12, 11). In this his first published monograph, Beckett is already conceiving of the alienated subject in terms of confinement. He compares Proust's narrator Marcel's inability to accommodate himself to the unfamiliar surroundings of a strange hotel room to 'the tortured body of [French cardinal] La Balue in his cage, where he could neither stand upright nor sit down' (*PTD*: 24).[5] The 'spacious annexe of mental alienation' from which 'Proust hoisted his world' foreshadows the monadic selves of Beckett's later prose (*PTD*: 32). Proust's characters, according to Beckett, are 'hermetic' and the only way for the writer to approach reality is through the imposition of solitary confinement within the 'imprisoned microcosm' of experience stored within the self (*PTD*: 74):

> The artistic tendency is not expansive, but a contraction. And art is the apotheosis of solitude. There is no communication because there are no vehicles of communication. [...] Either we speak and act for ourselves – in which case speech and action are distorted and emptied of their meaning by an intelligence that is not ours, or else we speak and act for others – in which case we speak and act a lie. (*PTD*: 64)

This leads Beckett to his quietist aesthetic manifesto: 'The only fertile research is excavatory, immersive, a contraction of the spirit, a descent' (*PTD*: 65). '[I]f I may add this nux vomica to an apéritif of metaphors', he begs of his reader, 'the heart of the cauliflower or the ideal core of the onion would represent a more appropriate tribute to the labours of poetical excavation than the crown of bay' (*PTD*: 29). In the years following the publication of *Proust*, contraction within the self became a byword for Beckett when referring to his own artistic creation. In 1937, he sent a letter to his friend Thomas MacGreevy in which he describes writing poetry as 'the frail sense of beginning life behind the eyes' (SB to TM, 16 February 1937,

---

[5] French cardinal Jean Balue was imprisoned by King Louis XI of France from 1469 to 1480 'but not, as has been alleged, in an iron cage' ('Jean Balue' 1998).

LSB I: 447). In 1932, he wrote of good poetry as that which goes 'into the burrow of the "private life"' and praised 'what I find in Homer & Dante & Racine & sometimes Rimbaud, the integrity of the eyelids coming down before the brain knows of grit in the wind' (SB to TM, 18 October 1932, *LSB* I: 134–5). In writing his first novel, *Dream of Fair to Middling Women*, Beckett would burrow into his own private life as well as the lives of those around him.

Dream's 'wombtomb'

The self-confinement in Beckett's early prose and poetry follows directly from the incommensurability outlined in his aesthetic writing between the subject and the world of objects. While Schopenhauer's 'veil of *māyā*' and Beckett's 'veil of hope' protect the self from the harsh light of the real by masking reality with individuated phenomena, it is the threatening exposure of social life that causes early Beckett protagonists, such as Belacqua, to turn inwards towards a supposedly truer form of self-expression. However, like Belacqua's retreats into his 'wombtomb' and the character's own professed 'aesthetic of inaudibilities', Beckett's aesthetic of alienation only makes sense in relation to what it avoids. Belacqua shrouds himself not in a veil of hope but in a mask of intellectual superiority displayed to his peers in order to escape the 'pestiferous sunlight' of social interaction, which shatters his mental retreat in *Dream* 'after the furious divers had hauled him out like a crab to fry in the sun' (*D*: 46, 122).

Beckett outlines his own quietist aesthetic in a discussion of portraiture which closes one of his letters on the art of Paul Cézanne:

> the individual feels himself more & more hermetic & alone & his neighbour a coagulum as alien as a protoplast or God, incapable of loving or hating anyone but himself or of being loved or hated by anyone but himself. (SB to TM, 8 September 1934, *LSB* I: 223)

Beckett's professed turn away from the world, announced in the very many letters which kept him involved in that world, was not an abandonment of social interaction. Similarly, the characters he created – from Belacqua, to Victor Krap (in *Eleutheria*, written in French, 1947; published 1995), to Krapp (in *Krapp's Last Tape*, 1958) – by closing themselves off in confined spaces exist in antagonistic relation with the societies in which they refuse to fully participate. Belacqua's wombtomb, Victor's room and Krapp's den are all spatially reduced zones which mirror the desired self-enclosure of these characters. However, just as Beckett's diary account of the 'veil of hope' which shields us from the reality of the phenomenal world emphasizes the existence of that phenomenal world; just as his mention of the veil of language in the letter to Kaun draws attention to the possibility of the 'something or nothing' which lies beyond language, so too do the confined spaces he creates always suggest other places beyond.

Dream's narrative voice highlights the gap between its central protagonist and society. Foreshadowing the pronominal politics of *The Unnamable*, Beckett uses a narrative voice that can be both singular and plural, with 'we, extenuate concensus of me' relating Belacqua's adventures in the dimly defined surroundings of Ireland, France and Germany (*D*: 112). However, the mental life of Belacqua, the 'great big, inward man', will not conjugate easily with this outside world:

> We find we have written *he is* when of course we meant *he was*. For a postpicassian man with a pen in his fist, doomed to a literature of saving clauses, it is frankly out of the question, it would seem to be an impertinence – perhaps we should rather say an excess, an indiscretion – stolidly to conjugate *to be* without a shudder. (*D*: 46; emphasis in original)

Belacqua himself discusses the difficulty of narrative composition with the Mandarin (based on Beckett's uncle Boss Sinclair) as they are celebrating the ringing in of the new year in Germany: 'The notion of an unqualified present – the mere "I am" – is an ideal notion. That of an incoherent present – "I am this and that" – altogether abominable' (*D*: 102). These two passages point to Beckett's own difficulty as he 'learnt to say "I"' over the course of the 1930s; the narrative voice of *Dream* is an important, if faltering, early step on the way to his doing so (Nixon 2011: 35).

Beckett's 'veil of hope' protects the self from facing the harsh light of the phenomenal world. In *Proust*, he advocates a retreat into the self as part of the process of artistic creation. When Belacqua performs a similar act of self-enclosure, his mind is described as being 'enwombed and entombed' (*D*: 6). The most extensive description of Belacqua's wombtombing comes after the narrator admits to an inability to compare the beauty of two of Belacqua's love interests – the Smeraldina-Rima (based on Boss Sinclair's daughter Peggy) and the Syra-Cusa (based on James Joyce's daughter Lucia) – using an altered phrase from Dante's *Paradiso*: '*Da questo passo vinti ci concediamo*' ['from this point on, we must admit defeat'] (*D*: 43; Pilling 2004: 63).[6] Beckett changes Dante's

---

[6] See Dante, *Paradiso* canto XXX, line 22. All references to *The Divine Comedy* are to Dante Alighieri (1999).

first-person singular 'concedo' to the plural 'concediamo' and his 'mi' to 'ci', so that Dante's declaration of his style's inability to describe Beatrice's beauty can be accommodated in *Dream*'s first-person plural narrative.

For Belacqua, this contemplation of female beauty is intimately bound up with the unbearable socialization that life on earth entails. Upon arriving in Paris, he performs his own personal 'anabasis' [retreat]:

> The labour of nesting in a strange place is properly extenuating. The first week and more went to throwing up a ring of earthworks; this to break not so much the flow of people and things to him as the ebb of him to people and things. It was his instinct to make himself captive, [...] for two months and more he lay stretched in the cup, sheltered from the winds and sheltered from the waters, knowing that his own velleities of radiation would never scale the high rim that he had contrived all around and about, that they would trickle back and replenish his rumination as marriage the earth and virginity paradise, that he could release the boomerangs of his fantasy on all sides unanxiously, that one by one they would return with the trophy of an echo. [...] If that is what is meant by going back into one's heart, could anything be better, in this world or the next? The mind, dim and hushed like a sick-room, like a chapelle ardente, thronged with shades; the mind at last its own asylum, disinterested, indifferent, its miserable erethisms and discriminations and futile sallies suppressed, the mind suddenly reprieved, ceasing to be an annex of the restless body, the glare of understanding switched off. (*D*: 43–4)

To Belacqua, the 'mind gone wombtomb' is 'real thought and real living, living thought' (*D*: 45). This mental 'enwombing' is 'assumption upside down': rather than the body ascending to immaterial paradise, the mind retreats into physical purgatory, as it does for the 'flesh-locked' protagonist of Beckett's debut short story, 'Assumption' (*D*: 181; *CSP*: 5). As well as enabling a retreat from society, Belacqua's wombtomb is also a place where material gathered from the outside world can sit and decompose in the 'dear slush' of Belacqua's mind (*D*: 181). Hence even a typically unsuccessful social encounter with the third of his fair to middling women, the Alba, can be salvaged as an occasion during which '[p]erhaps even he had got copy for his wombtomb' (*D*: 175). From the image in *Godot* of 'giv[ing] birth astride of a grave' to the opening line of *A Piece of Monologue* – '[b]irth was the death of him' – the enclosed spaces of birth and death remain in close proximity throughout Beckett's oeuvre (*CDW*: 83, 425).

The narrative of *Dream* avoids blending Belacqua's mental slush with the social detail fundamental to the work of realists like Balzac: 'Milieu, race, family, structure, temperament, past and present and consequent and antecedent back

to the first combination and the papas and mammas and paramours and cicisbei
and the morals of Nanny and the nursery wallpapers and the third and fourth
generation snuffles...'. As the narrator admits, '[t]hat tires us. [...] The only
perspective worth stating is the site of the unknotting that could be, landscape of
a dream of integration, prospective' (*D*: 12–13). This impossibility of narrative
harmony between protagonist and the world he inhabits is expressed in terms of
grammatical disjunction. When the narrator asks the reader regarding Belacqua,
'surely you see now what he am?' the clash between subject and verb anticipates
the more radical self-alienation of postwar protagonists such as the Unnamable
(*D*: 72).

Belacqua's 'being at home to nobody' allows him to distance himself from a
world of abortive social engagements, romantic relationships and parties, such as
the new year's celebration which precipitates the termination of his relationship
with the Smeraldina-Rima, during which he completely falls apart (*D*: 128). For
Beckett's early male protagonists, a woman's romantic love is a key part of the
process of socialization which they fail or refuse to participate in. Whereas in
the novels of the 'divine Jane [Austen]' (*D*: 119; SB to TM, 14 February 1935, *LSB*
I: 250), whose work Beckett admitted 'has much to teach me', central characters
progress towards accommodation with the social world through marriage, it is
Belacqua's lack of 'success' with women, his friends and 'the people' that marks
this novel of discontinuity (SB to TM, 14 February 1935, *LSB* I: 250; *D*: 127).[7]
Belacqua is 'doomed to leave no trace [...] on the popular sensibility' and as
the Cherbourg–Cobh ferry pulls into dock, class alienation combines with the
narrator's misogyny in a mocking description of what seems to be a prostitute
returning home (*D*: 127):

> Next to Belacqua the slut bawn is now weeping, she is weeping and waving a
> fairly clean portion of Bourbon bloomer. That is very meet, proper and, given
> her present condition, her bounden duty. Before Xmas she shall be in Green St,
> she shall be in Railway St under the new government. She was born well, she
> lived well and she died well, Colleen Cresswell in Clerkenwell and Bridewell.
> (*D*: 140)

These Dublin street names give the briefest of glimpses into the slide down
the social scale of a good many of the prostitutes Belacqua slinks off to visit on
Railway Street at the end of 'Ding-Dong' (*MPTK*: 39). In the 1920s and 1930s,
Green Street contained a courthouse a short walk from the cluster of brothels on

---

[7]   For Beckett's later, far more negative reaction to Austen's work, see Atik (2001: 76).

and around Railway Street (O'Brien 1986: 302). However, the narrator shows no real interest in the people that such legal institutions deal with. The final sentence is copied almost verbatim from a late nineteenth-century account of a prostitute's funeral, with 'Madame Cresswell' hibernicized as a Boucicauldian 'Colleen' Bawn in Beckett's version (*DN*: 55). Typical of the Joycean 'notesnatching' that marks Beckett's intertextuality of the period, this first mention of specific institutions of confinement in his fictional writing uses the names of two famous London prisons, 'Clerkenwell and Bridewell', primarily as a source of rhyming wordplay (SB to TM, early August 1931, Nixon 2011: 183). In two episodes of *More Pricks than Kicks* and his first published novel *Murphy*, institutions of confinement, penal and psychiatric, take a more important position in the narrative.

2

The Ethics of Writing Confinement

'Dante and the Lobster', 'Fingal', *Murphy*

While Beckett was drawn to 'heterotopias of deviation' as compositional material for his early prose, it was not to an asylum or prison that he directed scholar Sighle Kennedy in a letter of 14 June 1967 when she asked for scholarly guidance on *Murphy*. Instead, he famously advised her to start from Democritus' statement '[n]aught is more real [than nothing]' and Arnold Geulincx's '[u]bi nihil vales [ibi nihil velis]', translated by the editors of the recent English edition of his *Ethics* as 'wherein you have no power, therein you should not will' (*Dis*: 113; Geulincx [1675] 2006: 178). On receipt of Beckett's letter, Kennedy no doubt followed his direction and went back to her copy of *Murphy*, where she would have found the two phrases he mentioned in Chapters 9 and 11, which depict Murphy's employment in the Magdalen Mental Mercyseat asylum (*Mu*: 112, 154). Alongside the Geulincx quote, Beckett emphasized the epigraph to Chapter 9 of *Murphy* in a letter to Thomas MacGreevy of 16 January 1936. This epigraph, taken from one of the many existentialist self-reflections in André Malraux's *La Condition Humaine* (*Man's Fate*), points more directly to the problematic relationship between self and other that will be the focus of this chapter: 'Il est difficile à celui qui vit hors du monde de ne pas rechercher les siens' [it is difficult for one who lives outside the world not to seek out his own] (*LSB* I: 299; *Mu*: 99; Malraux 1946: 189). While Malraux's militant character Tchen reflects here on the difficulty of the necessary solitude of a terrorist, deliberately cut off from others in order to protect himself against informers, Murphy's attempted solitude is an escape from the world of love and commerce. Nevertheless, Murphy too is strongly drawn towards others who live 'outside the world' in his employment at the asylum. What ethical questions are raised when social outsiders like Murphy identify with figures whom they believe to be their 'own'?

For Shane Weller, postwar European philosophy is 'the history of the attempt to think a saving alterity' (2006: 2). This ethics of alterity has strongly influenced the so-called 'ethical turn' in literary studies, with ethical writing frequently defined as 'that which engages with, and is responsible to, Otherness' (Meffan and Worthington 2001: 131). Derek Attridge strengthens this claim, arguing not just that otherness is literature's subject matter but that 'the literary occupies, in the practices and understandings of Western culture, the place of the other' due to the 'openness to alterity' he sees 'at the heart of both artistic production and artistic reception' (2004: 137; 2017: 6). In Beckett's prewar prose, representations of confinement posit the confined other as someone who may be able to shake his protagonists out of their self-imposed 'wombtomb'. Yet the representation of incarcerated others raises particular ethical problems, as J. M. Coetzee notes in an essay on the state censorship of prison writing in apartheid South Africa: 'Since the time of Flaubert, the novel of realism has been vulnerable to criticism of the motives behind its preoccupation with the mean, the low, the ugly. If the novelist finds in squalor the occasion for his most soaring poetic eloquence, might he not be guilty of seeking out his squalid subject matter for perversely literary reasons?' (1986: 35). If we are to answer this question with regard to Beckett's early depictions of inmates, it is not enough to simply sum up Beckett's artistic interest in confinement by noting that '[t]he disadvantaged in society are special to Beckett' (O'Brien 1986: 225). For Laura Salisbury, in opposition to the idea that ethics are defined by judgements of value, the ethics of Beckett's late prose are seen in terms of 'the particular shape of the relationship of self to otherness' (Salisbury 2015: 173). We must seek to understand how the ethical relationship between self and other is given shape in Beckett's spaces of confinement if we want to understand the political effects of his writing.

In some of his earliest reading on the topic of ethics, Beckett reported a particular interest in Arnold Geulincx's 'fourth cardinal virtue, Humility', whose central procedures are an 'inspection of oneself' and 'disregard of oneself' (SB to Arland Ussher, 25 March 1936, *LSB* I: 329; Geulincx [1675] 2006: 183, 217). This might lead one to believe, as Beckett recorded in his early notes on Geulincx, taken from Wilhelm Windelband's *History of Philosophy*, that '[m]an has nothing to do in outer world' (TCD MS 10967: 189v, qtd in Tucker 2013: 23). However, his later notes on the *Ethics* itself include transcriptions of Geulincx's work that deal with the worldly obligations incumbent on the self leading an ethical life. These include the obligations not to commit suicide and to maintain a livelihood in order to submit to God's command to go on living. Since, for Geulincx, ethical decisions involve an interaction with human institutions, they also inform a politics, which Geulincx sees as being a subset of ethics:

> There are two divisions of Ethics, Monarchics and Politics. In Monarchics we are concerned with, and it teaches us, how a man, considered in the abstract and apart from other men, should conduct himself [...]. Politics teaches us how a man should conduct himself in the company of other men. (Geulincx [1675] 2006: 264)

Geulincx's recommended turning away from the world is a form of quietist protest against that world, a protest also evident in Murphy's failed attempt to 'surrender to the thongs of self' (SB, diary entry, 18 January 1937, qtd in Nixon 2011: 73). While Murphy, like his prose predecessor Belacqua, aims for 'an absolute withdrawal from the object world, which includes not just the human body, but the social, the historical, and the political', the interactions of these characters with inmates of prisons and asylums cannot be abstracted from the social relations of these institutions, however antisocial these interactions might be (Weller 2005: 79). This chapter takes three of Beckett's depictions of 'heterotopias of deviation' – in 'Dante and the Lobster' (1932), 'Fingal' (1934) and *Murphy* (1938) – in order to track the ethics of confinement in his early prose.

'Dante and the Lobster': Translating confinement

'Dante and the Lobster' demonstrates Beckett's early use of an actual heterotopia of deviation, Dublin's Mountjoy Prison, as an 'offstage' space in his first published story from *More Pricks than Kicks*. The story draws on detail from the real-life execution of gardener Henry McCabe in 1926, which Beckett, then a student in Trinity College, would almost certainly have been aware of at the time. McCabe was initially charged with the murder of six members of the family he worked for, whose bodies were found in their burning home in the North County Dublin suburb of Malahide. However, he was tried and convicted, on flimsy evidence, for just one of those murders. News of McCabe's execution prompted a public outcry (Kroll 1977). Beckett, in using the case as one of his sources, explores the extent to which a prisoner's experience can and should be translated into literary production.

As indicated in the title 'Dante and the Lobster', Beckett's narrative frames the McCabe material with two problems of translation: firstly, how does one translate a tricky pun from Dante's *Divine Comedy*? Secondly, how does one translate the suffering of a lobster about to be boiled alive into terms a human can understand? For Ioan Davies, 'translation is in many respects the central theme of prison writing' (1990: 5), which functions as an interpretation of incarcerated experience, allowing the reader – by implication 'on the outside' – to catch a glimpse of life on the inside. But the otherness of prison was more than just a compositional catalyst for Beckett. While waiting for *More Pricks* to be published, he used the prison scenario of its opening story to explore the affective ethics related to his own bouts of anxiety:

> If [...] I read in the paper that poor Mr. So-and-so is to be executed early in the morning, before I get out of bed, and immediately start to congratulate myself that I do not have to spend such a night, I deceive myself in as much as I compare two circumstances instead of two emotions. And it is highly probable that the man condemned to death is less afraid than I. At least he knows exactly what is at stake and exactly what he has to attend to, and that is a greater comfort than one is generally inclined to believe. (SB to Morris Sinclair, 5 May 1934, *LSB* I: 204–5)

This letter, written in German to help Beckett's cousin prepare for a Trinity College language exam, opens with Beckett complaining about those 'moralists' who 'are so terribly afraid of life that if there is any object from which they can draw no sure profit, they feel beaten, if not nearly murdered' (*LSB* I: 203). 'Dante and the Lobster' uses translation to ask how much literary 'profit' should be drawn from the execution of a convicted murderer and how much insight an outside observer might be expected to have into a prisoner's emotional state. While for Davies, prison literature acts as 'the eyes in a sightless world' (Davies 1990: 240), Beckett is interested in how such experiences are observed 'through a keyhole' of writing, particularly when that writing has to cross a linguistic or spatial boundary (SB to Morris Sinclair, 5 May 1934, *LSB* I: 205).

The prison cell is not the dominant space of 'Dante and the Lobster' – indeed, its protagonist's musings 'on McCabe in his cell' are done entirely from afar (*MPTK*: 10). Instead, the story begins with an invocation of the grand astral space of Dante's *Divine Comedy* and for the first paragraph, Beckett's first-time readers may have been hard-pressed to identify Beckett's principal character Belacqua as a Dubliner and not the figure that Dante meets in canto IV of the *Purgatorio*. To add to the initial topographic confusion, the first reference to the *Comedy* is not to the *Purgatorio* but to 'the canti in the moon' of the *Paradiso*, cantos II–V. It is only when his copy of Dante's *Commedia* is 'slammed [...] shut' that Belacqua Shuah is clearly differentiated from his medieval namesake and brought back to earth from his lunar exegesis into the much more restrictive 'bottled climate' of Beckett's story (*MPTK*: 3; SB to TM, 13 May 1933, *LSB* I: 157).

Though images of confinement abound in the text, the two carceral spaces used by Beckett are McCabe's prison cell and the 'cruel pot' into which the lobster has crept, sealing his own death sentence (*MPTK*: 14). The jail is introduced through McCabe's appearance in the *Evening Herald* newspaper. Having closed his *Commedia*, Belacqua opens his copy of the paper on which he cuts his bread for lunch and '[t]he rather handsome face of McCabe the assassin stared up at him' (*MPTK*: 4). In *Late Modernist Style*, Peter Fifield writes on the importance of the face-to-face encounter in Beckett's work in light of the philosophy of Emmanuel Levinas, for whom '[t]he face to face remains an ultimate situation' ['situation ultime'] in his view of ethics as first philosophy (2007: 81; 1961: 53). If, for Levinas, '[t]he immediate is the face to face' (2007: 52) and if proximity provides for 'the *immediacy* ["l'*immédiateté*"] of the other' (2006: 84; 1974: 106; emphasis in originals), then Belacqua's face-to-face with McCabe is, by contrast, heavily mediated. This is evident first in McCabe's appearance in the *Herald* newspaper; it is emphasized again when Belacqua hears the news, 'transmitted in a low tragic voice across the counter by Oliver the improver' that the petition appealing McCabe's execution has been unsuccessful and that he 'must swing at dawn in Mountjoy' (*MPTK*: 10). 'Dante and the Lobster' is not a text giving us a glimpse inside the confined space of a prison but one which reflects on the ethical difficulties of imagining that space from without.

Details from the speculative prosecution case against McCabe resurface later in *More Pricks*, providing a grim end to 'Draff' (1934) when, during Belacqua's funeral, his gardener rapes a servant girl named Mary Ann and sets the house on fire. Both before and after committing these crimes, the gardener shuts himself up in a tool shed, initially to escape from Mary Ann's 'opinions and impressions' which she 'commit[s]' on him from the garden (*MPTK*: 176). The same verb is used to describe Belacqua's aversion to social contact in 'Dante and the Lobster' as he makes his way to collect his gorgonzola: 'Now the great thing was to avoid being accosted. To be stopped at this stage and have conversational nuisance committed all over him would be a disaster' (*MPTK*: 6). For student and soon-to-be convicted felon alike, conversational intrusion into one's mental refuge is a serious crime. To prevent it, both men retreat into what the narrator of *Echo's Bones* (written 1933; published 2014) calls the 'uterotaph', a word which combines Latin root for 'womb' and the Greek root for 'tomb' (*EB*: 35, 97). It is in the light of this narrative framing of Belacqua's social withdrawal as an equivalent to McCabe's outsider status that Beckett's use of the 'Malahide murderer' case must be read (*MPTK*: 10).

In McCabe, Belacqua comes across someone whose dereliction almost shakes him out of his own self-absorption. However, his efforts to think in terms of how McCabe and the lobster feel facing their impending deaths are strictly circumscribed by his own appetites, whether they be intellectual or physical. Beckett structures Belacqua's contemplation of the McCabe hanging and his realization that the lobster he has bought his aunt for dinner will be boiled alive around a 'superb pun' taken from the eighth circle of hell in the *Inferno*, where Virgil rebukes Dante for his tears on seeing the suffering of the damned soothsayers. Belacqua asks his Italian teacher, Adriana Ottolenghi, to translate '*qui vive la pietà quando* [*sic*] *è ben morta*', which can be translated as 'here lives pity when it is quite dead', 'here lives piety when it is quite dead' or, as in Robert and Jean Hollander's translation of the *Comedy*, '[h]ere piety lives when pity is quite dead' (*MPTK*: 11).[1] Is Beckett's Belacqua closer to Dante in his pity than Dante's Belacqua in the latter's sloth? The passage in which Belacqua reflects on the cruelty of both divine and penal justice as he brings the unfortunate lobster to his aunt's house would seem to suggest so:

> Why not piety and pity both, even down below? Why not mercy and Godliness together? A little mercy in the stress of sacrifice, a little mercy to rejoice against judgement. He thought of Jonah and the gourd and the pity of a jealous God on Nineveh. And poor McCabe, he would get it in the neck at dawn. What was he doing now, how was he feeling? He would relish one more meal, one more night. (*MPTK*: 13)

McCabe's physical incarceration is here presented so as to make Belacqua's own mental self-imprisonment seem like a luxury in comparison. However, it is important to note that this expression of fellow-feeling is framed squarely in terms of the problem of translation Belacqua has been puzzling over since morning. He only finally engages with the injustice of capital punishment as a coda to his reflection on his Italian lesson, initiated by his recalling the words of the Ottolenghi, which signal stasis rather than personal development or ethical epiphany: 'where we were, as we were' (*MPTK*: 13). Earlier on in the day, Belacqua is too obsessed with his lunch for McCabe's case to be anything more than a visual backdrop to his culinary preparations or a garnish which renders his sandwich 'further spiced' (*MPTK*: 10). Indeed, in an earlier version of the story, Belacqua's reaction to the failure of the petition for McCabe's pardoning is anything but empathetic: 'If anything was wanted to crown that exquisite

---

[1] Slote (2010: 20); Dante, *Inferno* canto XX, line 28.

gastronomical experience, it was just such a piece of news' (Beckett 1932: 231). As Belacqua's aunt points out, he will also eat the lobster in spite of his protests against its treatment.

Beckett had already emphasized pity over piety in his translation of Dante's line in the poem 'Text 3' (1931): 'pity is quick with death' (*CPSB*: 39). The only pity Belacqua allows himself is a peculiar form of 'impersonal pity'. In 'What a Misfortune', the narrator explains Belacqua's lack of reaction to the death of his wife Lucy, 'his small stock of pity being devoted entirely to the living, by which is not meant this or that particular unfortunate, but the nameless multitude of the current quick, life, we dare almost say, in the abstract' (*MPTK*: 109). This form of pity is again evident in 'Yellow', when he worries that any tears he sheds will be interpreted as marks of his fear of undergoing surgery and not as a reaction to 'the follies of humanity at large' (*MPTK*: 156). We see it yet again in his cold response to the death of a girl under a tram in 'Ding-Dong', after which he wonders '[w]hether the trituration [grinding to a fine powder] of the child in Pearse Street had upset him *without his knowing it*' (*MPTK*: 36; emphasis added). Sitting in a nearby pub, 'the objects in which he was used to find [...] recreation and repose lost gradually their hold upon him, he became insensible to them little by little, the old itch and algos crept back into his mind' (*MPTK*: 37). The immediate cause of what seems to be some kind of mental breakdown may be hidden from Belacqua, but it seems clear to the reader that the witnessing of the death of a small child would penetrate even Belacqua's egotistical self-confinement. With similar ironic distance, the ending of 'Dante and the Lobster' critiques Belacqua's rueful rationalization of the lobster's impending death: 'Well, thought Belacqua, it's a quick death, God help us all.' The final line lifts us out of the bottled climate of Belacqua's world: 'It is not' (*MPTK*: 14). These occasional instances of narrative distancing in *More Pricks* serve to highlight Belacqua's lack of protest at the cruelty of the world he inhabits.

Rather than standing as a figure for the literary representation of confinement, in 'Dante and the Lobster', it is the failure of translation that best encapsulates Belacqua's ethical relationship with the condemned. For Beckett in *Proust*, it is not the true 'artist' but merely the artisanal 'writer' who is involved in the work of translation (*PTD*: 84). However, Belacqua is neither artist nor writer: he can translate neither the Dante passage nor the experience of McCabe's last night alive into terms he can understand. For him, the Dante passage remains untranslatable and his question about McCabe's emotional state unanswered. While Levinas, during his own incarceration in a Nazi prisoner-of-war camp, could empathize with none other than Marie Antoinette climbing the scaffold, 'separated from her little children' ['séparée de ses petits enfants'] (Levinas 2009: 74), the mediated encounter with a confined other in 'Dante and the Lobster' comes to an ethical dead end for Belacqua. If the novel Belacqua fantasizes about writing in *Dream* is to be experienced in the gaps left between the terms of expression, the most important gap in *More Pricks than Kicks* is the one between Belacqua and the objects of the world he inhabits – even those objects who should by rights be perceived as subjects. In 'Fingal', Belacqua's encounter with such subjects gains in narrative proximity.

'Fingal': Facing confinement

While it is the intertexts of 'Dante and the Lobster' that point beyond its inner-city setting to places as far apart as Malahide, Mountjoy Prison and the moon, the very title of 'Fingal' immediately identifies a specific district in North County Dublin. As in 'Dante and the Lobster', Beckett structures this short story around events in a heterotopia of deviation – Portrane Lunatic Asylum – the topography of which he researched in person: 'I was down at Donabate on Boxing Day and walked all about Portrane lunatic asylum in the rain' (SB to TM, 5 January 1933, *LSB* I: 150).[2] He returned at Easter: 'I wrote another [story] [...]. On [Easter] Saturday [15 April] I went off for the day on the bike, through Malahide & round the estuary to Portrane and back by Swords' (SB to TM, 23 April 1933, *LSB* I: 154). If the hypothesis is correct that the story Beckett refers to in the second letter as having been recently completed is indeed 'Fingal' (Pilling 2006: 42), it is highly likely that he was using the return visit to check details for an episode heavy on topographical features, including those of the local asylum.

Translating landscape

The landscape of 'Fingal' is by no means a neutral zone, with Belacqua's description of it as a 'land of sanctuary [...] where much has been suffered in secret, especially by women' more apt than he realizes (*MPTK*: 18). In this politically charged landscape, a carceral institution functions as a counter-space in which Belacqua is again drawn towards an exiled other. Belacqua's initial act

---

[2]   Beckett also used his trips to Portrane as the basis for his poem 'Sanies I' (*CPSB*: 12–13).

is to make his girlfriend Winnie suffer boredom by translating Fingal's landscape into terms she cannot understand. These include references to Romantic writer Alphonse de Lamartine, author of the poem 'L'Isolement' ('Solitude'), which contains the line 'Un seul être vous manque, et tout est dépeuplé' ['You lack a single person, and your whole world is empty'] (de Lamartine 1993: 4–5).[3] Against Lamartine's Romantic longing, Belacqua's world seems empty even with 'un seul être' in his company. Indeed, as in 'Dante and the Lobster', Belacqua is again happier engaging in problems of translation – this time drawing an improbable comparison between the landscape of North County Dublin and Lamartine's home region of 'Saône-et-Loire' (*MPTK*: 18) – or communing with an inanimate object such as a bike than making conversation with Winnie, the field labourer they meet or Winnie's friend Dr Sholto.

However, Belacqua is once again attracted to a particular kind of human company: namely, those who suffer involuntary confinement, this time in the nearby Portrane Asylum (later St Ita's Hospital).[4] Yet again, carceral images dominate the opening of this story, when Winnie's words of advice to Belacqua regarding the impetigo on his face come to him 'like a drink of water to drink in a dungeon' (*MPTK*: 18).[5] However, Belacqua soon decides to stop trying to persuade her of the merits of the district: 'He would drop the subject, he would not try to communicate Fingal, he would lock it up in his mind.' No sooner has he resolved to do so than he catches sight of the asylum: '"Do you know what that is" he said "because my heart's right there"', evoking the longing of the exiled Irishman in the popular music hall number 'A Long Way to Tipperary' (*MPTK*: 19). When they eventually reach an elevated viewing point, Winnie and Belacqua see some of the inmates exercising:

> Now the loonies poured out into the sun, the better behaved left to their own devices, the others in herds in charge of warders. The whistle blew and the herd stopped; again, and it proceeded. [...] Below in the playground on their right some of the milder patients were kicking a football. Others were lounging about, alone and in knots, taking their ease in the sun. The head of one appeared over the wall, the hands on the wall, the cheek on the hands. Another, he must have

---

3   Beckett adapted this line for the title of his prose piece *Le Dépeupleur* (1970; published in English as *The Lost Ones* in 1972).
4   I would like to thank Brendan Kelly for confirming that the asylum still had the earlier name at the time Beckett visited.
5   See Beckett's translation of André Breton's 'L'Union libre' as 'The Free Union' (1932), which includes the line: 'My woman whose eyes are water to drink in prison' (*CPSB*: 69). The simile is also used in *Dream* (*D*: 108) and in 'A Wet Night' the water is upgraded to 'a pint of Perrier' (*MPTK*: 70).

been a very tame one, came half-way up the slope, disappeared into a hollow, emerged after a moment and went back the way he had come. Another, his back turned to them, stood fumbling at the wall that divided the grounds of the asylum from the field where they were. One of the gangs was walking round and round the playground. Below on the other hand a long line of workmen's dwellings, in the gardens children playing and crying. Abstract the asylum and there was little left of Portrane but ruins. (*MPTK*: 22–3)

This passage is notable for both its categorization of the patients (first generally as 'loonies', then as 'better behaved', 'others' and 'milder patients') and its correlation with contemporary criticism of the asylum. The year after Beckett wrote his story, a 1934 report recommended more occupational therapy in Grangegorman Mental Hospital, of which Portrane was the auxiliary asylum (Kelly 2016: 180). But there is little occupation for Beckett's inmates, whom the narrator presents as being led through their exercises like imprisoned zombies (tramping round in 'gangs') or simply left to their own devices. Brendan Kelly reports that reform was 'excruciatingly slow' between 1925 and 1945 in the Irish asylum system: for instance, there was no voluntary admission procedure for asylums before the Mental Health Treatment Act in 1945 (2014: 74). This is important to remember when reading Beckett's story, particularly as it presents Portrane's inmates in an open space, seemingly at liberty. While the patients may appear free to roam, they would have been legally confined with little hope of release when Beckett wrote 'Fingal'.

The animalistic terms 'herds' and 'tame' in the descriptive passage of the Portrane inmates add to the air of a disturbing, anti-bucolic scene of institutional life. C. J. Ackerley points out that the term 'asylum' in *Murphy* has a 'double articulation [...] as both a place of madness and of sanctuary' (2008: 60). With regard to the way the asylum functions in 'Fingal', asylum needs to be understood in terms of the exile of incarceration, which was the position of all Irish asylum inmates in a system heavily dependent on institutionalization. After Belacqua abandons Winnie to the company of Dr Sholto, who works in the asylum, she hears yet another story of incarceration – the local legend of Jonathan Swift locking up his 'motte' Stella in a local tower, which Beckett had heard while visiting Portrane (*MPTK*: 25–6; SB to TM, 5 January 1933, *LSB* I: 150). Swift himself is closely associated with the Irish asylum system, having been instrumental in the establishment of 'the first formal asylum in Ireland' (Kelly 2016: 110). The additional allusion in the Dublin slang word for girlfriend to Madame de la Motte, who is named in Beckett's poem 'Sanies II' and was the last woman to be publicly flogged in France, adds a further sadistic layer to these institutional references (*CPSB*: 14). Belacqua's earlier description of Fingal as 'a land of sanctuary [...] where much has been suffered in secret, especially by women' now appears much more sinister.

'Landscapes', we are told, 'were of interest to Belacqua only in so far as they furnished him with a pretext for a long face' (*MPTK*: 23). Beckett was interested in representations of landscape which portrayed the observer's separation from the countryside and described his admiration for Cézanne as an artist who 'leaves landscape maison d'aliénés' ['lunatic asylum']. This he contrasted with the 'anthropomorphised landscape' of pre-modernist painting (SB to TM, 8 September 1934, *LSB* I: 222, 226). In the asylum scene of 'Fingal', instead of animating the landscape, the narrative animalizes the inmates, turning individual subjects into narrative objects. Winnie expresses surprise at their 'docility' and Belacqua agrees with her, but thinks that 'the head over the wall told a tale' (*MPTK*: 23). In 'Dante and the Lobster', the mediation of the tale of McCabe through the text of the newspaper and the discussion overheard in the pub means that he may as well be as distant from Belacqua as the soothsayers in Dante's eighth circle of hell. The encounter in 'Fingal' gives Belacqua at least a view into the grounds of an actual institution of confinement, provoking curiosity regarding the stories of its inmates. Beckett's next novel, *Murphy*, engages at a proximity with such tales that raises important questions about the ethics and politics of representation.

'Light in the monad': *Murphy*

At a party in Dresden on 18 February 1937, Beckett was asked what he most wished to create (Nixon 2011: 162). He recorded his response in his diary: 'I say light in the monad. That the book, picture, music, etc. is incidental, what matters, the primary, is the illumination of which they are the vulgarisations, falsifications, etc.' (qtd in Tonning 2007: 210). While Beckett's attempts to 'find a form that accommodates the mess' received their most stark spatial manifestation in the enclosures of his later prose and drama, his use of confinement as a formal means to deal with the 'mess' of the world began to bear important results with the composition of *Murphy* (qtd in Driver 2005: 243). As his diary writings show, the monad gave Beckett a key spatial figure for the incommunicability of experience, as when using confined spatial imagery to describe the relationship between Rainer Maria Rilke and Paula Modersohn-Becker in a diary entry of 15 January 1937: 'I say "Die Monade ist doch Fensterlos"' ['But the monad is windowless'] (Nixon 2011: 163). In *Murphy*, Beckett used the windowless monad as a means of conceptualizing both the architecture of the cells of a psychiatric hospital and the minds of those who occupy them, allowing him to shape his novel around the imagined impenetrability of specific kinds of mental alienation. What results is a critique of both institutional confinement and the unquestioning valorization of the experience of an asylum inmate.

Uhlmann's concept of a philosophical image as something which is 'transformed in the process of translation' is a particularly apt way of thinking of Beckett's use of Leibniz, whose conviction that we live in the best of all possible worlds is about as far as one can get from the pessimism that attracted Beckett to Schopenhauer (see SB to TM, *c.* 18 to 25 July 1930, *LSB* I: 32–3). The social dynamics of confinement in Beckett's early structural plan for *Murphy* is underpinned by Leibnizian imagery. This plan contains two elements: X, who later becomes Murphy, and H, which becomes the horoscope which Murphy lives by, described as a 'force to be obeyed' by X. Both are characterized as '[m]onads in arcanum of circumstance, each apperceiving in the other till no more of the petites perceptions that are life' (UoR MS 3000: 1r, qtd in Ackerley 2010: 22). For Leibniz, monads are indivisible, self-sufficient mental entities which are the only true substances in the world. In Beckett's *Murphy*, the monad provides a model not only for the self but also for the institutional space that confined selves occupy.

What is interesting in Beckett's early plan for the novel is his explicit link between what for Leibniz is the self-reflexive knowledge of apperception ([1714] 1898: 208) and 'the other'. Granted, this 'other' is a horoscope in Beckett's sketch, but this idea was developed for the published text, in which Murphy also attempts to see himself through an exiled other – asylum inmate Mr Endon. Like Belacqua, Beckett's early version of Murphy is determined to avoid social interaction: 'X is realised by his failure to encounter & his progress depends on this failure being sustained. If he made terms with people the story would come to an end' (UoR MS 3000: 3r, qtd in Pilling 2004: 138). In the published text, Murphy's unwillingness to attain 'attunement' with the social world leads to a situation in which – in the words of Beckett's early plan – his 'quasi-vocation' does indeed 'threaten[...] to incarcerate him' (UoR MS 3000: 2r, qtd in Feldman 2006: 65). But as Laura Salisbury points out, Murphy's 'need for the other precisely demonstrates that he is not himself closed' (2015: 139), a contention that will support my reading of Murphy's time in the asylum.

In line with his remark regarding his reading of Schopenhauer that he was 'not reading philosophy, nor caring whether he is right or wrong or a good or worthless metaphysician', Beckett, rather than building on Leibniz's work to construct a coherent metaphysical system, as a philosopher might do, draws on the windowless image of one of what he called the 'splendid little pictures' in Leibniz's *Monadology* to create a model of the self, an important architectural space as well as a central formal gap in his own literary text (SB to TM, *c.* 18 to 25 July 1930, *LSB* I: 33; SB to TM, 5 December 1933, *LSB* I: 172).

Boswell's Bedlam; Beckett's Mercyseat

From the opening description of Murphy tied to a chair in 'a medium-sized cage of north-western aspect' to his circuits as he paces around Pentonville Prison to waste time instead of jobhunting, *Murphy* is yet another Beckett text in which carceral imagery proliferates (*Mu*: 3, 48). Though largely set in London, the novel's first reference to an institution of coercive confinement relates to the mental health system of 1930s Dublin. When Neary attempts to headbutt the statue of Cuchulain, erected to commemorate the leaders of the 1916 Rising in the General Post Office, his former student Wylie pleads insanity to the on-duty Civic Guard:

> Wylie turned back, tapped his forehead and said, as one sane man to another: 'John o' God's. Hundred per cent harmless.' [...] 'Stillorgan,' said Wylie. 'Not Dundrum.' [...] 'John o' God's,' said Wylie. 'As quiet as a child.' (*Mu*: 29–30)

The implication is that Neary is a 'harmless' rather than a 'criminal' lunatic who would have been kept in the Saint John of God Hospital in Stillorgan rather than the Central Criminal Lunatic Asylum, Dundrum. Such fine institutional distinctions are again at play when Murphy, newly hired as a psychiatric nurse, is shown around the Magdalen Mental Mercyseat (M.M.M.) for the first time: he is told in no uncertain terms that, contrary to appearances, the institution is not an asylum but 'a hospital for the better-class mentally deranged' (*Mu*: 56).

Beckett's own experience of mental healthcare would have made him acutely aware of the roles class and money play in the kind of treatment received. Funded by his mother, Beckett spent almost eighteen months visiting psychotherapist Wilfred Bion in London's Tavistock Clinic between 1934 and 1935. In spite of his resistance to overly prescriptive forms of mental health treatment, derided by the narrator of *Murphy* as 'therapeutic voodoo' and 'the text-book attitude' towards asylum patients (*Mu*: 148, 111), Beckett's craft as a writer was deeply affected by his time with his therapist, during which he read voluminously in the fields of psychology and psychoanalysis.[6] Having drawn on Robert Burton's sprawling seventeenth-century treatise *The Anatomy of Melancholy* as the most frequently used source in his *Dream* Notebook, and having noted the antisocial nature of Burton's life in his 'Whoroscope' Notebook (UoR MS 3000: 84r), Beckett moved on to study other laureates of mental disorder as part of his programme of philosophical, psychoanalytic, linguistic and literary self-education in the 1930s. Foremost among these was Samuel Johnson, who reportedly said that Burton's *Anatomy* 'was the only book that ever took him out of bed two hours sooner than he wished to rise' (Boswell 1848: 217). In the personal library Beckett held at the time of his death, 'the largest number of books […] is dedicated to the work of Samuel Johnson' (Van Hulle and Nixon 2013: 32). This is symptomatic of the interest he expressed in the unreason that haunted the 'age of reason':

> The 18th century was full of ahuris ['bewildered people'] – perhaps that is why it looked like the age of 'reason' – but there can hardly have been many so completely at sea in their solitude as he [Johnson] was or so horrifiedly aware of it – not even [William] Cowper. Read the <u>Prayers & Meditations</u> if you don't believe me. (SB to TM, 4 August 1937, *LSB* I: 529, 531)

As early as 1929, in 'Dante … Bruno . Vico .. Joyce', Beckett had called Joyce's critics 'monodialectical arcadians', who mistook an emerging masterpiece, 'Work in Progress', for 'the "ravings of a Bedlamite"', thus drawing on a long tradition of Anglophone writing on mental disorder which saw 'bedlam' enter the *OED* to denote 'a scene of uproar and confusion' (*Dis*: 31). Central to this tradition of literary melancholy, madness and, in Beckett's day, neurosis and psychosis, was London's Bethlem Royal Hospital, whose status as a national institution of mental illness Beckett came across in his reading. For instance, Beckett would have encountered Jonathan Swift's vicious satire on the confinement of the insane when reading *A Tale of a Tub*, whose narrator claims to have been an inmate in Bethlem (Swift [1704] 2004: 98; see Smith 2002: 30). In Boswell's *Life of Johnson*, Beckett read a passage from the *Tatler* describing Bethlem Asylum in the eighteenth century as 'one of the sights of London, like the *Abbey* and the *Tower*' (qtd in Boswell 1848: 455 n. 2). Beckett, like his eighteenth-century predecessors, drew on Bethlem as a 'resource of spectacular material' for his novel (Andrews et al. 1997: 132). Reversing the function of the 'Judas-hole' in *Dream* which Belacqua fashions with his knees in order to view only a restricted

---

[6] Beckett's nickname for Bion, 'the covey', comes from the Sean O'Casey character who backs up all views on human existence by referring to a socialist textbook (SB to TM, 8 and 16 September 1934, *LSB* I: 222, 227; O'Casey 1998).

portion of the outside world (*D*: 52), *Murphy* is particularly concerned with the representation of coercive confinement from without.

Beckett greeted the news of his friend Geoffrey Thompson's installation as senior physician in Bethlem with interest: 'Perhaps it will be somewhere to go in the spring' (SB to TM, 8 February 1935, *LSB* I: 246). Like Johnson before him, Beckett paid multiple visits to the hospital, which had recently moved to a new location in south-east London. A letter to Thomas MacGreevy relates that he 'was down at Bedlam this day week & went round the wards for the first time, with scarcely any sense of horror, though I saw everything, from mild depression to profound dementia' (SB to TM, 22 September 1935, *LSB* I: 277). As well as clarifying certain aspects of mental health treatment, these visits gave Beckett access to people who were suffering from some of the conditions he was reading about at the time. For Beckett, as for Boswell 160 years earlier, 'the general contemplation of insanity was very affecting' (1848: 456) and in a 1962 interview with Lawrence Harvey he still recalled one such encounter with a patient suffering from schizophrenia: 'There was no one there. He was absent' (qtd in Knowlson 1997: 209). This deep interest in mental alienation is also evident in *Murphy*.

For Foucault, heterotopias are liminal spaces, whose positions on the outskirts of the city reflect the marginal positions of those who inhabit them. *Murphy's* M.M.M. is quite literally liminal, lying as it does 'a little way out of town [...] on the boundary of two counties' (*Mu*: 99), as Bethlem Asylum did when Beckett visited in 1935 (Ackerley 2010: 146). In his transmutation of Bethlem for his novel, Beckett was sensitive to the liminal position of asylum inmates as well as the limits imposed on them by institutional space. For instance, the description of patients and their symptoms in *Murphy's* M.M.M. displays the detailed knowledge Beckett accumulated in his research notebooks as he made his way around Bethlem. He took notes on the procedure for putting patients on suicide watch, the practice of patients 'bein [*sic*] bullied' by the staff, the specific terminology used to describe the asylum cells, the hierarchy among the staff and the living arrangements for nurses (UoR MS 3000: 11r–13r). As well as these organizational aspects of the asylum, Beckett also drew on mental disorders he had seen during his visit to Bethlem when portraying the patients in the M.M.M.:

> Melancholics, motionless and brooding, holding their heads or bellies according to type. Paranoids, feverishly covering sheets of paper with complaints against their treatment or verbatim reports of their inner voices. A hebephrenic playing the piano intently. A hypomanic teaching slosh to a Korsakow's syndrome. An emaciated schizoid, petrified in a toppling attitude as though condemned to an

eternal *tableau vivant*, his left hand rhetorically extended holding a cigarette half
smoked and out, his right, quivering and rigid, pointing upward. (*Mu*: 106)

This passage goes beyond the categorization of asylum inmates in 'Fingal' to
provide a literary dissection of madness reminiscent of Burton's opening to his
Anatomy, which tells of Democritus cutting up various animals in order to find
'the seat of this *atra bilis*, or melancholy', an image noted by Beckett when reading
the book (Burton 1912: 16; UoR MS 3000: 84r). In spite of his assertion that
Proust contained 'no allusion [...] to the legendary life and death' of its subject,
Beckett did like to get under the skin of writers he admired and, like Johnson, put
an emphasis on 'the biographical part of literature' (*PTD*: 9; Boswell 1848: 145).
This was certainly the case during his most intensive period of study on Johnson,
from 1937 to 1940, when he was doing research for a never-to-be-completed
play entitled *Human Wishes* (written 1940; published 1983), centred around the
love triangle of 'the Lexicographer', Henry Thrale and Henry's wife Hester (SB
to TM, 8 September 1934, *LSB* I: 223). In Beckett's own creative process, the
decantation of personal experience into art took the form not of autobiography
but what H. Porter Abbott calls 'autography', which includes a plurality of
forms of self-writing, rather than just the narrative of one's own life. A study of
texts of self-writing, argues Abbott, must take into account the 'autographical
action' of the writing of these texts (Abbott 1996: x). With regard to Beckett's use
of confined space, this 'autographical action' can be fruitfully studied through
his reading notes.

Beckett noted Johnson and Boswell's asylum visit of 8 May 1775 in one of
his research notebooks: 'He [Boswell] calls the cells in Bedlam the "mansions"
(& the corridors the galleries)' (UoR MS 3461/1: 15r, qtd in Smith 2002: 24). As
Ackerley points out, the detail in parentheses is taken from a footnote added
by John Wilson Croker to his edition of Boswell's *Life*, with Beckett incorrectly
attributing the word 'galleries' to Boswell himself (2010: 150). In *Murphy*'s
description of the architecture of the M.M.M., Beckett explicitly references
Boswell in an addition made at typescript stage: 'There were no open wards in
the ordinary sense, but single rooms, or as some would say, cells, *or as Boswell
said, mansions*' (*Mu*: 105).[7] This reference shows Beckett filtering the London
architecture he knew through the literature he was reading and then decanting
the finished product of that experience into his novel. The narrator's description

---

[7] Emphasis added. The words in italics were added at typescript stage (HRC SB MS 5/2: 114). I follow
the pagination on the typescript.

of 'the padded cells, known to the wittier as the "quiet rooms", "rubber rooms" or, in a notable clip, "pads"', all of which are terms Beckett picked up on his visits to Bethlem, demonstrates Beckett's preoccupation with the process of finding words to describe the physical structure of institutions of confinement (*Mu*: 105; UoR MS 3000: 11v). However, in mirroring the enclosure of the asylum cell in his description of Murphy's mind, Beckett goes further than mere mental health nomenclature; instead, the monadic cell becomes a crucial symbolic space in the novel.

Murphy's monadic mind

As well as drawing heavily on Anglophone literary tradition, *Murphy* became, following the publication of its French translation in 1947, 'le premier roman bilingue' [the first bilingual novel] in Beckett's canon (Montini 2007: 66). One significant change in the French version is an addition regarding the claustrophobic garret that Murphy is so keen to have as his lodging in the M.M.M.:

> Fewer years ago than he cared to remember, while still in the first cyanosis of youth, Murphy had occupied a garret in Hanover, not for long, but for long enough to experience all its advantages. Since then he had sought high and low for another, even half as good. In vain. [...] But the garret that he now saw was [...] a genuine garret, not half, but twice as good as the one in Hanover, because half as large. (*Mu*: 102)

In Beckett's translation, the garret is specified as having been found 'dans la belle maison renaissance de la Schmiedestrasse où avait vécu, mais surtout où était mort, Gottfried Wilhelm Leibniz' ['in the beautiful Renaissance house on the Schmiedestrasse, where Gottfried Wilhelm Leibniz had lived, and above all had died'] (Beckett 2013d: 140; Ackerley 2010: 148). Beckett had visited this house while travelling around Germany in late 1936, at the same time that *Murphy*'s English typescript was doing the rounds of different publishing houses, and this trip provided him with the extra detail when he came to translate the novel. Showing a keen awareness of the restricted lighting in Leibniz's room, Beckett wrote on a postcard entitled 'Hannover: Leibniz-Haus':

> This is where, for fifty years, he formed distinct ideas, or, worse, let them form in him. [...] Solidly seated in a north light he did his deleting and striking out over an open tomb ['il barrait à tombeau ouvert']. (SB to Brian Coffey, 5 December 1936, *LSB* I: 395, 394)

Murphy's garret, as well as being one of a series of enclosed spaces in *Murphy* itself, is an early instance of the single-windowed rooms which come to populate Beckett's oeuvre (see Mori 2004).[8] Creating 'light in the monad' requires an aperture, however restricted, through which such light may pass.

In addition to providing him with extreme instances of psychological dereliction and an institutional link with the history of writing madness, Bethlem Royal Hospital, specifically its padded cells, gave Beckett an architectural form through which he could represent Murphy's ideal mental state of detached self-confinement, represented in a spatial model of the mind: 'what he called his mind functioned not as an instrument but as a place', elsewhere termed his 'mental chamber' (*Mu*: 112, 70). The Leibnizian monad provides a crucial conceptual nexus between *Murphy*'s confined architectural spaces, specifically the asylum cell, and the representation of Murphy's mind as an enclosed space, his mind being the narrative and structural centre of the book around which everything else revolves. Following Windelband's claim that Leibniz's monads prefigure the 'unconscious mental states' of twentieth-century psychology, Beckett himself linked Leibniz's philosophy of mind with modern theories of psychoanalysis in his Philosophy Notes.[9] Crucially, the monad also serves as a model for the clinical space in which modern mental disorder was treated in prewar London.

In the seventh section of his *Monadology* Leibniz describes the monad, a simple, unalterable entity which underpins the existence of everything in the universe, as having 'no windows, through which anything could come in or go out' ([1714] 1898: 219). Beckett noted down this feature when reading the section on Leibniz in Windelband's *History of Philosophy*, in which the 'windowlessness' of the monads is put down to their 'metaphysical impenetrability' (Windelband 1907: 423; see TCD MS 10967: 191r–191v).[10] When describing the asylum cells which Murphy inspects in the M.M.M., Beckett draws on Windelband directly:

---

[8] A single-windowed room also appears in the first *Watt* notebook (HRC SB MS 6/5/104). I follow the HRC numbering.

[9] 'In the language of to-day the *petites perceptions* would be *unconscious mental states* (*Vorstellungen*)' (Windelband 1907: 424; emphasis in original). When taking notes from Windelband on Leibniz's theory of 'the development [of the soul] from unconscious to conscious, obscure to clear', Beckett added '[c]f. psychoanalysis', which is not in Windelband (TCD MS 10967: 205r, qtd in Tonning 2007: 208).

[10] Though Windelband's Leibniz is undoubtedly the major influence on Beckett's use of the monad in *Murphy*, his earlier notes on Pythagoreanism also contain a description (TCD MS 10967: 16r). Beckett also uses Giordano Bruno's concept of the monad in 'Dante ... Bruno . Vico .. Joyce' (1929) (*Dis*: 21).

The compartment was windowless, like a monad, except for the shuttered judas in the door, at which a sane eye appeared, or was employed to appear, at frequent and regular intervals throughout the twenty-four hours. Within the narrow limits of domestic architecture he had never been able to imagine a more creditable representation of what he kept on calling, indefatigably, the little world. (*Mu*: 114)

In the M.M.M., the judas hole is the only means of visually penetrating the closed, windowless cell. What is more, unlike many windows, the judas hole is a device designed according to an asymmetrical power relation: while the observer can see in, the patient cannot easily get a clear picture of what is outside. Confinement here entails a politics of vision which reverses the perspective of Belacqua's view of the world from the willed enclosure of his wombtomb in *Dream*.

As well as constituting a key gap in the novel's narrative, during which the reader is made to wait to find out what 'shocking thing' has caused Celia to abandon her domestic chores (*Mu*: 68), Chapter 6 of *Murphy* is the book's most striking example of Beckett's attempt to shine a narrative light in 'the cell of [the] mind' (*Mu*: 94). In doing so, it anticipates the confinement of the asylum cell which Murphy will find so attractive in the M.M.M.: 'Murphy's mind pictured itself as a large hollow sphere, hermetically closed to the universe without' (*Mu*: 69). Murphy's mind sees itself as a 'closed system' within which there are three zones: 'light, half light, dark', recalling the 'trine' mind of Belacqua in *Dream of Fair to Middling Women*: 'centripetal, centrifugal and not' (*Mu*: 70, 71; *D*: 120). While the light and half-light allow some form of detached mental activity, Murphy favours retreat into the darkness of the third zone, a 'successor to the wombtomb' (Love 2005: 481), in which he can be 'a mote in the dark of absolute freedom' (*Mu*: 72). In a letter written while trying in vain to get *Murphy* published, Beckett describes his own version of this retreat, again referencing the monad:

There is an end to the temptation of light, its polite scorchings & consolations. [...] The real consciousness is the chaos, a grey commotion of mind, with no premises or conclusions or problems or solutions or cases or judgements. I lie for days on the floor, or in the woods, accompanied & unaccompanied, in a coenaesthesia of mind, a fullness of mental self-aesthesia that is entirely useless. The monad without the conflict, lightless & darkless. (SB to Mary Manning Howe, 30 August 1937, *LSB* I: 546)

If the monad was completely sealed, it would be pitch dark, and therefore of no interest to the outside observer. But in spite of being 'windowless', Beckett's monads do contain some light. Speaking in a 1961 interview about the problem of life and death in *Godot* and *Endgame*, Beckett again reflected on the difficulty of artistic representation in terms of light and darkness: 'If life and death did not both present themselves to us, there would be no inscrutability. If there were only darkness, all would be clear. It is because there is not only darkness but also light that our situation becomes inexplicable' (qtd in Driver 2005: 244). It is the attempt to shine a light in the monad of another human being's seemingly 'imperturbable' psyche that marks the relationship between Murphy and Mr Endon (*Mu*: 116).

'Seen and unseen': Murphy and Mr Endon

Murphy's disdain for 'the complacent scientific conceptualism that made contact with outer reality the index of mental well-being' signals his preference for the 'little world' of psychotic mental experience over the 'outer reality' privileged by the psychiatric community (*Mu*: 111, 112):

> The issue therefore, as lovingly simplified and perverted by Murphy, lay between nothing less fundamental than the big world and the little world, decided by the patients in favour of the latter, revived by the psychiatrists on behalf of the former, in his own case unresolved. In fact, it was unresolved, only in fact. His vote was cast. 'I am not of the big world, I am of the little world' was an old refrain with Murphy, and a conviction, two convictions, the negative first. (*Mu*: 112)

Ackerley notes that '"[a] little world" is used for the microcosm' in Burton's *Anatomy* and Swift's *Tale of a Tub* (2010: 156). Gaining access to the 'little world' of Mr Endon, 'a schizophrenic of the most amiable variety', becomes Murphy's primary focus and acts as a narrative catalyst that propels the novel towards its conclusion of the death by fire of its central protagonist (*Mu*: 116).

Anna McMullan has rightly observed that 'the concern with being seen, as either need or coercion, haunts Beckett's characters' in the theatre (McMullan 1998: 133). There is also a concern with the politics of visual interpretation in *Murphy*, as is evident in the detailed notes Beckett took on visual aspects of Bethlem during his visits to the hospital, such as the procedure for the surveillance of a suicidal patient – nicknamed a 'tab' (UoR MS 3000: 11r; *Mu*: 115) – and the frequency of inspections required through the judas hole on a nurse's night round (UoR MS 3000: 11r, 12r). These arrangements are an important part of the decisive final encounter between Murphy and the patient

Mr Endon. But in *Murphy*, '*percipere*' [to perceive] is as important as '*percipi*' [to be perceived] and the phenomenological aspects of the act of seeing are crucial to the novel's power relations (*Mu*: 154). This is the case in Murphy's encounter with his favourite patient, which hinges on a problem of perception and is the novel's structural climax.

When Murphy peers through the judas hole to check on his suicide 'tab' Mr Endon and sees a chessboard laid out for a game, he is glad (*Mu*: 115–16): 'Mr. Endon had recognised the feel of his friend's eye upon him and made his preparations accordingly.' The narrative interpretation of Mr Endon's response takes Murphy's estimation of himself down a peg or two:

> Friend's eye? Say rather, Murphy's eye. Mr. Endon had felt Murphy's eye upon him. Mr. Endon would have been less than Mr. Endon if he had known what it was to have a friend; and Murphy more than Murphy if he had not hoped against his better judgment that his feeling for Mr. Endon was in some small degree reciprocated. Whereas the sad truth was, that while Mr. Endon for Murphy was no less than bliss, Murphy for Mr. Endon was no more than chess. Murphy's eye? Say rather, the chessy eye. Mr. Endon had vibrated to the chessy eye upon him and made his preparations accordingly. (*Mu*: 150)

Through his identification with the insane, Murphy wants to turn himself from a voyeur on the little worlds of psychosis into a '*voyant*' [seer] who can view such worlds from within (*Mu*: 58). He would presumably agree with French Surrealist poet Robert Desnos, who wrote that 'it is us [*sic*] who are locked up when one shuts the door to the asylum: the prison is outside, liberty within' (qtd in Mooney 2011: 60). In the Surrealist volume Beckett translated, it is argued: 'the complete indifference of lunatics to the way the rest of us criticize their behaviour [...] allows one to suppose that they find their imagination to be a great comfort and sufficiently enjoy their delirium to be able to put up with its being valid for them alone' (qtd in Breton and Éluard 1932: 101). *Murphy*, while drawing on material directly related to the experience of psychological alienation, questions the notion that Murphy can gain direct access to the experience of an inmate. Instead of the transparent communicative model that allows Surrealists to presuppose liberty in confinement, in *Murphy*, there is no representation of incarceration (of the subject) without a necessarily mediated interpretation (of that subject position).

Murphy's chess games with Mr Endon typically are non-competitive, non-communicative affairs. At the end of their final game, after forty-three moves each, almost all of Mr Endon's pieces are back in their original positions. Having realized that competitive interaction over the chessboard is impossible, Murphy concedes defeat by laying down his king and fixes his gaze on Mr Endon's remarkably coloured clothes. The passage which follows describes Murphy's perception of a 'big blooming buzzing confusion', then 'the Nothing, than which in the guffaw of the Abderite naught is more real' (*Mu*: 153–4), drawing directly on his philosophy and psychology reading to describe Murphy's encounter with the perceptual void that replaces his projected 'brotherhood' with Mr Endon (*Mu*: 111).[11] While putting him to bed it becomes clear to Murphy not only that 'the most biddable little gaga in the entire institution' is a solipsistic chess player but that any form of communication with this exemplar of 'the race of people he had long since despaired of finding' is impossible (*Mu*: 149, 106). Murphy stares at the vacant eyes of his patient 'across a narrow gulf of air, the merest hand's-breadth of air' (*Mu*: 155):

> Kneeling at the bedside, the hair starting in thick black ridges between his fingers, his lips, nose and forehead almost touching Mr. Endon's, seeing himself stigmatised in those eyes that did not see him, Murphy heard words demanding so strongly to be spoken that he spoke them, right into Mr. Endon's face, Murphy who did not speak at all in the ordinary way unless spoken to, and not always even then.
>
> > 'the last at last seen of him
> > himself unseen by him
> > and of himself'
>
> A rest. 'The last Mr. Murphy saw of Mr. Endon was Mr. Murphy unseen by Mr. Endon. This was also the last Murphy saw of Murphy.' A rest. 'The relation between Mr. Murphy and Mr. Endon could not have been better summed up than by the former's sorrow at seeing himself in the latter's immunity from seeing anything but himself.' A long rest. [...] 'Mr. Murphy is a speck in Mr. Endon's unseen.' (*Mu*: 156)

The proximity of Murphy and Mr Endon is such that they are 'all set [...] for a butterfly kiss', in which the eyelashes of one kisses the skin of another (*Mu*: 156). The eyes here prove to be inadequate as organs of interpersonal perception and, as in Beckett's dramatic work, 'when vision falters the sense of touch comes to the fore' (McTighe 2013: 9). In both the minutely physical description of Mr Endon's eye and the near butterfly kiss, the eye becomes almost an organ of

---

[11] Beckett took down the phrase 'big blooming buzzing confusion' in his notes on Robert S. Woodworth's *Contemporary Schools of Psychology* (TCD MS 10971/7/12, qtd in Feldman 2006: 103). He noted the description of Democritus of Abdera as the laughing philosopher in TCD MS 10967/78. Beckett would also have come across this description of Democritus in Burton (1912: 48–54).

touch rather than of sight. Instead of being a passage through which Murphy can perceive 'light in the monad', Mr Endon's 'fleshly eye[s]' are simply part of the world of objects from which he feels so alienated (Merleau-Ponty 1993: 127). Murphy's alienation foreshadows the disconnected encounters at the climax of *Ohio Impromptu* and *Catastrophe*. Both in the latter play and in *Murphy*, communicative failure is used to refashion the kind of direct sociopolitical critique which depends on giving voice to voiceless. While Murphy gets closer than Belacqua ever did to an actual inmate, his hero-worship of Mr Endon is ultimately shown up as a fetishization of difference.

Murphy's final scene, which depicts Mr Kelly's kite-flying in Kensington, provides a counterpoint to Murphy's vision of unseeing seeing in the eyes of Mr Endon. The scene is another example of Beckett's 'autographical action', drawing on the author's own kite-watching while writing the novel, after which he decided that '[m]y next old man, or old young man, not of the big world but of the little world, must be a kite-flyer (SB to TM, 8 September 1935, *LSB* I: 274). In contrast to Murphy's despair at seeing Mr Endon not seeing him, when Mr Kelly's kite disappears from view, he is 'enraptured. Now he could measure the distance from the unseen to the seen, now he was in a position to determine the point at which seen and unseen met' (*Mu*: 174). This space beyond the limits of immediate perception anticipates the spatial dynamic of Beckett's theatre writing, in which the 'big world' of offstage space plays a crucial role in the interpretation of confined space onstage. Before turning to the actual heterotopia of the stage, Beckett would again use institutions of confinement in his prose, notably when constructing a derelict psychological perspective to explore the boundary zone between seen and unseen, known and unknown, in his novel *Watt*.

3

'Vaguening' Confinement

Watt

In a diary entry for 19 November 1936, in response to his reading of texts by German Expressionist painter Franz Marc, Beckett returned to the image of the 'no-man's-land' used in 'Recent Irish Poetry', stating that his interest was 'not in the relation between subject & object [...] but the alienation (my nomansland)' (qtd in Nixon 2011: 164). Having used the monadic cells of Bethlem Asylum to portray the 'nomansland' of mental alienation in *Murphy*, Beckett returned to a space of coercive confinement in order to create the gap-filled narrative of his next novel. *Watt* (written 1941–5; published 1953) is presented as a compositional manuscript, riddled with question marks in place of missing words and, increasingly, as the novel progresses, spaces marked 'Hiatus in MS' or 'MS illegible (*W*: 207, 209)'. Discussing the work of Henry Fielding, which Beckett greatly admired (see SB to TM, 8 October 1932, *LSB* I: 129), Wolfgang Iser argues that 'the deliberate gaps in the narrative are the means by which the reader is enabled to bring both scenes and characters to life' (1978: 38–9). According to Iser, Beckett is the ne plus ultra of authors whose narrative gaps continually demand new interpretations, keeping the reader active through his refusal to provide closure: 'Beckett's works are a continual (though never completed) "exit", and each stage of the exit is only a starting-point for more "exiting"' (1978: 258). Through his 'vaguening' of a space of coercive confinement, Beckett's use of gaps in *Watt* not only opens up the hermeneutic field for his reader, allowing for the potentially endless creation of meaning, but also draws attention to what Beckett described in 'Recent Irish Poetry' as the 'rupture of the lines of communication', already explored as an ethical impasse in Murphy's encounter with Mr Endon (*Dis*: 70).

In the typescript of *Watt*, marked '[i]ncomplete' and created in stages as Beckett composed his novel in six manuscript notebooks and on loose leaves, Beckett's narrator considers the problem of gaps in cultural archives (HRC SB MS 7/5/1, qtd in Admussen 1979: 92).[1] The reflection is prompted by an account of a series of dog sex shows promoted by the perennially ailing Lynch family, guardians of the famished dog who eats the leftovers of the evening meal of Watt's master Mr Knott (in this draft still called Quin). The narrator tells us that 'similar spectacles' exist 'in other parts of the country' (HRC SB MS 7/5/295). But while these other spectacles can trace their origins, the Lynch dog sex show has left no such record of its foundation. Without a trace 'in the annals, or archives', the origin of this particular staging of canine copulation is something the narrator cannot pin down with precision, despite discussing records from 'the British Islands', 'the European mainland', 'Africa, Asia, Australia, America' and elsewhere (HRC SB MS 7/5/295–6). However, in a salutary warning on the dangers of archival positivism, the narrator expresses scepticism regarding the hypothesis that a lack of archival evidence from former civilizations proves definitively that similar dog sex shows did not take place there:

> Nor did the old accounts of Atlantis and Hy Brasil allude to any entertainment of the kind. But what does this prove? For traces cannot endure for ever, but the time comes, for every trace, when it must disappear and leave no trace behind, to tell where it had been. For as things vanish, so must traces vanish, and the traces of traces as the traces of things. And old accounts are notoriously incomplete. (HRC SB MS 7/5/296, qtd in Bolin 2013: 85)

The focus of this chapter is on the effects that the 'vaguening' of confined spaces, and these spaces' resulting traces, have on the sociopolitical dynamics of *Watt*. The representation of institutional confinement which gives the sprawling text its compositional anchor is comparatively vague when compared to the parodic realism of *Murphy*. Focusing on *Watt*'s manuscript genesis, I contend that the introduction of this asylum during the drafting process was a key compositional turning point for Beckett. *Watt*'s two principal aesthetic strategies – a 'vaguening' process and the development of a poetics of missing parts – allowed Beckett to give greater focus to the 'nomansland' of alienated experience rather than the attempt (already satirized in *Murphy*) to recuperate the experience of the 'little world' of the asylum inmate. Key to this is the heterotopic nature of the

---

[1] See Lake (1984: 75–9) and Admussen (1979: 90–2). I follow C. J. Ackerley in numbering the notebooks 1–6.

asylum space itself. As Kevin Hetherington points out, the literal translation of the medical term 'heterotopia' is 'place of otherness' and it is this sense of alterity which Beckett outlined in his responses to visiting Bethlem in 1935 (2003: 8). In much recent social theory, these '"Other places" have become the space of Other voices' (Hetherington 2003: 7). But how does this spatially defined otherness inflect the voice of a writer at a crucial period in the development of his craft? I will argue that Beckett's shaping of the narrative voice of *Watt* – the single most important work in Beckett's process of 'learn[ing] to "say I"' (Nixon 2011: 35) – is intimately related to the 'vaguening' of a confined space which, through its association with marginalization and social exclusion, has political implications for Beckett's representation of alterity.

'Vaguening'

Critics have long discussed the hermeneutic richness of the spaces that are hinted at, or half seen, in Beckett's work. As early as 1966, Theodor Adorno wrote of the 'image ban' he saw as being operative in the spaces of Beckett's theatre and interpreted this as a response to the horror of Second World War concentration camps (2004: 380). Two decades later, theatre critic Rosemary Pountney characterized Beckett's poetics in terms of 'vaguening', based on a manuscript note she found in a draft version of *Happy Days* (1961). Pountney sees the term 'vaguen' in the play's second typescript as 'explicit testimony to Beckett's policy of "vaguening" the later drafts of his plays' (1988: 149).[2] However, in terms of its challenge to the representation of place in stage realism, Winnie's situation was vague from very early on in the compositional process.[3] While there were topographical details erased elsewhere in the drafts – most notably regarding rocket attacks on places such as Ireland – the principal 'vaguenings' to the stage space of *Happy Days* concerned not the place of action as such but rather the stage measurements.[4]

---

[2] Four *Happy Days* typescripts are stored in OSU, Spec.Rare.MS.Eng.28. I follow the OSU numbering of TSS 1–4.

[3] The stretching of realist convention outlined in the stage directions – '[v]ery pompier trompe-l'oeil backcloth to represent unbroken plain and sky receding to meet in far distance' (*CDW*: 138) – is already a feature of the earliest extant draft: 'The back cloth represents unbroken plain and cloudless sky receding to meet in the far distance' ('Été 56' Notebook, UoR MS 1227/7/7/1 (henceforth NB 1): 35r, *BDMP* III).

[4] See *Happy Days* compositional notebook (OSU, Spec.Rare.MS.Eng.28; henceforth NB 2): 9r; TS 1: 4r.

The example of *Happy Days* shows that 'vaguening' is a concept which needs to be treated with caution. However, it can still be very useful when analysing *Watt*, particularly if we take into account not only how each individual work was composed but also what Beckett called the novel's 'place in a the series' of his oeuvre (SB to Reavey, 14 May 1947, *LSB* II: 55, 56 n. 2). Pountney sees the process of 'vaguening' as taking place not just in each individual performance text but also across Beckett's body of work: 'The process of drafting each play [...] may be seen as a microcosm of the development of Beckett's oeuvre as a whole, a refining and scaling down of the text' (1988: 195). In this model, there is a move from 'the Dublin-landmarked stories of *More Pricks Than Kicks* to the nameless spaces of his later fiction and drama' (Grene 2014: 129). But again, this needs to be nuanced. While acknowledging that Pountney's 'conclusions are sound and indeed indisputable', Erik Tonning has warned that 'the trajectories mapped out – from realist detail and plotting to formalism and ambiguity – may [...] be overly linear' (2007: 74). My subsequent chapters will analyse the myriad ways in which Beckett arrived at the 'nameless spaces' of his later texts. But what of *Watt*? How does this novel fit the paradigm of Beckett the 'vaguener'? And how does Beckett's 'vaguening' shape the politics of his writing? It is my contention that, due to the 'vaguening' of the asylum setting already encountered in much greater detail in 'Fingal' and *Murphy*, Beckett's changing treatment of confinement can give us a unique insight into the political effects of his aesthetic development.

Gaps

In a letter to Mary Manning Howe, written while still trying to get the book published, Beckett reacted furiously to publisher Houghton Mifflin's proposed cuts to *Murphy*:

> I am exhorted to ablate 33.3 recurring to all eternity of my work. I have thought of a better plan. Take every 500th word, punctuate carefully and publish a poem in prose in the Paris Daily Mail. Then the rest separately and privately, with a forewarning from Geoffrey [Thompson], as the ravings of a schizoid, or serially, in translation, in the Zeitschrift für Kitsch ['Magazine for Kitsch']. (14 November 1936, *LSB* I: 382–3, 385)

Beckett's satirical reaction to the publisher's proposed imposition of gaps in *Murphy* links his style of writing to mental disorder as well as anticipating the punctured textual surfaces through which he would explore the psychological 'nomansland' of *Watt*. Daniela Caselli has made the point that Beckett's entire oeuvre can be read in terms of gaps, with titles like *From an Abandoned Work* (1956), *A Piece of Monologue, Abandonné* [Abandoned] (1972), *Rough for Theatre I* (*Fragment de théâtre I*, 1974) and collections such as the *Faux départs* [False Starts] and *Six Residua* (1978) advertising the incompletion of his works (2005: 86). The asylum gives Beckett a space from which to create his residual poetics, which in turn provides his work with a new relationship with the politics of institutional space. Instead of reducing his texts to 'distilled essences' (Gontarski 1995: xi), Beckett created pieces of writing which, like his marginalized characters, appear as draff, left over from the distillation undergone in the writing process. In its use of the asylum as the central locus of an obsessional narrative style which increases, rather than decreases, the gap between subject and object and results in a fragmented world which fails to meaningfully cohere, *Watt*'s 'vaguened' confinement is crucial to the politics of Beckett's work, reshaping narrative perspective to create 'an expression [which] does not find its place in the system of visible coordinates where it appears' (Rancière 2011a: 63).

When Murphy reaches the apogee of his alienation in the M.M.M., realizing that he is merely a 'speck on Mr Endon's unseen', he does so from the outside looking in (*Mu*: 156). In using the ex-inmate Sam as its narrator, *Watt* stages an attempt at portraying such alienation from the inside looking out. Beckett arrived at this alienated narrator through a centrifugal development of the narrative perspective, recorded in his manuscripts. In the first two notebooks, the central character of Beckett's draft novel is called James Quin, whose story is told by a first-person narrator. It is only in NB 3 that this narrator himself becomes the narrative focus. Initially unnamed, he develops into Johnny Watt, one of Quin's servants. Then Beckett moved a step further from his narrative centre by using Sam as a means of further filtering Watt's story of life as a servant in the big house. In spite of this shift of perspective away from Quin, *Watt* is structured around, and draws most of its material from, Watt's period of service with his master. Without the magnetic pull of the house in which he is employed, Watt would have no reason to start his quest, Mr Hackett and the Nixons would spend an unremarkable evening at the tram stop and Watt's narrative as we know it would have neither material nor structure.

Watt's gaps not only structure the narrative; the distance between Beckett and his reading material while writing the book on the run from the Gestapo in the south of France during the Second World War was also central to the missing parts that came to pockmark the text. It is worth noting, however, that Beckett started and finished work on the manuscripts within reach of his reference materials.[5] This makes his decisions to leave gaps in the narrative all the more interesting. So, for instance, towards the end of the novel, the reader misses out on a quotation from *Homeward: Songs by the Way*, the first published collection of poetry by Irish theosophist Æ (aka George Russell), which is being read by a railway worker: 'Mr Case, his head flung back, held this book out at arm's length. Mr Case had a very superior taste in books, for a signal-man. Mr Case read:

?' (*W*: 197)

In NB 6, Beckett wrote the word '([q]uotation)' in this gap (HRC SB 7/3/53, qtd in Ackerley 2005: 191). Another such instance involves a missing piece of philosophical scaffolding. In NB 4, when accompanying Watt in their unnamed institution, Sam describes his mental faculties, 'faculties properly so called of (- - - Locke - - - -)' (HRC SB MS 7/1/138). In the published text, the brackets containing Locke's name are replaced by a series of spaces and question marks (*W*: 145). These gaps in the manuscript suggest that Beckett had planned to come back to these passages and fill them in with material from Æ's and Locke's works but that, by the time *Watt* was published in 1953, he decided to keep these ruptures in the textual surface.[6]

The introduction of the narrator Sam in NB 4 seems to have been a crucial point in the creation of a narrative based on gaps. As it is in the published text, the opening of the section based in the asylum is initially narrated in an anonymous first person (*W*: 129; HRC SB MS 7/1/93). Sam is inserted a few pages later, when the narrator describes the weather conditions under which he was likely to meet Watt outside, now that they were in separate parts of the asylum: 'But whereas for Watt the important thing was the wind, the sun was the important thing for me Sam' (HRC SB MS 7/1/97).[7] Ackerley posits that 'part II [was] presumably revised at this time to bring him [Sam] in incrementally'

[5] Beckett fled his Paris apartment on 16 August 1942, returning on 12 October 1944 (Pilling 2006: 90, 93). On a loose page in NB 1, Beckett wrote: 'Begun evening of Tuesday 11/2/41' (HRC SB MS 6/5/1, qtd in Ackerley 2005: 17). On the cover of NB 1, he wrote: 'Watt was written in France during the war 1940–5 and published in [xxx] 1953 by the Olympia Press' (HRC SB MS 6/5/front cover, qtd in Ackerley 2005: 17). On one of the loose leaves stored with NB 6, he wrote 'Dec 28th 1944 / END' (HRC SB MS 7/3/119, qtd in Ackerley 2005: 18) but the cover of NB 5 contains the words 'Watt V / Suite et fin / 18.2.45', indicating that revision continued into 1945 (HRC SB MS 7/2/front cover, qtd in Ackerley 2005: 18).

[6] Beckett even created gaps in the published text that were not there in the manuscript. In a draft of Part IV, Watt sees a picture of a horse with 'an inscription of unusual [xxx] height, width + distinctness' (HRC SB MS 7/3/91). In the published text, this becomes 'an inscription of great   ?   ' (*W*: 205).

[7] As this insertion is made on the same line as the rest of the sentence, we can assume that Beckett made it as he composed the passage, not afterwards.

(2005: 244). From my analysis of the notebooks, it would indeed appear that Sam acted as an anchor around which Beckett could shape his increasingly unwieldy material. At the end of NB 4, Beckett wrote a note to himself: 'Present dogs, food, picture, etc. as told by W. as Committee told' (HRC SB MS 7/1/175, qtd in Ackerley 2005: 240). In NB 6, Beckett gave more detail on the function of 'the long story of com[m]it[tee]–Nacibal. Present as told by Phelps to Mr Gomez, and overheard by Watt, on the only occasion, during his service on 1st floor, that he [? went], after Mr Knott, to the garden' (HRC SB MS 7/2: 91v, BDMP V). In other words, having inserted Sam in NB 4, it would now be necessary to present episodes from the first two parts in a narrative frame so that it was clear they had been told to him by Watt, just as the story of the academic committee examining Louit and Nackybal is framed by a narrator telling this story in the garden to others.[8] Gérard Genette calls such a narrative structure 'metadiegetic', containing stories within stories; in this case, *Watt* contains stories which were told to Sam by Watt (and often told to Watt by others) (1983: 231–2).

Genette also uses the terms 'homodiegetic' and 'heterodiegetic' to distinguish between narratives in which the narrator is present in the story and those in which the narrator is not (1983: 245). Sam's insertion as a character in *Watt* gave Beckett the means of turning what he has already composed – the stories about the 'dogs, food, picture, etc.' – into material for Sam's homodiegetic narrative. Having contextualized the narrative voice using the figure of Sam, Beckett then rewrote the first two parts of the novel on loose pages stored with NB 4 and in NB 5. In the revised draft version of Part II, Beckett added evidence of Sam's presence as the receiver of Watt's story by alluding to 'the material conditions in which these communications were made' in the institution grounds where Watt meets Sam (HRC SB MS 7/2/19; see below). Such instances point to the importance of Beckett's insertion of the asylum as his narrative's nodal space in NB 4.

How does the genesis of the character Sam relate to *Watt*'s gaps? On the most basic level, Sam uses the material conditions of the asylum as an excuse for the gaps in his narrative. But there are even more important gaps that started to emerge as Beckett wove Watt's story around the confined space in which it was ostensibly told to Sam. These gaps point to Beckett's decision to play with – indeed, to break – the limits of the homodiegetic narrative he was creating. The most glaring narrative omission is caused by the fact that the version of *Watt*'s opening passage in NB 4 starts without Watt or Sam on the scene. Instead, we find a draft

---

[8]   In NB 4 and the typescript, it is Watt who tells the Louit–Nackybal story; in the published text, it is Arthur, with Watt as one of his audience (HRC SB MS 7/1/25; HRC SB MS 7/6/367; W: 146).

version almost identical to the novel's opening line, setting up a section which focuses on a character who is marginal to Watt's story: 'Mr Hackett turned the corner and saw, in the failing light, at ~~a distance of~~ [x] ^some^ little distance, his seat' (HRC SB MS 7/1/177; see *W*: 1). On another set of loose squared pages stored with the notebook, Beckett continued a draft of Part IV he had commenced in NB 6 which is close to the version in the published text. The notebook version, like the published ending, tells of Watt being woken up in the waiting room of a train station before being kicked off the premises by the railway staff, who enjoy the morning light together after he departs (HRC SB MS 7/3/97–120; see *W*: 206–14). What is key is that neither the opening nor the closing sections of the novel, drafted on these notebook pages, could have been told to Sam by Watt. Such episodes cannot be subsumed into a homodiegetic narrative structure based on the metadiegetic recounting of stories to the narrator.

The versions of the opening and closing sections drafted after Sam's appearance in NB 4 therefore form important gaps in the narrative structure. Following the insertion of Sam in NB 4, Beckett started 'imposing blank spaces on the text that he did not intend to fill and that could not have been left by Sam' (Bolin 2013: 93). The existence of these key gaps suggests that, having rewritten parts of his huge manuscript, and anchored the narrative with Sam's appearance in Part III, Beckett then added an opening and ending which he knew would not fit with the narrative schema of the rest of the text. It is here, after all the pyrotechnics of his previous prose, that Beckett reshapes the aesthetic structures associated with realist writing, which demands that the central narrative voice retain a basic level of coherence. The asylum was therefore crucial, not only as a narrative space that was 'vaguened', bringing Beckett away from the kind of forensic attention to detail of *Murphy*, but as a means by which Beckett constructed his poetics of ignorance through textual gaps, thus redefining the field of the sensible in which Watt appears. As I will now show, the function of *Watt*'s asylum goes beyond simply a rational explanation for what the narrator of *Malone Dies* calls 'a mad world, in the midst of strangers' (*MD*: 18). Rather, the asylum plays a deeply political role in 'undoing the relations between the visible, the sayable, and the thinkable' (Rancière 2011a: 65).

In the asylum

As shown in Chapter 2, questions around the ethics and politics of representation were posed ever more insistently in Beckett's writing of the 1930s through an increased narrative proximity to carceral spaces: firstly, Mountjoy Prison is an unseen space evoked by the image of McCabe's face in the *Evening Herald* newspaper in 'Dante and the Lobster'; next, Belacqua comes face to face with an inmate over the wall of Portrane Asylum; then, using an omniscient third-person narrator, the M.M.M. is meticulously described in *Murphy*. *Watt* is the first of Beckett's prose works to use a first-person narrator coming out of an institution of confinement, making the asylum a crucial element in the process of representing social as well as psychological alienation.

Though the asylum was not the compositional starting point for *Watt*, specific institutions of coercive confinement were on Beckett's mind as he was writing the novel. In one draft version, the piano tuner Green tells his master of his time spent incarcerated in Dublin:

> the roses of my prime withered in Windy Arbour [site of the Central Criminal Lunatic Asylum, now the Central Mental Hospital], Beggar's Bush [site of a barracks used for internment during the Irish Civil War], Richmond [Asylum], Portrane [Asylum], Stillorgan [site of Saint John of God Hospital] and Foxrock. (HRC SB MS 7/5/7)[9]

At this stage in the narrative, Green is the principal interlocutor of Quin and Beckett uses the spaces of coercive confinement as a useful way of explaining Green's change from a 'fine lovely boy [...] to the little wizened blind old bugger that you may have happened to have noticed before you to-day' (HRC SB MS 7/5/7). In the published text, confinement becomes even more important, though the place-names which would locate the novel's institutional confinement are gone, having been 'vaguened'. To understand how this closed space functions, it is important to understand its role in constructing a narrative perspective based on the otherness of those who inhabit it.

The first two of *Watt*'s four numbered parts contain a narrative voice that flickers briefly in the foreground, before being given a marginalized figure (the hitherto unmentioned narrator Sam) and a heterotopic place (an unnamed asylum) from which to speak. To understand the social politics of the novel, we must give due attention to the otherness of the place in which Sam receives Watt's story. John Bolin argues that 'Beckett's dilemma [...] is always the writer's question: "comment dire?"' [literally 'how to say?'] (2013: 169). Going beyond the title of Beckett's last published poem, we might pose the question more accurately as 'comment écrire?' [literally 'how to write?'] in order to investigate

---

[9]   Foxrock, Beckett's birthplace, is the only one of these Dublin townlands not to feature a carceral institution, though it is close to Saint John of God Hospital.

how Beckett creatively shapes his carceral spaces during the compositional process. This will help us to explore the politics of Beckett's work not according to the author's level of political engagement, but rather on the work's ability to reshape existing modes of representation. For Rancière, 'political art' – which remains for him a 'dream' – would contain 'a double effect: the readability of a political signification and a sensible or perceptual shock caused, conversely, by the uncanny, by that which resists signification' (Rancière 2011a: 63). The politics of *Watt* are not simply a matter of Beckett once again using a heterotopia of deviation as a liminal narrative space in which a character tries to make contact with the other; rather, because of the narrative structure of the text, the politics of that space are interwoven with the emerging role of 'vaguening' as an important aesthetic strategy in his work.

The reader can discern the presence of a shaping narrator from the novel's very first footnote, found where Mr Hackett's hypothesizes about the couple kissing on 'his' seat: 'Tired of waiting for the tram, said[1] Mr Hackett, they strike up an acquaintance.' The accompanying footnote explains: 'Much valuable space has been saved, in this work, that would otherwise have been lost, by avoidance of the plethoric reflexive pronoun after *say*' (*W*: 4; emphasis in original). Matthew Winston contends that this footnote marks the narrative as other: 'Watt is a tale told by a madman and its initial footnote is the first indication of his strangeness' (1977: 73). Though I will contest Winston's reading that *Watt*'s narrative strangeness can be put down simply to mental disorder, further indications of strangeness do indeed follow, including the comparison of Watt's reasoning with that of Nackybal, a character who only arrives on the scene thirty-eight pages later (*W*: 111, 149), and the narrator's self-references (*W*: 57, 65, 98, 102, 106–9), each of which undermines the initial supposition that we are reading a tale told by a heterodiegetic narrator. As mentioned above, before we even meet Sam as a named character, he gives us his excuses for the disjunctive form in which Watt's experiences are presented:

> For when Watt at last spoke of this time, it was a time long past, and of which his recollections were, in a sense, perhaps less clear than he would have wished, though too clear for his liking, in another. Add to this the notorious difficulty of recapturing, at will, modes of feeling peculiar to a certain time, and to a certain place, and perhaps also to a certain state of the health, when the time is past, and the place left, and the body struggling with quite a new situation. Add to this the obscurity of Watt's communications, the rapidity of his utterance and the eccentricities of his syntax, as elsewhere recorded. Add to this the material conditions in which these communications were made. Add to this the scant

aptitude to receive of him to whom they were proposed. Add to this the scant aptitude to give of him to whom they were committed. And some idea will perhaps be obtained of the difficulties experienced in formulating, not only such matters as those here in question, but the entire body of Watt's experience, from the moment of his entering Mr Knott's establishment to the moment of his leaving it. (*W*: 62)

The 'scant aptitude' of speaker and listener here suggests that *Watt*'s narrator possesses 'a mind alienated – or emancipated – from the causal sequence of our world' (Cohn 1961: 159). But this is only confirmed when the space of narration shifts to the asylum at the start of Part III, a shift accompanied by the first sustained use of the first-person pronoun in Beckett's prose.

Beckett had previously used a first-person voice in 'Ding-Dong' and in ten of the thirteen poems of *Echo's Bones and Other Precipitates* (1935). However, Part III of *Watt* features a concentration of first-person pronouns hitherto unseen in Beckett's prose. Note how the opening sentences of this section immediately link the narrative voice (and its subject, Watt) to a particular kind of space:

It was about this time that Watt was transferred to another pavilion, leaving me behind in the old pavilion. We consequently met, and conversed, less than formerly [...]. For we seldom left our mansions, Watt seldom left his mansion and I seldom left mine. (*W*: 129)

Though Sam and Watt's place of meeting is never named, the 'pavilions' which constitute their site of confinement, and the fact that an unnamed authority 'transfers' Watt between buildings, strongly suggest some kind of medical facility (*W*: 185).

If, for Umberto Eco, the best way of verifying any interpretative conjecture is to 'check it against the text as a coherent whole' (1994: 59), the best way to verify that Watt and Sam are in an asylum is to check *Watt* against a text which relatively few people would have read when the novel was published in 1953. In the denouement of *Murphy*, Beckett refers directly to James Boswell's use of the term 'mansions' to describe Bethlem's asylum cells. As shown in Chapter 2, Beckett added the explicatory detail of Boswell's name to the *Murphy* typescript, providing his readers with a clear pointer back to Boswell's description of Bethlem in his *Life of Johnson*. *Watt* uses the same compositional material in a way which demonstrates a 'vaguening' of Beckett's source. Instead of the walking tour of the asylum provided in *Murphy*, *Watt*'s use of the word 'mansion' is the first in a series of interpretative breadcrumbs, which leads the reader back to Bethlem via the description of the madhouse cells in the Magdalen Mental Mercyseat. *Watt* never uses the words 'inmate' or 'patient', making the intertextual link to *Murphy* a key tool for the reader attempting to identify the novel's narrative locale.

Raymonde Debray-Genette describes intertextual self-references, such as Beckett's use of 'mansion', using the term 'autotextuality' ['autotextualité'] (1979: 33). There are other elements in *Watt*'s autotextual trail. Reference to Sam and Watt's 'windowlessness' recalls the monadic isolation of the asylum inmates in the M.M.M., confined in their 'windowless' cells. Mention of the 'bloodheat' of the cells recalls the term used by Wylie to describe Neary's fictional incarceration in a Dublin asylum, returning once more to the images of intrauterine confinement of *Dream*, Beckett's reading of psychoanalysis texts as well as his own sessions of psychoanalysis (*W*: 129; see *Mu*: 30). This is far from the topographically specific confinement of *Murphy*, which mentions by name the Saint John of God Hospital near which Beckett grew up and explicitly draws on Bethlem Asylum which he visited.

What of clues in the surrounding landscape? Can the traces of Dublin's spaces, scattered throughout the novel, be used to pinpoint the asylum in which Sam and Watt are held? In C. J. Ackerley and S. E. Gontarski's plot summary, 'Watt arrives, by tram, to what in SB's world was the Harcourt Street Station, where he will take a train to what etc. is Foxrock. [...] Watt arrives at Knott's house, the model for which is Cooldrinagh [Beckett's family home]' (2004: 629–30). Because of the elements of Dublin that appear in the novel, it is tempting to triangulate other locations in the text using Beckett's biography. According to this paradigm, the asylum would be Saint John of God's Hospital, in spite of the fact that none of its topographical features map onto the Irish institution in the same way as the asylum in *Malone Dies* (Ackerley 2005: 143; Ackerley and Gontarski 2004: 494). But, as the qualifier 'in SB's world' suggests, we also have to take into account the fact that, with notable exceptions such as Glencullen and Leopardstown (*W*: 10; 215), Dublin place-names are largely absent from the text. David Addyman rightly objects: 'If the setting of the novel is as clear as Ackerley and Gontarski suggest, then there is surely no need to make the point. However, the recourse to Dublin as a source of stability is only made necessary because the novel's locations are so *vague*' (2010a: 113; emphasis added). This exemplifies 'a more sophisticated use of secondary material, whereby references are absorbed rather than overtly visible' (Nixon 2011: 187).

Beckett's 'vaguening' of the asylum setting, which he initiated in *Watt*'s English-language genesis, continued in the text's French-language epigenesis, defined as 'the continuation of the genesis after publication' (Van Hulle 2019: 47). For the reader of the French translation in 1968, the reference would have been even less visible. In this version, the 'mansions' of the English-language *Watt* have all been translated into 'pavillons' (Beckett 1969: 155). While this word recalls the 'pavillons de convalescence' [convalescent houses] of the M.M.M.M. (La Maison Madeleine de Miséricorde Mentale) in the French version of *Murphy*, including 'Pavillon Skinner' ['Skinner's House'], the French *Watt* lacks the clear intertextual trail of its English counterpart which evokes Boswell's Bethlem (Beckett 2013d: 143; *Mu*: 104). Does this lack of intertextual continuity make my focus on institutional confinement in readings of *Watt* an act of undue hermeneutic constraint? I would argue, rather, that it gives us an important example of Beckett's poetics in development, a trajectory of progress which, in his increasingly vague delineation of topographical detail, also involved regress.[10] Beckett's 'vaguening' process is also central to the politics of his work. The 'vaguened' asylum space, to return to Rancière's terms, allows for 'a political signification' which nonetheless 'resists signification' (2011a: 63). As can be seen in his experience of confinement in a train station, Watt's very position in society is defined by such resistance to signification.

On the outside

The asylum is a key locale in setting Watt apart from mainstream society, and in Mr Hackett's suggestion that Watt is 'off his head', there is already a hint of the social stigma that faces former asylum inmates (*W*: 14). But before being held in the asylum, Watt is locked into the waiting room of a railway station, an event which is nevertheless depicted after the narrative of his psychiatric confinement in the novel. An examination of the circumstances surrounding Watt's confinement in the train station will give a better idea of how his sheer otherness presents an unacceptable affront to the society in which he lives.

In a chapter entitled 'Railway Navigation and Incarceration' ['Naval et Carcéral'], Michel de Certeau highlights the collision of contraries brought about by rail travel. This collision includes the mixing of social hierarchies, which we can see in the novel between, on the one hand, the daily commuters and staff of the train station and, on the other hand, Watt, who is considered a stain on shared social space that must be removed as swiftly as possible. De Certeau describes

---

[10] Strengthening the idea of *Watt* as being part of a 'series', Beckett mistakenly inserted Murphy's name into a draft of Part IV of *Watt*, a slip which he later corrected (HRC SB MS 7/3/101). In the same letter to Reavey in which he describes *Watt* as being part of a 'series', Beckett responded positively to Reavey mixing up *Murphy* and *Watt*: 'I am glad to see you confusing them' (14 May 1947, *LSB* II: 55).

train travel in terms of 'the immobility of an order', 'a module of imprisonment ["enfermement"] that makes possible the production of an order, a closed and autonomous insularity', the final phrase describing particularly well the version of postcolonial Ireland presented by Beckett in *Watt* (1988: 111; 1990: 165). Though we never get to see Watt's second journey on the train, and though his confinement in the waiting room is voluntary, de Certeau's analysis of the spatial order of the railway can help us understand the social dynamics at play at the close of the novel, given that railway stations, like heterotopias themselves, are 'spaces of alternate ordering' (Hetherington 2003: 39–54), which benefit some more than others through particular distributions of social space.

The characters of *Watt* live in the same kind of modernized, suburban world which Beckett came to know growing up in early twentieth-century South County Dublin. But Watt is an outsider in this world. Mr Cox and Mr Waller, who commute daily 'to and from the city', are the kind of suburbanites one can set a watch by; indeed, the stationmaster Mr Gorman knows when to expect each of his early-rising customers (*W*: 213). This is what makes Watt's appearance in the train station such a scandal: in spite of the fact that he does nothing but sleep in the waiting room, buy a ticket and leave, his mere presence is a threat to a carefully constructed social order.

The reason the train station can function as a social nexus in Beckett's novel is due to the public nature of the space: quite simply, nowhere else does Watt have the chance to interact with so many people at the one time – indeed, it is the only place we get an instance of non-inverted direct speech from the novel's eponymous hero (*W*: 212). But this experience of socialization is not a happy one for Watt and both his visits to the train station result in his blood being shed. The first wound is the result of an unprovoked attack by Lady McCann, who throws a stone at him hard enough to leave a scar for 'five or six years' (*W*: 25). The second is the result of what is initially an act of kindness.

When Watt returns to the train station following his time spent in Mr Knott's house, the signalman Mr Case allows him to stay for the night locked in the waiting room. Emphasizing the extent to which Watt's request to stay in the waiting room presents a problem of spatial politics for Mr Case, Beckett meticulously sketched and resketched the railway station building in his notebook so as to outline a specific spatial justification for Watt's incarceration (see Figure 1). He must be locked into the waiting room to prevent him accessing the booking office and, most importantly, the 'sanctum' of stationmaster Mr Gorman (*W*: 198).

When Watt is found the next morning lying on the waiting-room floor, having been injured by another railway employee's overzealous opening of the waiting-

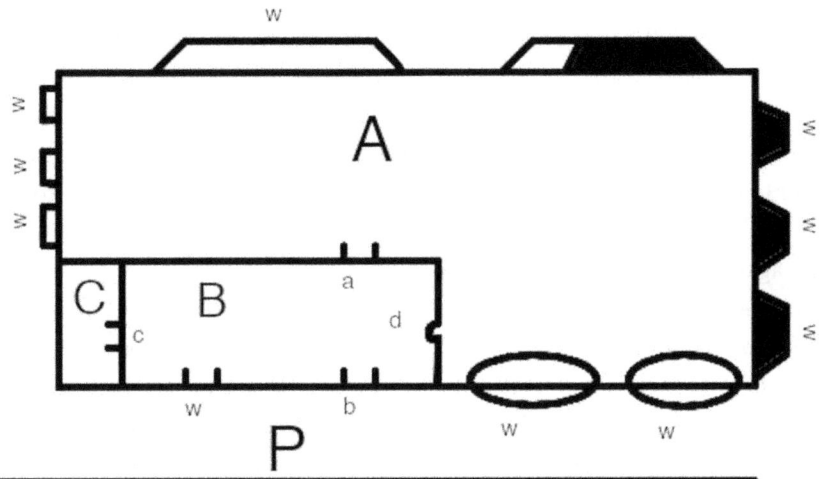

Figure 1 Beckett's second sketch of the railway station in *Watt* NB 6 (HRC SB MS 7/3/56): A marks the waiting room; B the booking office; C the stationmaster's sanctum; and P the platform. The lowercase a, b, c and d denote the doors of the booking office, while w marks the windows.

room door, the first instinct of Mr Gorman is to call for a policeman rather than a doctor. Indeed, Mr Gorman is part of a series of Beckettian authority figures who control characters' movements by ordering them to '[h]old on there' and '[m]ove on', as Belacqua is told to do by the Civic Guard in *Dream* (*D*: 226). Or, as the Civic Guard in *Murphy* puts it: 'Howlt on there, youze […]. Come back in here owwathat. […] Move on' (*Mu*: 29–30). For Rancière, the term 'police' designates not just these officers of the peace but a system of political distinction which identifies some members of society as having no share in the social order.[11] The reaction of other users of the train station clearly marks Watt as one such figure.

The stationmaster, Mr Gorman, is extremely perturbed by Watt's presence, as evidenced by his unhabitual spitting and impatience. As primary authority over the social space of the station, Mr Gorman is more concerned about 'soiling the floor' than he is about the injured Watt (*W*: 209). Similarly, he is more worried about the state of Mr Case's copy of Æ's *Songs by the Way* than he is about Watt's health: 'Mr Case picked his way, to where Watt lay. Bending he scraped, with

---

[11] 'The police is, essentially, the law, generally implicit, that defines a party's share or lack of it' ['qui définit la part ou l'absence de part des parties'] (Rancière 1999: 29; Rancière 1995: 52).

his book, a little mire from the face. Oh, you'll spoil your nice book, cried Mr Gorman' (*W*: 210). Indeed, the only compassion shown to the bleeding Watt is by Cack-faced Miller, another outsider who never talks to any of the other passengers. Miller 'knelt down beside Watt and inserted his hand under the head. In this touching attitude he remained for some time' (*W*: 211), coming closer to the tenderness of Watt's embraces with Sam in the asylum than to Lady McCann's missiles or Mr Case's use of his book to avoid physical interaction. Here again, Beckett underlines Watt's position as an outcast.

Mr Gorman's behaviour presents a picture of a harsh, hierarchical social order. This is a world in which the class system is rigorously maintained, where even convicted criminals retain their former social status: 'You remember Grehan? said Mr Hackett. The poisoner, said the gentleman [Mr Nixon]. The solicitor, said Mr Hackett' (*W*: 5–6). But where precisely might someone like Watt find a place in this hierarchy? Mr Nixon believes it 'highly probable' that he is a 'university man' (*W*: 17). The gardener Mr Graves takes off his hard hat when speaking to Watt – as Mr Graves always does when conversing with 'his betters' – suggesting that Watt is not quite on the bottom rung of the ladder (*W*: 124). What is more, Sam's vicious differentiation of himself and Watt from the other patients in the asylum suggests a further class bias towards those belonging to a lower social stratum:

> No truck with the other scum, cluttering up the passageways, the hallways, grossly loud, blatantly morose, and playing at ball, always playing at ball, but stiffly, delicately, out from our mansions, and through this jocose this sniggering muck, to the kind of weather we liked, and back as we went. (*W*: 130)

Watt and Sam may be socially segregated in their confinement, but according to the narrator Sam, they still have a perch from which they look down on 'other scum'.

In spite of their friendship being the only source of any real tenderness in the novel, one of Sam and Watt's favourite pastimes is to feed rats with birds' eggs, frogs and even their own young, during which they agree that they come 'nearest to God' (*W*: 133). These acts of cruelty again undermine any attempt to read Sam and Watt simply as persecuted outsiders. However, outsiders they most definitely are – and for figures of authority such as Mr Gorman, such outsiders are best disposed of as soon as possible.

Watt arrives at a station empty of other passengers. From a narrative point of view, it is crucial that he stay lying on the waiting-room floor long enough for a crowd to gather when he is injured the following morning. The situation of people standing around and discussing possible courses of action while others lie suffering on the ground, rendered comic in *Godot* (*CDW*: 72–9), is here used to spell out the disregard – even disgust – of a group who cannot wait to get rid of Watt from the station. He rises from the ground to general hostility, headed up by his former attacker, Lady McCann, who underlines Watt's outsider status by asking whether he is a white man and commenting on his 'extraordinary accent'. The pronoun in her question '[i]s *it* a white man?' (*W*: 212; emphasis added; see Bixby 2009: 156) betrays a racialized politics which identifies Watt as an objectified outsider not even worthy of belonging to the 'same species' as herself, to borrow a phrase of Pozzo's in *Godot* (*CDW*: 24). She sums up the dawn events to a messenger boy:

> Return, my little man, said Lady McCann, to him that sent you. Tell him that —
> has been the scene of terrible events, but that now all is well. Repeat now after
> me. The scene … … of terrible … … terrible … … events … … but that now … …
> all is well … … Very good. Here is a penny. (*W*: 211)

This last action shows that whatever disruption Watt may have caused, the social order is close to being restored: as in 'The End' and *All That Fall* (1957), but unlike in *Godot*, the messenger boy gets his tip. The man ironically called 'our friend' has been sent on his way and will eventually end up in a psychiatric institution, where he will find a similarly marginalized companion with whom he can share his story. Meanwhile, Mr Gorman, carefully watched by his two subordinates, is free to enjoy staring out over the suburban countryside at 'nothing in particular' (*W*: 214). Mr Gorman has cleaned out his social space, but the world which he is left to reign over is disturbingly empty, with the narrative detachment of the final scene underlining the function of narration in the novel as 'a failed exercise in asserting the authority of the detached observer and the ability to speak for the Other' (Bixby 2009: 150).

Conclusion

In his depiction of Watt's two episodes of confinement, Beckett uses the figure of a marginalized inmate to stage his critique of a very specific kind of social order, albeit one that has been 'vaguened' beyond easy recognition. Through this important shift in Beckett's poetics, he shaped a new kind of politics in writing about the social alienation of confinement. What results is more than the normalized eccentricity presupposed by Matthew Winston's claim that *Watt's* discontinuities can be rationalized as 'a tale told by a madman'. Take, for example, the final pages of *Watt*, which are more gap-ridden than any other part of the novel, an aspect which Frederik Smith links to Beckett's reading of Swift's *Tale of a Tub* (2002: 41). Swift uses '*Hiatus in MS*' and '*Desunt nonnulla*' ['something is missing'] as rhetorical tools for his polemical text ([1704] 2004: 9, 117; emphasis in original). In NB 6 of *Watt*, Beckett uses a similar metatextual tactic, writing '(nonnulla desunt)' to create a gap in the conversation between two railway staff regarding Watt's situation on the waiting-room floor (HRC SB MS 7/3/100, qtd in Ackerley 2005: 244). This Latin phrase then becomes '(Hiatus in MS)' in the published text (*W*: 207). However, as Bolin rightly points out, Beckett goes further than Swift in the deployment of textual gaps. Swift's can be explained away through the conceit that what we are reading is the narrator's manuscript (Bolin 2013: 90–1). *Watt* fits no such schema, fragmenting into closing Addenda which are impossible to assign to any one narrative voice. Similarly, Beckett goes beyond *A Tale*'s use of a mad narrator, formerly an inmate of Bethlem, whose madness would explain the eccentricity of the text.

The lack of any such focalizing key for the reader makes *Watt*'s politics other than the polemics of an other's voice. While the novel's 'vaguened' landscape brings to mind Beckett's 1938 claim in a review of a poetry collection by Denis Devlin that 'art has nothing to do with clarity, does not dabble in the clear and does not make clear', the politics which result are far from vague (*Dis*: 94). This is a writer accepting what Murphy never could – that the 'little world' of mental alienation is not to be represented using rational narrative structures, such as those associated with realist form. This poetics of missing parts would bear significant fruit after the Second World War, when Beckett continued to produce various forms of closed space while steering clear of the representational politics involved in portraying recognizable institutions of coercive confinement.

4

'Undoing' Confinement

'The End', 'The Expelled', *Molloy*, *Malone Dies*

Watt is a good example of Beckett's 'vaguening' of coercive confinement: in the English text, the asylum identifiable as Bethlem in *Murphy* is reimagined as a space foreign to both Dublin and London; in the French translation, this becomes even more vague in Beckett's use of the word 'pavillon' to translate the space of confinement even further away from its source. However, bearing in mind Beckett's own admonition to literary critics that '[t]he danger is in the neatness of identifications' (*Dis*: 19), this chapter is attentive to those instances of spatial 'undoing' which demonstrate a wider variety of compositional strategies than the word 'vaguening' suggests.

The term 'undoing' was introduced to the critical field by S. E. Gontarski's *Intent of Undoing* (1985) and has proved a durable concept for Beckett critics analysing his poetics.[1] Like Pountney, Gontarski based his research on the pre-publication manuscripts of Beckett's performance texts, developing an influential analytic model according to which concrete details are progressively erased from successive drafts. Gontarski notes that

> the plays most often emerge from and rest on a realistic and traditional substructure, against which the final work develops dialectically. While Beckett labors to undo that traditional structure and realistic content, he never wholly does so. The final work retains those originary tracings and is virtually a palimpsest. (1985: 2)

---

[1] In a recent collection of essays on Beckett, Gontarski's term is used by five of the thirty-five contributors (Herren 2014: 248; Nixon 2014: 300; Rabaté 2014: 141; Riquelme 2014: 404; Van Hulle 2014: 307, 309, 312, 315) and his book is referenced by two others (Maude 2014: 52; Slote 2014: 62).

Whereas 'vaguening' suggests a fixed 'policy' of removing detail in the drafting process (Pountney 1988: 149), 'undoing' pays attention to the dual dynamic of addition and subtraction. As Gontarski puts it: 'Beckett's creative process is marked not only by gestation, by accretion, but by deletion – disappearance as well as appearance' (1985: xiii). Nevertheless, following Gontarski's own emphasis on Beckett 'deleting detail' (1985: 17) in the compositional process, it is deletion and subtraction that have received greater attention in subsequent critical use of the term 'undoing'.

If 'undoing' focuses on what happens in the development of each work, 'vaguening' suggests a disintegration of detail that takes place across the entire oeuvre. Though the verisimilar representation of the asylum in *Malone Dies* (*Malone meurt*, 1951) bucks this trend, 'The End' (1954) and 'The Expelled' ('L'Expulsé', 1946) follow on from the 'vaguening' of confinement in *Watt*. This development of Beckett's aesthetics also has implications for the politics of his work. In Coetzee's words, the challenge for a writer representing spaces of confinement is to avoid being 'impaled on the dilemma proposed by the state, namely, either to ignore its obscenities or else to produce representations of them. The true challenge is how not to play the game by the rules of the state, how to establish one's own authority, how to imagine torture and death on one's own terms' (1986: 13). In a very different historical context to the apartheid South Africa to which Coetzee was responding, 'undoing' confinement provided Beckett with a means of establishing his own authority as a writer, critiquing the social order in the aftermath of the Second World War without confining interpretations within a limited sociocultural frame.

As markers of recognizable institutions decompose in Beckett's postwar prose, the relations between his narrators and society become increasingly oppressive. From the first line of 'The End' onwards – '[t]hey clothed me and gave me money' – these first-person narrators are persistently opposed to a threatening, unidentified 'they' who impose limits upon their freedom of movement (*CSP*: 78; see Slote 2011: 206; Cohn 2008: 129). This affects movement in open as well as closed spaces. Alain Badiou has divided the geography of Beckett's work into 'spaces of wandering' and 'closed places', opposing the 'closed space' of Malone's room in *Malone Dies* to the 'open, geographical space' of 'The Expelled' (2003b: 5–6). In many of the prose pieces composed during Beckett's self-styled 'frenzy of writing' following the war – during which he wrote four novellas, four novels and two plays – these spaces work in tandem (qtd in Knowlson 1997: 358). Beckett's first six works of prose fiction in French – the novellas 'The End', 'The Expelled', 'First Love' ('Premier

Amour') and 'The Calmative' ('Le Calmant') and the novels *Mercier and Camier* (*Mercier et Camier*) and *Molloy* – are stories in which wandering in open spaces is punctuated by different forms of enclosure, both self-imposed and imposed from without.[2] In 'The End' and 'The Expelled', such enclosure is identifiably institutional, even though the exact type of institution is not identifiable. In *Murphy*, the asylum acts as a key destination for both protagonist and narrative; in *Watt*, it serves as a turning point in the narrative form. 'The End' and 'The Expelled' use the barest shells of such institutions as a means of kick-starting their narrative journeys.

Strange spaces

In a letter to George Reavey following the completion of 'The End', Beckett compared his new text to Albert Camus's *L'Étranger* (1942):

> I have finished my French Story, about 45:000 words I think. The first half is appearing in the July <u>Temps modernes</u> (Sartre's canard). I hope to have the complete story published as a separate work. In France they dont bother counting words. Camus's <u>Etranger</u> is not any longer. Try and read it, I think it is important. (27 May 1946, *LSB* II: 32)[3]

The word count may be way off (the published text of 'La Fin' is about 8,000 words long; its translation only slightly longer), but the comparison between the two stories is instructive: firstly, 'stranger', as well as its derivatives, becomes an important word for describing othered experience in Beckett's postwar work, suggesting those who come from beyond a certain social group, as well as those who are kept confined in carceral spaces.[4] 'Humans are truly strange', the narrator of 'First Love' tells us (*CSP*: 29). But it is Beckett's protagonists who

[2] *Mercier et Camier*, 'Premier Amour' and 'Le Calmant' were written in 1946. *Mercier et Camier* was first published in 1970; *Mercier and Camier* in 1974. 'Le Calmant' was first published in 1955; 'The Calmative' in 1967. 'Premier Amour' was first published in 1970; 'First Love' in 1973. *Molloy* was written in French in 1947 and published in 1951.

[3] Beckett started writing 'The End' in English but drew a line across the middle of a page of his compositional notebook and continued in French (JBL SB MS 11/9/28r). I follow the Burns Library numbering. The first part of 'La Fin' was published in 1946 as 'Suite' in *Les Temps modernes*. An English translation of the full story was published in 1954 in *Merlin*, translated by Richard Seaver in collaboration with Beckett. The French version appeared in full in *Nouvelles et Textes pour rien* (1955). In 1960, Beckett revised the English translation for publication in the *Evergreen Review* but retained the credit for Seaver (details from Van Hulle 2011; Cohn 2008: 129; Slote 2011: 206).

[4] Beckett made more accurate calculations in his compositional notebook (JBL SB MS 11/9/back fly leaf v; /30v). Beckett would almost certainly have been aware of the publication of Stuart Gilbert's translation of *L'Étranger* as *The Stranger* in April 1946 (Lewis 1977: 18).

are marked as strangers in the social worlds they inhabit, following on from the interest shown by Belacqua and Murphy in outsiders who are locked up in institutions of confinement.

Secondly, in spite of his admiration of Camus's story, Beckett's postwar work uses very different aesthetic strategies when situating their alienated protagonists in relation to such institutions. Whereas the setting of *L'Étranger* is immediately fixed by reference to a specific institution – the Marengo Old Folks Home – the opening of 'The End', in which the protagonist is kicked out of an unidentified building, avoids any such contextualization (Camus 2005: 44). We know that the place is some sort of 'charitable institution', that it has other branches, that people die there and that it is staffed by men dressed in white (*CSP*: 80). Based on the cloister in which the protagonist waits for the rain to ease, we might assume it is a religious institution. Beyond this, however, any desire on the part of the reader to fix the narrative action in a specific, recognizable place is frustrated. In the earliest extant draft, the previous owner of the clothes which are donated to the narrator is described as having arrived at the institution as an outpatient before becoming an inmate (JBL SB MS 11/9/2r). However, this level of specificity is absent from the published text, where the predecessor's appointment is the less specific 'consultation' (Beckett 1954: 144; 2014c: 72). This is Beckett applying the lightest touch of 'undoing' to the details of his narrative world. While 'consultation' is slightly vaguer than 'outpatient', both the draft and the published text describe some kind of medical institution, but neither version specifies what kind. What is certain is that Beckett's spaces of confinement become stranger in his postwar prose, just like his characters who inhabit them.

'The Expelled' opens with such an intense focus on the steps which the protagonist is thrown down that the nature of the place they belong to is ignored. As in 'The End', this building is a nondescript residential institution, a fitting starting point for the protagonist's journey in a world where he is not in the same 'category' as those he meets (*CSP*: 52). As he leaves his dwelling place, he looks back to see the window of his former room 'outrageously open': 'A thorough cleansing was in full swing. In a few hours they would close the window, draw the curtains and spray the whole place with disinfectant. I knew them' (*CSP*: 49). In the eyes of the narrator, this is eviction with an authoritarian streak, fumigating a space that has been made unclean by his very presence, a practice also mentioned after the eviction of the narrator in 'First Love' (*CSP*: 29). 'The Expelled' continues with an interesting reference to the space itself:

I wasn't afraid to look, for I knew they were not spying on me from behind the curtains, as they could have done if they had wished. But I knew them. They had all gone back into their dens and resumed their occupations. (*CSP*: 49)

The indeterminate nature of the building is pointed up even further in the original French version of the story. Here, the 'dens' to which the staff members retreat are referred to as 'alvéoles', a word more commonly used to describe an anatomical cavity, such as the 'alvéole' [tooth socket] in *Malone meurt* (Beckett 2012b: 148; 2014c: 17; *MD*: 95). There is no mention in 'The Expelled' of the more explicitly institutional 'cellule' ['cell'], which Macmann inhabits in *Malone meurt* (Beckett 2012b: 132, 163; *MD*: 85). This is certainly a 'vaguening' of location, albeit in a different category to that described by Pountney and Gontarski.[5] If the 'realistic and traditional substructure' that Gontarski claims is standard in the composition of Beckett's drama was present in the conceptualization of this institution, it is not available to the reader. Rather, Beckett seems to have decomposed this particular in the process of composing something very close to the published text.

As Addyman argues, the 'loss of the sense of place' in Beckett's postwar writing is key to generating the portraits of displaced selves that populate his work from *Watt* onwards (2010a: 114). Upon being driven out of the cloister, the narrator of 'The End' expresses both topographical disorientation and an existential crisis:

In the street I was lost. I had not set foot in this part of the city for a long time and it seemed greatly changed. Whole buildings had disappeared, the palings had changed position, and on all sides I saw, in great letters, the names of tradesmen I had never seen before and would have been at a loss to pronounce. (*CSP*: 81)

Not only is the protagonist a stranger in this town, but the previously familiar urban space has become strange to him. The protagonist of 'The Expelled' reacts in a remarkably similar manner to his counterpart in 'The End' on being kicked out into the street: 'I did not know the town very well, scene of my birth and of my first steps in this world'; he feels 'ill at ease with all this air about me, lost before the confusion of innumerable prospects' (*CSP*: 49). On leaving Lulu/ Anna's residence, the narrator of 'First Love' is similarly lost: 'I was not sure where I was' (*CSP*: 45). The 'topophobia' of the narrators of the novellas does not consist in a complete detachment from place, but an uneasy relationship with it, central to which are the institutions of confinement from which they start their wanderings (Addyman 2010a: 125). With so little other contextual

---

[5] For Gontarski's discussion of the term 'vaguen' on TS 2 of *Happy Days*, see Gontarski (1985: 76–7).

information on offer, interpretations of Beckett's stories must take account of these confined spaces of initial eviction.

As well as their institutions of confinement, Beckett's novellas feature narrators questing to be confined in spaces such as a boat, bare rooms, a cloister, a cave, a stable and a cab. One way of interpreting these closed spaces is to read them in terms of a primal psychodynamics. To take but one example, we could see the narrator of the 'The End' as throwing himself onto the psychoanalyst's couch when he expresses his desire to be enclosed: 'I longed to be under cover again, in an empty place, close and warm, with artificial light, an oil lamp for choice, with a pink shade for preference' (*CSP*: 82). In the psychoanalytic critical paradigm, such spaces are a further development of the 'wombtomb' which serves as Belacqua's self-confined retreat from social interaction in the early prose. After having already used these intrauterine images of confinement in *Dream* and *More Pricks*, Beckett came across an influential account of 'the mythical womb' when reading Otto Rank's *Trauma of Birth* in 1935, part of the reading he did while attending psychoanalytic sessions with Bion (Baker 1997: 64). Beckett picked up some important images from his reading in psychoanalysis, such as Rank's remark regarding the 'tendency to identify the analytic situation with the intrauterine state' (1929: 6), which Beckett duly marked in his reading notes: 'Analytic situation identified with intrauterine one, patient back in position of unborn' (TCD MS 10971/8/34, qtd in Feldman 2006: 107).[6] In 1989, Beckett himself used the same image when describing his analysis with Bion, telling James Knowlson that the sessions provoked 'extraordinary memories of being in the womb, intra-uterine memories. I remember feeling trapped, being imprisoned and unable to escape, of crying to be let out, but no one could hear, no one was listening' (qtd in Knowlson and Knowlson 2006: 68).[7] The question is to what extent Beckett's engagement with psychoanalysis should be used as an interpretative paradigm for his creative work.

Both prior to and after Beckett's notes on psychology and psychoanalysis were made accessible to scholars, psychoanalytic readings have been influential in Beckett criticism. Phil Baker interprets the interdiction on the narrator of 'The Expelled' going out without wearing his hat as part of the story's treatment of the 'trauma of expulsion', which he connects to Rank's 'trauma of birth' (1997: 76–7). Using evidence of Beckett's knowledge of Rank's work, Matthew Feldman likewise

---

[6] Beckett also came across images of intrauterine confinement in Ernest Jones's *Papers on Psychoanalysis* (see TCD MS 10971/8/6, /11–/12).

[7] Elsewhere in his notes on Rank's book, Beckett wrote: 'Anxiety of child left alone in dark room due to his unconscious being reminded (er-innert) of *intrauterine* situation, terminated by frightening severance from mother' (TCD MS 10971/8/34, qtd in Feldman 2006: 107; emphasis added).

links the inability of *Murphy*'s Cooper to take off his hat to 'a corresponding inability to master the birth trauma' (2006: 113), citing Beckett's notes on Rank: 'The crown, noblest of all head coverings, goes back to embryonal caul, as also our modern hat, the loss of which in a dream signifies separation from part of one's Ego. "I'm back in the caul when I don my hat!"' (TCD MS 10971/8/35, qtd in Feldman 2006: 113; see Rank 1929: 91 n. 2). Shane Weller points out that Murphy's aversion to wearing hats comes from this same psychoanalytic source (2006: 186; see *Mu*: 48). Following these approaches, one could read the father's imposition of a hat upon his son in 'The Expelled' as an enforced arrested development, which does not allow the narrator to mature and adapt to society – an interpretation that would be supported by the fact that his boyhood companions 'mocked me' while he was wearing the hat (*CSP*: 48). However, even within the bounds of a Rankian interpretation, other readings are possible. In his analysis of mythical heroes, Rank connects their permanent wearing of hats to 'heroic *invulnerability*', interpreting this object 'as a kind of permanent uterus, which the hero brings with him into the world as armour, horny skin or helmet (magic hood), but which still betrays in the single mortal place, as, for example, Achilles' heel, how strongly even the hero was once purely physically attached to the mother' (1929: 107; emphasis in original). Now, Beckett could be seen as subverting Rank's analysis by keeping a hat on one of the most vulnerable heroes in postwar literature, dependent first on the care of the institution that expels him, then the cabman who shelters him. This would be in line with Beckett's 'detached intellectual irony' with regard to psychoanalysis and its forms of treatment (Nixon 2011: 41), evident in Beckett's ironic interjections throughout his Psychology Notes. But there is more to Beckett's hats than Rankian cauls.

Hats are crucial objects in his work, no more so than in 'The Expelled', in which the protagonist takes over half a page to describe the purchase, in the company of his father, of the first one he ever owned. As in Beckett's development of the asylum space, there is an autotextual aspect to such apparel, as can be seen in the reference of the narrator of 'First Love' to the storyline of 'The End': 'I wrote somewhere, They gave me…a hat' (*CSP*: 35, 78). Despite this seeming importance, the narrators of Beckett's novellas both draw attention to and ignore their hats, telling us, in 'First Love', 'I'll treat of my hat some other time perhaps' (*CSP*: 40) and, in 'The Expelled', that a description will be given '[s]ome other time, some other time' (*CSP*: 48).[8]

---

[8] Though there is a long additional passage on the hat in the manuscript draft of 'L'Expulsé', describing how his father made him tie with a piece of string in his buttonhole and predicting its eventual demise (HRC SB MS 3/6: 4v–6r), this passage ends without having described the hat itself in any detail and concludes by saying the narrator will describe it another time or perhaps never.

As noted by Julie Bates, the clothing that Beckett's characters wear 'signals their place in the world' (2017: 25). This is particularly true of hats. For instance, the manuscript version of 'L'Expulsé' states that before the narrator's father bought him a hat, he had only owned 'casquettes' [caps], an indication of his juvenile status (HRC SB MS 3/6: 4r). *Casquettes* can also refer to kepis, not the habitual garb of young boys but hats worn by French police and military personnel. Kepis are of significant importance in the novellas. In a detail which does not appear in the English translation, the policeman in the French version of 'The Expelled', who kicks the narrator off the street and onto the sidewalk, wears a 'képi', a piece of headgear which has a particular sociopolitical resonance given that it was part of the uniform of the French police in the postwar period and headgear of choice for General Charles de Gaulle, the paradigmatic authority figure of postwar France (Gibson 2010). The narrator of 'First Love' is convinced of the importance of this article of clothing but avoids wearing one himself: 'Kepis [...] exist beyond a doubt, indeed there is little hope of their ever disappearing, but personally I never wore a kepi' (*CSP*: 35). In the version of 'The End' published in *Merlin* in 1954, the narrator wears a 'British Kepi', the nationality of which disappeared when Beckett came to revise the story (1954: 148).[9] In a story in which so little is made explicit, a strange object like the kepi has connotations of political authority even as its meaning remains open. Seán Kennedy sees such objects as 'resisting interpretation, even as they provide condensed expression of repressed historical materials'. 'History has not disappeared', he argues, 'it just cannot readily be accounted for' (2015: 198, 188). In a similar way, the political dynamics of socialization did not disappear from Beckett's writing with his 'undoing' of institutional space. Instead, the sense of oppression increases as this 'undoing' develops.

Subscribing to the 'underlying assertion of the womb as paradigm' in Beckett's novellas misses out on the multiple interpretations they suggest (Baker 1997: 90). Beckett noted that for Rank '[w]hole circle of human creation equals attempt to materialize primal situation, i.e., to undo primal trauma' of separation from the mother (TCD MS 10971/8/35, qtd in Van Hulle 2008: 143; see Rank 1929: 103). Rank includes the artist as one involved in his model of 'undoing'. As we have seen, there is a difference between the psychoanalytic 'undoing' of Rank, who 'tended to reduce the complexity of the (psychic) world to one single source' (Van Hulle 2008: 163) and Beckett's forms of creative 'undoing', which lead to his closed spaces generating a multiplicity of possible interpretations. If one consequence

---

[9] The hat is a mere 'kepi' in *Stories and Texts for Nothing* (1967: 53) and *CSP*: 83.

of a widespread acceptance of the idea of 'undoing' in Beckett's poetics is the popularity of the idea that '[a]bsent in Beckett's writing are social and domestic relations' (Bates 2017: 24), then a more nuanced understanding of Beckett's poetics can lead to a new understanding of his politics of confined space.

'Freedom of movement': *Molloy*'s law

When accosted by a park ranger in the first chapter of their story, Mercier asks Camier: 'Can it I wonder be the fillip we needed, to get us moving?' (*MC*: 9). As Beckett's early postwar prose features a contrast between spaces of wandering and closed spaces, it is very frequently official figures of authority who impede their 'freedom of movement' (*Mo*: 129). For characters like Molloy, 'the unavoidable police constable' is always just around the next corner and this is indicative of a wider policing of these outsider figures by the social structures they inhabit (*Mo*: 31). 'On' carries an ontological imperative in late prose works like *Worstward Ho*: 'On. Say on. Be said on. Somehow on. Till nohow on. Said nohow on' (*NHO*: 101). In Beckett's prewar prose, it has a different kind of imperative force when spoken by one in official authority due to the particular social matrix in which the protagonist is reluctantly imbricated, as is emphasized in the heavy Dublinese of *Murphy*'s Civic Guard when he tells Neary and Wylie to '[m]ove on'. In contrast to this localized accent, the policeman in 'The Expelled' speaks something close to a pure dialect of the law: 'The street for vehicles, the sidewalk for pedestrians' (*CSP*: 51). But the sociocultural matrix is still crucial to Beckett's early postwar prose, however much it has been 'undone'.

When Molloy is accosted by a policeman for violating 'public order, public decency', he is reminded, like his predecessor in 'The Expelled', that there is a common law for all (*Mo*: 17). Like the novellas, *Molloy* features a threatening 'they' who form part of a society heavy on surveillance, as is evident when Molloy is released from the police station: 'They were watching me through the bars, I felt their eyes on me' (*Mo*: 23). As his later description of the town's justice mob demonstrates, 'they' do more than simply watch:

> Morning is the time to hide. They wake up, hale and hearty, their tongues hanging out for order, beauty and justice, baying for their due. Yes, from eight or nine till noon is the dangerous time. But towards noon things quiet down, the most implacable are sated, they go home, it might have been better but they've done a good job, there have been a few survivors but they'll give no more trouble, each man counts his rats. (*Mo*: 67)

Molloy's experiences of confinement spring directly from his status as an outsider to this social order. When he is first locked up in the police station, he is subject to what David Garland has termed 'penal modernism', a system of disciplinary correction developed in the late nineteenth century usually involving imprisonment rather than fines as well as a 'specialized differentiated' way of dealing with violators (2003: 48). The uniformed policeman and public 'official' ['fonctionnaire'] in the police station signal that Molloy is confined by just such a system, one of a few markers that can help the reader to roughly date the text to the twentieth century (*Mo*: 18; Beckett 2012c: 27).[10] How did Beckett arrive at the institutions which confine Molloy in the novel? And how can an examination of Beckett's creative process help us better understand the politics of his early postwar prose?

If his reports are to be believed, Molloy's social interactions are intensely oppressive: like Estragon in *Godot*, he reports being beaten (*CDW*: 11, 55); like Watt, the narrator tells us he has been spat at (*Mo*: 19). Molloy is confined twice, firstly in the guardroom of a police station for having no papers, secondly in a room with a barred window in Lousse's house, where, in an early draft, Molloy describes himself as a 'prisonnier' (HRC SB MS 4/6: 20r, *BDMP* IV). The degree to which the politics of such instances of confinement are 'undone' in *Molloy* can be fruitfully examined by comparing Beckett's novel to another writer of 'stranger' stories to whom he felt very close.[11] When reading Franz Kafka's *The Castle*, Beckett reported to Hans Naumann 'I felt at home ["chez moi"], too much so' (17 February 1954, *LSB* II: 464, 462). One can see why. Like Molloy and Moran, many of Kafka's characters find themselves in the midst of vast, inexplicable legal institutions.[12] Molloy, having been arrested and released without charge by the police – like Josef K. at the beginning of *The Trial* (2009b: 14–15) – and then suddenly, inexplicably released again from Lousse's house, would presumably subscribe to Kafka's statement in 'The Problem of Our Laws' that 'it remains a vexing thing to be governed by laws one does not know' (2015: 23). But there are differences in the forms of judicial oppression at work in the two writers' novels, and these forms are arrived at in different ways.

---

[10] Others include products such as Baume Bengué and *thermogène* wool (O'Reilly, Van Hulle and Verhulst 2017: 355–6).

[11] K. is repeatedly referred to as a 'stranger' in Kafka's *Castle* (2009a).

[12] See *The Trial* and *The Castle* as well as the short stories 'The Refusal', 'The Knock at the Manor Gate' and 'Advocates'. Beckett was aware of these two Kafka novels and some of his short prose (Van Hulle and Nixon 2013: 101).

Pondering his sudden release by the police, Molloy outlines the haphazard nature of the legal system to which he is subject: 'To apply the letter of the law to a creature like me is not an easy matter. It can be done, but reason is against it. It is better to leave things to the police' ['aux agents'] (*Mo*: 21; Beckett 2012c: 31). Molloy is of course tracked by his own 'agent', Moran, who claims to belong to a 'vast organization', though also he admits he and his messenger Gaber may be acting alone (*Mo*: 111). Because of this lack of information, it has been hypothesized that Moran is 'a sort of private detective' (Solomon 1967: 84). But there is little in the novel to indicate precisely what kind of institution Moran works for.

Crucially, there is also no evidence in the *avant-texte* which would help us solve this mystery. This proves that Beckett's process of 'undoing' was a complex affair. As shown by O'Reilly, Van Hulle and Verhulst, Beckett did remove 'some of the more explicit references to Ireland in the original manuscript' when drafting the French text of *Molloy*, such as Molloy's reference to a town starting with 'D'. On the other hand, he inserted into the French drafts units of currency (pounds, shillings and florins) and measurement (miles) which brought the novel's setting closer to his country of birth (2017: 353–5). Such balancing results in what Gerry Dukes, in relation to the topography of the novellas, has called the 'double exposure or montage' of Irish and French elements in Beckett's bilingual writing of this period (2000: 3). For Dukes, an important Irish element in this double exposure is the narrator's mention of the city's two canals in 'First Love', recalling the Grand and Royal Canals of Beckett's home city (*CSP*: 30). In the context of Beckett's 'undoing', it is interesting to note that this reference was added to the typescript (HRC SB MS 5/6: 7r), just as a reference to there being two canals in Molloy's town was added relatively late in the compositional process of that novel.[13] These instances go against a more general model of stripping away, with Beckett instead achieving an effect of vagueness and cultural instability by balancing different elements in different languages. While the overall idea of 'undoing' is helpful when studying Beckett's manuscripts, political readings of the texts must avoid the temptation to trace back vague institutional references to a 'realistic substructure' in the *avant-texte*. In the case of the organization to which Moran belongs, such a substructure simply does not exist in the drafts.

Based on manuscript research, Kafka could be classed with Beckett as another modernist 'undoer'. Mark Harman has used the draft versions of *The*

---

[13] https://www.beckettarchive.org/molloy/comparesentences/0562.

Castle to show how 'Kafka pruned back his fictional alter ego' K., removing biographical references and references to K.'s self-awareness in the course of the compositional process (2002: 325). Similarly, while writing *The Trial*, Kafka 'undid' references to the state, removing them from his description of policemen that Josef K. sees on his way to his execution (Robinson 1982: 142–3). While, according to Robinson, 'Kafka recognized, followed, and commented on the reality of the criminal law and theory of his day in <u>The Trial</u>' (1982: 128), there is no manuscript evidence that Beckett used a particular state institution which he then 'vaguened' when creating the police station of *Molloy* – not even the kepi of the novellas, with its associations of military and French state authority, makes an appearance. Rather, this seems to have been another form of confinement which was already relatively vague when Beckett sketched it out in his first draft.

Beckett was famously reported as saying that, in comparison to Kafka's alienated protagonists, '[m]y people seem to be falling to bits' (qtd in Shenker 1956: 1). Because of their indeterminate nature, the same can be said of the institutions these people interact with. As with his interest in mathematics, Beckett was interested in systems not because they are overarching and impervious to penetration; rather, he liked to describe such systems in states of breakdown, as when Molloy gives up on the many permutations he has tried for using his sucking stones: 'the solution to which I rallied in the end was to throw away all the stones but one, which I kept now in one pocket, now in another, and which of course I soon lost, or threw away, or gave away, or swallowed' (*Mo*: 75). In his letter to Naumann, Beckett stressed his uncertainty about the systematic nature of Kafka's portraits of alienation: 'I am wary of disasters that let themselves be recorded like a statement of accounts' ['qui se laissent déposer comme un bilan'] (SB to Hans Naumann, 17 February 1954; *LSB* II: 464–5, 462). Beckett wrote this letter less than a year after publishing *L'Innommable*, in which the radical undermining of any fixed place of confinement would be central to the 'disaster' which that novel's protagonist experiences. The various forms of 'undoing' in his postwar prose are important steps towards this radical disintegration of space.

'The charitable gesture'

While relations between narrators and the world they live in become more oppressive in Beckett's early postwar prose, it is also notable just how many characters try to help these protagonists. To take only the novellas: the narrator of 'The End' is offered food and lodging by a friend; the protagonist of 'The Expelled' is housed by the cabman he meets; that of 'First Love' by the prostitute who takes him home; and even the narrator of 'The Calmative' is offered a sweet by a little boy he meets on his journey. By accepting the charity of others, the narrators feel themselves sucked into an inescapable web of social relations, of which charitable institutions form a central part.

Due to the frequent imposition of charity upon them against their will, the narrators of Beckett's prose hold figures from such institutions in as low esteem as the policemen who bully them about. For example, in *Malone meurt*, Macmann is 'stunned' when he is addressed using the informal second person 'tu' in the House of Saint John of God: 'Étonné par ce tutoiement torrentiel, ayant jusqu'alors échappé à la charité, Macmann ne comprit pas tout de suite que c'était à lui qu'on s'adressait' (Beckett 2012b: 132).[14] 'Charity', according to an early version of this sentence, 'gives one the right to "tutoyer" people', enforcing a social gap ['Charité donne le droit de tutoyer les gens'] (HRC SB MS 7/4: 70v, *BDMP* V). There are other examples of the narrator's critique of institutional charity. In spite of Malone's claim that he was only 'going to' use the term 'prisoners' to describe the asylum inmates, both versions contain this term, which emphasizes the carceral nature of psychiatric confinement in mid-century Europe (see below). What is more, the numbering of inmates calls to mind the then recent confinement of prisoners in Nazi concentration camps, where many fellow members of Beckett's French Resistance cell Gloria SMH had been incarcerated (Knowlson 1997: 314; Morin 2017: 147–8).

In 'Le Calmant', the narrator conflates the police order and networks of charitable institutions by grouping together in a list an imagined Samaritan, Salvation Army member and police officer.[15] But it is Molloy who expresses the aversion towards institutional charity most eloquently:

> Let me tell you this, when social workers offer you, free, gratis and for nothing, something to hinder you from swooning, which with them is an obsession, it is useless to recoil, they will pursue you to the ends of the earth, the vomitory

---

[14] This is given the non-literal translation: 'Stunned by this *torrent of civility*, for he had eluded charity all his days, Macmann did not immediately grasp that he was being spoken to' (*MD*: 85; emphasis added).

[15] 'Je dis, Reste là, étalé sur ces dalles amicales ou tout au moins neutres, n'ouvre pas les yeux, attends que vienne le Samaritain, ou que vienne le jour et avec lui les sergents de ville ou qui sait un salutiste' [I said, Stay where you are, down on the friendly stone, or at least indifferent, don't open your eyes, wait until the Samaritan comes, or until day comes and with it police officers or, who knows, a Salvationist] (Beckett 2014c: 69; trans. based on *CSP*: 76). Beckett deleted these institutional references in translation.

in their hands. The Salvation Army is no better. Against the charitable gesture
there is no defence, that I know of. You sink your head, you put out your
hands all trembling and twined together and you say, Thank you, thank you
lady, thank you kind lady. To him who has nothing it is forbidden not to relish
filth. (*Mo*: 21)

But in the end, Molloy is not forced to digest the 'filth' that is offered him by
the woman he supposes to be a social worker. Instead, he throws her food and
drink on the ground of the guardroom. Likewise, when the narrator of 'The End'
becomes the target of political objectification by a left-wing orator, he folds up
his begging board and walks away.

He was bellowing so loud that snatches of his discourse reached my ears.
Union … brothers … Marx … capital … bread and butter … love. It was all Greek
to me. […] All of a sudden he turned and pointed at me, as at an exhibit. Look
at this down and out, he vociferated, this leftover. If he doesn't go down on all
fours, it's for fear of being impounded. Old, lousy, rotten, ripe for the muckheap.
And there are a thousand like him, worse than him, ten thousand, twenty
thousand – […]. Every day you pass them by, resumed the orator, and when
you have backed a winner you fling them a farthing. […] It never enters your
head, resumed the orator, that your charity is a crime, an incentive to slavery,
stultification and organized murder. (*CSP*: 94)

The narrator's considered reflection turns the tables on his antagonist: 'He
must have been a religious fanatic, I could find no other explanation. Perhaps
he was an escaped lunatic. He had a nice face, a little on the red side' (*CSP*: 95).
If the face-to-face encounters with institutional inmates are central to the
ethical questions posed in Beckett's writing of confinement in the 1930s,
then his postwar protagonists demonstrate that turning one's back is also a
legitimate political gesture, whether this be on Marxist rhetoric or charitable
support.

Charity does indeed lead to murder in *Malone Dies*, but not in the way the
Marxist orator in 'The End' might have expected. As they do in *Watt*, Beckett's
postwar protagonists frequently carry out unexpected acts of violence: Molloy
kills a charcoal burner, Moran an unidentified man by beating his head to a pulp;
even the bedridden Malone has a club mysteriously stained with blood. When
Mercier and Camier, having received the order to '[m]ove on' from a constable,
kill him by bashing in his skull, this is not presented as an inexplicable act but
as a furious reaction to the pain he causes Camier in arresting him (*MC*: 75–6).
Uhlmann, citing Foucault's account of charitable institutions as being part of a

network of social discipline, argues that this murder, as well as the axe-murders that close *Malone Dies*, in which two male assistants to the philanthropic Lady Pedal are killed by asylum keeper Lemuel on a day trip to a local island, is an act of resistance against an oppressive social order (Uhlmann 1999: 134–5; Foucault 1995: 212). Is Lemuel a rebel with a cause? Certainly, he is subject to the rules of the asylum and also has to enforce them, something he is not keen to do:

> One evening Macmann went back to his cell with a branch torn from a dead bramble, for use as a stick to support him as he walked. Then Lemuel took it from him and struck him with it over and over again, no, that won't work, then Lemuel called a keeper by the name of Pat, a thorough brute though puny in appearance, and said to him, Pat, will you look at that. Then Pat snatched the stick from Macmann who, seeing the turn things were taking, was holding it clutched tight in his two hands, and struck him with it until Lemuel told him to stop, and even for some little time afterwards. All this without a word of explanation. (*MD*: 105–6)

This use of epanorthosis – '[a] figure of speech in which something said is corrected or commented on' – shifts the responsibility for the violence onto Pat and could also be read as Malone's way of trying to conceal Lemuel's impending murders from his reader (Cuddon 1984: 224). Lemuel is unwilling to mete out corporal punishment, but beats himself violently and is 'subject to almost hypomaniacal fits of good-humour' (*MD*: 96). The murderous rampage which closes the book would therefore seem more likely to stem from the psychological pressure Lemuel is under, rather than being a conscious act of rebellion against an oppressive institutional system. Otherwise, why would Lemuel spare the injured Lady Pedal after murdering her two assistants?

Lady Pedal is certainly a normative figure who gains self-affirmation from her charitable work. In a nod to the hyper-rational social order which she represents, we are told that she is a member of society 'who was all right in her head and to whom life had always smiled or, as she had it herself, returned her smile, enlarged as in a convex mirror, or a concave, I forget' (*MD*: 111). By implication, her self-satisfied mental state is opposed to the overt mental disorder of the asylum patients. But it would be a stretch to see her as part of a network of charitable organizations involved in disciplining the inmates of the House of Saint John of God. Though she encourages the inmates to '[s]it back!' and '[s]ing!' (*MD*: 115–16), there is nothing in the novel to indicate that her charitable act is an effort to shape the behaviour of the inmates. Nor do the inmates respond to her orders: 'Nobody stirred' (*MD*: 115).

Malone decomposes

As the last of Beckett's novels to contain an identifiable asylum, *Malone Dies* is a fitting work through which to examine the final stages of the decomposition of recognizable forms of institutional confinement in his writing. To describe Beckett's poetics, Dirk Van Hulle uses the term 'decomposition', which is interesting with regard to the topographical disintegration that occurs in much of Beckett's postwar work, given that 'decompose' has its roots in the French verb *poser*, meaning 'to place'. Van Hulle cites Malone, a victim of physical decay himself, who claims to have 'lost the faculty of decomposing' the buzzing he hears, a buzzing caused by the sounds of the world merging into one (*MD*: 33, qtd in Van Hulle 2008: 169). Decomposition is here for Malone an 'analytical activity' which separates out elements of information and tries to follow them back to their sources in order to make sense of them (Van Hulle 2008: 172). Because the spaces of *Malone Dies* contain non-textual traces in the genetic dossier, it is necessary to combine approaches drawn from historicism and genetic criticism in order to analyse them.

Towards the beginning of the novel, Malone distances himself from fictional predecessors such as Mr Endon by describing his room: 'It is not a room in a hospital, or in a madhouse, I can feel that' (*MD*: 7). The fact that this needs to be pointed out to the reader demonstrates the extent to which such institutions became staples of Beckett's creative process. Just after this line, Malone hypothesizes that, were it not for the fact that he could feel himself dying, he may have thought he was 'in one of heaven's mansions' (*MD*: 8), repeating the term used to describe the asylums of *Murphy* and *Watt* but emphasizing its biblical echoes rather than the intertextual link to Boswell.[16] In spite of these narrative shifts away from the heterotopias of deviation which populate the earlier prose, the final section of *Malone Dies* is located unambiguously in an asylum, where the last of Malone's own fictional creatures is confined. In the manuscript notebook, this section is preceded by the note 'Bout MacMann' [end of MacMann] (HRC SB MS 7/4: 70v, *BDMP* V). As in *Murphy*, Beckett puts one of his characters in a confined space to bring an end to the narrative of *Malone Dies*:

> One day, much later, to judge by his appearance, Macmann came to again, once again, in a kind of asylum. At first he did not know it was one, being plunged within it, but he was told so as soon as he was in a condition to receive news.

---

[16] 'In my father's house there are many mansions' (John 14.2).

They said in substance, You are now in the House of Saint John of God, with the number one hundred and sixty-six. Fear nothing, you are among friends. Friends! Well well. Take no thought for anything, it is we shall think and act for you, from now forward. We like it. (*MD*: 84)

Eoin O'Brien has outlined the correspondences between the asylum in Beckett's text and the Saint John of God Hospital in South County Dublin, a psychiatric institution less than fifteen minute's cycle from Beckett's childhood home (1986: 240–5). However, it is not possible to trace a textual trail back to where this particular was picked up for inclusion in *Malone Dies*, though the level of descriptive detail in the novel suggests that Beckett, in line with his previous reconnoitring of psychiatric institutions for inclusion in 'Fingal' and *Murphy*, may well have made a trip there on one of his postwar visits home.[17] There is no surviving notebook for the early postwar fiction of a kind similar to the 'Whoroscope' Notebook, in which the written descriptions of Beckett's visits to Bethlem Royal Hospital form part of the genetic dossier of *Murphy*. However, the Saint John of God Hospital is nevertheless a crucial element in the book's composition. Bailey notes a similar issue when he argues that studying the Bible in Beckett's work necessarily takes us beyond the tracing of evidence in what Grésillon, discussing the benefit of knowing the exact editions that writers used when reading for their own work, calls a 'manière sûre' (Grésillon 1994: 216, qtd in Bailey 2010: 90). As my analysis of Beckett's notes on Boswell demonstrated, such information is extremely useful. But we must also be able to track the function of elements in the compositional process which do not provide a detailed trail as part of the chronologically reconstituted *avant-texte*. In taking into account the social function of an institution like the Saint John of God Hospital, as Wylie encourages the Civic Guard to do when opposing it to the Dundrum Criminal Lunatic Asylum in *Murphy*, we can enrich our interpretation of the closing section of the *Malone Dies* by tracking Beckett's production of space using a historicist approach which complements the genetic study of his written traces.

The hospital setting would have had an interesting resonance for the novel's earliest readers when it was first published in 1951 as *Malone meurt*, in which Macmann is found in 'l'asile Saint-Jean-de-Dieu' (Beckett 2012b: 132). Only the most dedicated of Beckett's tiny cadre of early readers would have recognized this as the same hospital mentioned by Wylie in *Murphy*, the French translation of which was published in April 1947 and which had sold no more than 285

---

[17] Beckett spent part of 1947 in Dublin and wrote the asylum section of *Malone Dies* in 1948 (Pilling 2006: 101; *BDMP* V).

copies by May 1951 (Pilling 2006: 100–1). Certainly, Francophone readers
would have been less likely to recognize the topographical details taken from the
surroundings of the Dublin hospital than their later Anglophone counterparts.
But given the strong international presence of the Order of Saint John of
God – with branches in France, the UK and the United States – the name of
the institution is likely to have had a similarly vague association with some
form of clerical medical care for the early readers of *Malone meurt* and those
of *Malone Dies*. The reference ends up working in a similar way to the request
of the lost narrator of 'The Expelled' that a cabman bring him to the zoo. 'It is
rare for a capital to be without a Zoo', he tells us, thereby keeping the possible
topographical interpretations of the story open (*CSP*: 53). Moran uses the same
trick when confronted by a farmer, who angrily accuses him of trespassing, by
telling him that he is on a pilgrimage to the local statue of the Virgin Mary: 'To
the Turdy Madonna, I said. The Turdy Madonna? he said, as if he knew Turdy
like the back of his hand and there were no Madonna in the length and breadth
of it. But where is the place in which there is no Madonna?' (*Mo*: 181). It may be
rare for a capital to be without a zoo or for a Christian, particularly a Catholic,
country to be without a Marian statue; it is equally rare for a Western European
country not to have a psychiatric institution named after a Christian saint. In
spite of having a very specific, local source, the function of the reference to the
House of Saint John of God becomes hermeneutically open in reception and
translation, taking us beyond the certainty of a one-to-one identification.

Beckett's varied methods of 'undoing' are again evident in his use of another
Dublin institution of religion, Glasnevin cemetery, which is mentioned by name
and receives a footnote in *Malone meurt* as 'un cimetière local très estimé' [a
highly regarded local cemetery] but is translated in *Malone Dies* as '*the nearest
cemetery*'. This reference appears in a poem written by Macmann to his lover
Moll: 'La main dans la main vers Glasnevin / C'est le meilleur du chemin' [Hand
in hand towards Glasnevin / It is the best of ways] (Beckett 2012b: 143). In the
iambic English translation, 'the nearest' could have easily been replaced by
the three-syllable 'Glasnevin'. That Beckett chose not to draws our attention to
the proper noun's absence:

> To the lifelong promised land
> Of the nearest cemetery
> With his Sucky hand in hand
> Love it is at last leads Hairy. (*MD*: 92)

Seán Kennedy rightly sees this topographical change between French and English versions of the novel as evidence of Beckett's 'undoing' in translation, part of the author's 'way of situating himself in oblique relation to his own personal and cultural history' (2005: 22). However, by using 'cemetery' in the English text, Beckett is actually returning to the vague 'cimetière' used in the earliest extant draft of the poem, which was then itself changed to the more specific 'Glasnevin', before being 'undone' again in translation (HRC SB MS 7/4: 79v, *BDMP* V). Along with the translation of 'l'asile Saint-Jean-de-Dieu' into English, which brings a topographical reference closer to home, this process of first making the cemetery reference more specific and only later subjecting it to 'undoing' in translation shows that Beckett did not have a fixed method of 'vaguening' place.

Another way in which Beckett decomposed the asylum setting was to make the staff who administer it lay rather than clerical (O'Brien 1986: 244). However, this decomposed space retains many details of the local scenery taken from its source. In outlining the panoramic view of the countryside surrounding the asylum, Malone recalls the critique of Romantic descriptions of landscape from the earlier asylum story 'Fingal':

> From here a fine view was to be obtained of the plain, the sea, the mountains, the smoke of the town and the buildings of the institution, bulking large in spite of their remoteness and all astir with little dots or flecks forever appearing and disappearing, in reality the keepers coming and going, perhaps mingled with I was going to say with the prisoners ['prisonniers']! For seen from this distance the striped cloak had no stripes, nor indeed any great resemblance to a cloak at all. So that one could only say, when the first shock of surprise was past, Those are men and women, you know, people, without being able to specify further. A stream at long intervals bestrid – but to hell with all this fucking scenery. (*MD*: 107–8; Beckett 2012b: 167)

As Sam Slote points out, the last line of the English translation is far more violent than its French counterpart: 'Une rivière qu'enjambaient de loin en loin – mais il s'agit bien de la nature' (Beckett 2012b: 167; Slote 2011: 210). This makes it possible to read the passage as a focused attack on Beckett's own prewar English prose, such as the similar passage describing the asylum grounds in 'Fingal'. In *Malone Dies*, it is not only the narrator who is decomposed but also a prose style centred on verisimilitude which Beckett had critiqued in the highly fastidious realism of 'demented particulars' in *Murphy* (*Mu*: 11). Having then marked an important turning point in the composition of *Watt*, it is fitting that an asylum should be at the centre of Beckett's two-fingered farewell to the 'fucking scenery' of realist fiction, which he had criticized since his time as a lecturer in Trinity College in 1930–1, where he focused his attack on Balzac for 'transcribing surface' (qtd in Le Juez 2008: 29).[18]

As well as killing off realism in the asylum of *Malone Dies*, Beckett put versions of his previous characters at risk of being killed off by Lemuel. A note in the second manuscript notebook of *Malone meurt* shows that Beckett was thinking of former characters of his 'series' of novels as Malone's narrative came to a close:

> Murphy
> Watt–Quin
> Mercier–Camier
> Molloy–Moran
> ~~Macmann~~
> Malone–Macmann (HRC SB MS 7/4, 100v, *BDMP* V)[19]

Having drawn an equivalence between Malone's relationship with Macmann and the relationships of his earlier 'pseudocouple[s]' (*U*: 7), Beckett drafted the description of the four inmates taken on Lady Pedal's excursion in the following pages of the notebook. All resemble former protagonists, two of whom are asylum-dwellers: the first inmate is found in a rocking chair, like Murphy, and we are told he is 'dead young' ['mort jeune'], recalling Murphy's own early death (*MD*: 112; Beckett 2012b: 174). The second dreams of 'that bloody man Quin again' and, like Watt, is described as having a strange accent (*MD*: 113; see *W*: 212). This accent gains him the nickname of 'the Saxon, though he was far from being any such thing' (*MD*: 113), which, in the Irish cultural context of the novel's English version, would correspond with the Nixons' presumption that Watt is university educated.[20] The third is called 'Mamier' in an early draft and owns an umbrella which features heavily in *Mercier and Camier* (HRC SB MS 7/4: 103r, *BDMP* V). The fourth echoes precisely Moran's description of Molloy in being huge and 'misshapen' (*MD*: 113; *Mo*: 118). Having rounded up these characters with a homicidal keeper, whose violence is already foreshadowed in the first draft by the remark that for Lady Pedal, the trip 'was going to cost her dear' ['allait lui coûter cher'] (*MD*: 111; HRC SB MS 7/4: 100r, *BDMP* V), Beckett may

---

[18] Van Hulle and Verhulst argue that 'realism à la Balzac is put to rest' in *Malone Dies* (2017b: 29).

[19] In another note, Murphy is paired with Mr Endon and Macmann with Samuel (an early name for Lemuel which recalls the narrator of *Watt*) (HRC SB MS 7/4: 152r, *BDMP* V).

[20] In *Malone meurt*, the Saxon speaks English in a Francophone milieu; in *Malone Dies*, he speaks a distinctly upper-class variety of Hiberno-English.

have considered numbering these versions of his protagonists among Lemuel's victims. But the four inmates are allowed to float on in their boat past the end of novel. Similarly, though recognizable institutions disappear in Beckett's writing after *Malone Dies*, his engagement with confinement continues, albeit in different forms.

Conclusion

In the first draft of *Molloy*, the eponymous protagonist remarks following his departure from the police station: 'Décidément j'ai du mal à m'arracher à cette prison' (HRC SB MS 4/5: 67r, *BDMP* IV) [Decidedly I had trouble tearing myself away from that prison]. On a thematic level, the same can be said of Beckett himself, in spite of the various forms of 'undoing' to which carceral spaces were subjected in his postwar prose. The varieties of 'undoing' analysed in this chapter demonstrate that institutional confinement, fundamental as it is to Beckett's work in this period, is similarly not simply a substructure which has been 'vaguened' in the writing process but an element which is open to decomposition and recomposition through strikingly varied compositional techniques. After the death of the verisimilar asylum in *Malone Dies*, Beckett stopped writing *about* 'heterotopias of deviation' and started to create an art *of* confinement in the theatre. My next chapter tracks the politics of that shift.

5

Political Pentimenti

Waiting for Godot, Endgame

A portrait of the playwright as a middle-aged man

Having put most of his young energy into forging a career as a poet, prose writer and essayist, the sum total of Beckett's theatrical creations by the time he started his 'frenzy of writing' in 1946 was a co-authored spoof of Corneille (*Le Kid*, performed 1931), the silent character Horace Egosmith in Mary Manning's *Youth's the Season-?* (performed 1931), a dramatic fragment in German entitled 'Mittelalterliches Dreieck' ['Medieval Triangle'] (written 1936; see Van Hulle and Verhulst 2017a: 30–5) and an unfinished play about Samuel Johnson called *Human Wishes*.[1] In 1947, Beckett completed *Eleutheria* in French, but this was never staged during his lifetime.[2] It was only with the stage premiere of *En attendant Godot* in 1953 that Beckett's writing finally found an audience in the spatial art of the theatre. Why did he make such a move?

Beckett's own responses in interviews point to the aesthetic possibilities of working with space. In 1961, the year he premiered the confined scenario of *Happy Days*, Beckett told a group of Swiss students that he wanted to create drama which 'makes a new start in a new room-space' (qtd and trans. in Knowlson 1997: 477). Confinement was central to the new forms of performance space Beckett created. In 1983, he is reported to have highlighted the importance of confined space in his early theatre aesthetic: 'When I was working on *Watt*, I felt the need to create for a smaller space, one in which I had some control of where people stood or moved, above all of a certain light. I wrote *Waiting for Godot*' (qtd in

---

[1] Mary Manning married in 1934 and then went by Mary Manning Howe.
[2] There have been a number of staged readings and one full staging of *Eleutheria*, in Tehran in 2005 (Tucker 2011: 239, 241).

Brater 1987: 176). He told Lawrence Shainberg: 'I wanted walls I could touch, rules I had to follow' (Shainberg 2019: 77). If the 'smaller' space of the theatre was a new and welcome creative impetus for Beckett, the space of the prose page often was not. To Colin Duckworth, Beckett contrasted his theatre writing with the prose he had been working on just after the Second World War: 'I began to write *Godot* […] as a relaxation, to get away from the awful prose I was writing at that time' (qtd in Duckworth 1966: xlv). With his early plays written closely together, it is unsurprising that Beckett's stage aesthetic is evident in this 'awful prose'.

On 26 September 1948, Beckett told Thomas MacGreevy that he had 'finished typing out Malone meurt (may he never come back)' (*LSB* II: 105). Very soon after, on 9 October 1948, he started writing *En attendant Godot* (BnF MS MY 440: 1r, *BDMP* VI). A recently published fragment in the second *Malone meurt* notebook, written after Beckett had finished his first manuscript draft of the novel, sheds light on the importance of space in Beckett's aesthetics at this key stage in his development. In doing so, it echoes the spatial concerns in Beckett's essay-writing of the period while putting into operation yet again the image of the veil outlined in his early writing. There is a heavy focus in the prose fragment on an image which would 'make appear the blank it covers', with a long paragraph simply subtitled '[i]mage' (qtd and trans. in Van Hulle and Verhulst 2017b: 306). This focus on invisible elements in a visual aesthetics echoes his contemporaneous definition of the painting of the brothers Geer and Bram van Velde, which he conceptualizes as an 'art of confinement':

> An endless unveiling, veil behind veil, plane after plane of imperfect transparencies, light and space themselves veils, an unveiling towards the unveilable, the nothing, the thing again. And burial in the unique, in a place of impenetrable nearness, cell painted on the stone of cell, art of confinement ['art d'incarcération']. (Beckett 2011b: 880; *Dis*: 137)[3]

An alternative draft translation of part of this text in Beckett's 'Été 56' Notebook has 'art of incarceration' instead of 'art of confinement', underlining the importance of carceral imagery in his aesthetic formulations in the postwar years (UoR MS 1227/7/7/1: 22v, *BDMP* III). The theatre would give Beckett a place in which to give these images of confinement his own spatial forms, as in the 'Petit Odéon' fragments (written 1967–8), abandoned theatre drafts which feature the concept: 'Réduction Espace' (UoR MS 2927: 13r, qtd in Nixon 2014: 294). Elsewhere in this same manuscript, it is suggested that this confinement be

---

[3] Beckett composed the essay in March 1947 (Pilling 2006: 100).

achieved by very thin sheets (UoR MS 2927: 6r, qtd in Jeantroux 2004: 210). This would have created a physical, theatrical version of the veil described in his aesthetic writing, suggesting a spatial beyond rather than a 'something or nothing' beyond language (SB to Axel Kaun, 9 July 1937, *LSB* I: 518). Beckett's use of invisible, offstage space would likewise be crucial to both *Waiting for Godot* (*En attendant Godot*, 1952) and *Endgame* (*Fin de partie*, 1957).

The impending concretization of such spatial figures in the theatre is evident in the *Malone meurt* fragment. Just before the narrator expresses annoyance at the way in which trying to make sense of life through self-denial 'gives an annoying impression of 2 people' (Van Hulle and Verhulst 2017b: 307), Beckett tried and then struck out the line 'je suis plus à mon aise dans la fiction de 2 endroits que dans celle de 2 personnes' [I am more at ease in the fiction of 2 places than in that of 2 people] (HRC SB MS 7/4: 112r, *BDMP* V). '[T]he fiction of 2 places' is an apt description of Beckett's own theatrical 'art of confinement', particularly because his heterotopic theatre spaces stress the relationship between the here and now of what is on the stage and the beyond 'of other places'. Joanne Tompkins defines heterotopic theatre as that which 'reflects or comments on a site in the actual world' (2014: 1). In Beckett's case, we can observe specific ways in which he uses the invisible otherness implied by visible theatre space to stage political themes associated with confinement.

Stage politics

'Not concerned with politics' (TCD MIC 60/59). 'Politics […] hardly mentioned' (TCD MIC 60/75, qtd in Le Juez 2008: 58).[4] While these comments read like many reviews of Beckett's own plays, they are in fact taken from the notes of his student Rachel Burrows at Trinity College Dublin, who assiduously copied what her young lecturer had to say about the plays of Jean Racine while Beckett held a post in the Department of French in late 1930. For the twenty-four-year-old Beckett, Racine's characters remain wrapped up in their '[s]olitary needs', unable to achieve any kind of 'mutual state' until the turning point which precipitates the dramatic conclusion (TCD MIC 60/57, /65): 'Then catastrophe + play ends' (TCD MIC 60/65, qtd in Le Juez 2008: 60). Indeed, he went so far as to label *Bérénice* 'most unracinian', due to the fact that the 'love interest [is] subordinate to [the] political' in Titus' rejection of the eponymous heroine and her rejection

---

[4] I follow the TCD numbering.

of Antiochus (TCD MIC 60/83, qtd in Le Juez 2008: 65). It was for this reason that Beckett somewhat unfairly labelled *Bérénice* a 'compromise', in which Racine 'makes the best of a bad job' (TCD MIC 60/86).[5] From the three-act *Eleutheria* to the two-act *Godot* to the one-acters and 'dramaticules' which followed, the form of Beckett's theatre would reduce until it was nothing but 'catastrophe', and in the play of that name in 1982, it did so in forcefully political terms. But Beckett's stage politics are not a late aberration; rather, they are fully present on his earliest stages. In *Godot*, the specificities of sociopolitical oppression are made 'concrete and particular' in the material connection between Pozzo and Lucky (McMullan 2010: 121). The first stage entrance in Beckett's revised versions of his debut play is made by Lucky, tied by a rope around his neck to his master Pozzo, who drives him on with a whip, on his way to sell him at market (*TN* I: 21).[6] So how does one align the anti-political stance in Beckett's early aesthetic statements with the forcefully political dynamics of his work?

Beckett's remarks on Racine's theatre are echoed in a well-worn critical paradigm for the Irishman's own writing. According to *New York Times* critic Mel Gussow, 'Beckett is the consummate artist, undeterred by sentiment, popular fashion, *politics*, theatrical rules of order or literary influences' (1969: 32; emphasis added). Such criticism is in line with Beckett's own comments on his writing, both public and private. When travelling through Nazi Germany before the Second World War, Beckett wrote in his diary that he wished to record '[n]o social or political criticism whatever, apart from what the fact as stated implies' (qtd in Nixon 2011: 122). To Lawrence Harvey in the early 1960s, he famously described himself as 'revolted but not revolting' (qtd in Knowlson and Knowlson 2006: 137). While such aversion towards direct political commentary is also an important feature of Beckett's use of confined space in his theatre work, the specific kinds of 'revolt' implied by the spatial 'fact[s]' of his oeuvre are far from being unimportant. Rather, they are crucial to Beckett's stage aesthetics.

Just as the various forms of confinement in the closed rooms of 'The End', 'The Expelled' and *Malone Dies* point beyond themselves to spaces of narrative wandering, so too do the different forms of physical restriction Beckett used to create images of confinement onstage point towards the multiple contexts which frame the dramatic action. In 'La peinture des van Velde' (1945), Beckett

---

[5] Beckett later revised this opinion (see SB to TM, 27 September 1953, *LSB* II: 407).
[6] In the original version of the play, Beckett had Estragon sitting onstage alone, with Vladimir joining him from offstage, but he changed this when directing the 1975 production in Berlin, putting both main characters onstage together from the start (Knowlson 1993: xiii).

praises Bram van Velde for presenting '[l]a chose immobile dans le vide, voilà enfin la chose visible, l'objet pur' [the immobile thing in the void, here at last the visible thing, the pure object] (*Dis*: 126). Beckett's turn to theatre allowed for a deeper engagement with the aesthetic problems involved in the creation of visual images. His stages frequently feature 'immobile thing[s]' in apparently empty spaces. However, as I have already shown with regard to his prose fiction, 'Beckett's wonted austerity as an artist […] has much to do with crafting spaces that are anything but empty' (Abbott 2004: 15). My argument regarding Beckett's theatre is that the relations between his plays and the world in which they exist prevented him from ever achieving the purity of image he aspired to in his postwar writing on art. Rather, the theatre provided Beckett with a necessarily impure spatial form in which he made striking use of what is unseen or half-seen. The heterotopic space of the proscenium-frame stage was central to Beckett's representations of elements – such as carceral spaces – that are 'undone' in his plays. The success of any political reading of Beckett's drama depends on constructing a feasible paradigm for the interpretation of such elements.

Pentimenti

It is perhaps no surprise that the two major early manuscript studies of Beckett's work were written by a pair of scholars, S. E. Gontarski and Rosemary Pountney, who both had experience in the inherently mutable form of theatre, in which one can step into a rehearsal room and see changes being made to the work in real time.[7] In his early postwar prose work, Beckett used multiple forms of 'undoing' to create atmospheres of social alienation which arise out of spaces of institutional confinement. Though these institutions would not appear on Beckett's stages, there are also key examples of different strategies of 'undoing' in his theatrical oeuvre, which become clearer if we study the text's theatrical epigenesis. As Jean-Loup Rivière puts it, '[l]'inachèvement n'est […] pas seulement un critère du texte dramatique, c'est plus précisément sa *définition*' [incompletion is […] not only a criterion of the dramatic text, it is more precisely its *definition*] (2005: 11). Therefore, the study of Beckett's work as a director can help us better understand the function of those carceral elements which are found in different layers of what Gontarski calls Beckett's palimpsestic texts.

---

[7] See McAuley (2008) and Heron et al. (2014).

In his preliminary notebook for the 1975 production of *Godot* which he directed in Berlin, there is evidence of Beckett's idea to project a '~~[f]aint shadow of bars on stage floor~~'. In the same notebook, he wrote: 'gen[eral] effect of moves, esp[ecially] V's [Vladimir's] though apparently motivated that of those in a cage' (UoR MS 1396/4/3: facing page 1, qtd in Knowlson 1993: xxii). He crossed the earlier phrase out and put an 'X' beside it, and the image of the cell bars did not appear in the production. But the structural concept of confinement carried over into another of his production notes as a means of giving 'form to the confusion' of the play (qtd and trans. in McMillan and Fehsenfeld 1988: 88). Having detailed the stage business of the opening sequence, Beckett outlined Vladimir and Estragon's tightly controlled movements using the same metaphor: 'Thus establish at outset 2 caged dynamics, E sluggish, V restless. + perpetual separation and reunion of V/E' (*TN* I: 187). The striped trousers and jacket, reminiscent of prison uniform, that the two actors swopped during the interval of this production are typical of the residues of confinement in Beckett's work as playwright and director: they gesture towards – but refuse to provide – a fixed institutional context for the play (Asmus 1975: 21 and Cohn 1980: 260–1).

The trace of the cell bars in *Godot*'s epigenesis can be regarded as a conceptual pentimento, following Dirk Van Hulle's six-part model of conceptual, structural, biographical, textual, translational and intertextual pentimenti. As James McNaughton puts it, such pentimenti 'remind[] us that the artwork is haunted by historical production' as they both 'interrogate and model the relationship between art and historical concerns from which it inevitably distances itself' (2018: 19–20). This term is borrowed from art criticism, where it describes the layers of a painting that the artist later painted over, but which still 'contribute to the colour and texture of the final result' (Van Hulle 2019: 39). For Paisley Livingston, pentimenti are 'options that were actively experimented with and then rejected' which constitute 'a world visited by the artist, but deliberately left behind' (2003: 99). By providing a model for interpreting those stage elements which are not immediately present to the audience, the pentimenti model gives us a way of taking into account the various layers of what Gontarski describes as Beckett's 'palimpsest[s]' without the teleological assumptions which come with the term 'undoing', which can suggest a reduction of the texts to 'distilled essences' (Gontarski 1995: xi). The pentimenti model also gives us a new way of conceptualizing the politics of Beckett oeuvre, particularly when a politically charged spatial configuration like confinement is repeatedly central to the meanings of this work. In this chapter, because of the political dynamics of carceral space, I will regard instances of the inclusion and subsequent rejection of institutional confinement in the course of the compositional process – such as the above example from *Godot* – as political pentimenti, whether they appear in the pre-publication *avant-texte* or the post-publication *après-texte*.

Doing and undoing 'la Roquette'

While Beckett was still conceptualizing *Godot* in terms of confinement as he directed the play in Berlin nearly three decades after its initial composition, some of the political pentimenti involving the use of carceral space were present before the play was published in print.[8] On 2 March 1952, Beckett sent a typescript of the play to his French publisher Jérôme Lindon, asking for help with a particular change he wanted to make:

> I would have liked to replace 'reformatory' ['la maison de correction'] [...] by the name of a well-known one, and cannot find any. Perhaps you could help me (no insinuations). If you find anything, make the correction yourself. If not, just leave it. (*LSB* II: 325–6)

As well as continuing the references to institutions of coercive confinement found in his prose works, this shows Beckett's awareness of the spatial specificity of theatre as an art form. His play would debut to a Parisian audience; it would therefore make sense to refer to carceral institutions they knew. Other examples of Beckett's spatial awareness can be found in *Godot*'s genetic history. There is a draft fragment in which Didi and Gogo pun on the verb 'pocher' [to sketch] and it has been convincingly suggested that this was written at the time *Godot* was being considered for performance at the Théâtre de Poche (Van Hulle and Verhulst 2017a: 49–51). We also know that Beckett later altered the text to better fit its performance conditions. When Estragon gave Vladimir directions to the toilet during *Godot*'s debut run, he guided him to the bathroom of the Théâtre de Babylone. In Beckett's 1975 production in Berlin, the line was modified and Vladimir was directed to the Schiller Theater backstage toilets (*TN* I: 124; Cohn 1980: 257). These instances, drawn from both the *avant-texte* and the epigenetic *après-texte*, demonstrate that Beckett was an artist fully engaged with theatre space. Furthermore, they signal a spatial particularity that disintegrates in his postwar prose, as when the narrator of the sixth of the *Texts for Nothing* (*Textes pour rien*, 1955) asks: 'Elsewhere perhaps, by all means, elsewhere, what elsewhere can there be to this infinite here?' (*CSP*: 123).[9] If on the stage 'it is always here' (Carlson 2013: 16), Beckett's dramaturgical 'heres' are not 'infinite', but multiple and particular.

---

[8]   Though *Godot* was not published in book form until the autumn of 1952, extracts from the first act were broadcast on French radio on 17 February 1952 (Van Hulle and Verhulst 2017a: 146).
[9]   This text was first published in French along with two other *Textes pour rien* in 1953 in *Les Lettres Nouvelles*.

In the case of the addition of the name of a Parisian carceral institution, it seems Lindon did indeed help. On the typescript Beckett sent him, 'Roquette' (a set of prisons in the 11th arrondissement which included a reformatory) is inserted in pencil – not in Beckett's hand – replacing the generic term 'maison de correction' (ML MS 5071/1: 6r, *BDMP* VI). The change in question occurs in the passage where Vladimir asks Estragon about his knowledge of the Bible:

> VLADIMIR: Did you ever read the Bible?
> ESTRAGON: The Bible … [*He reflects.*] I must have taken a look at it.
> (*CDW*: 13)

In the French version, there follow lines which Beckett cut when translating the play into English:

> VLADIMIR (*étonné*) [*astonished*]. – A l'école sans Dieu? [At a godless school?][10]
> ESTRAGON. – Sais pas si elle était sans ou avec. [Don't know if it was without or with.]
> VLADIMIR. – Tu dois confondre avec la Roquette. [You must be confusing it with La Roquette.]
> ESTRAGON. – Possible. [It's possible.] (Beckett 1973: 13–14)

Vladimir suggests that the education system might not be all that distinguishable from the criminal justice system, echoing a key concept of Foucault's disciplinary modern society, albeit in strongly comic form. Though this passage was cut in the 1954 translation, it remained in the French text Beckett revised for Lindon in the 1970s (Van Hulle and Verhulst 2017a: 103–5). So the 'la Roquette' pentimento has a double trajectory which once again complicates a one-way model of 'undoing': absent from the English translation, where the paring away of carceral detail corresponds with Gontarski's model, the topographical detail found in the French version, where the pentimento remains visible in texts published to this day, goes in the other direction, increasing specificity. Interestingly, when advising his Dutch translator Jacoba van Velde on the matter, Beckett suggested, having outlined that La Roquette 'corresponds to Borstal in England' ['correspond à Borstal en Angleterre']: 'If there's no such place in your fair country, you have only to put in the equivalent of reformatory' ['maison de correction'] (SB to Jacoba van Velde, 24 June 1953, *LSB II*: 382–3). Why did Beckett not follow his own advice when translating the play into English? Van

---

[10] Trans. based on Van Hulle and Verhulst (2017a: 178).

Hulle and Verhulst suggest that the English translation may have given 'too much realistic background' to the character of Estragon (2017a: 279). Yet he was not averse to providing such background in the French or Dutch versions. There are clearly diverse aesthetic strategies at work in different versions of this one text. While 'undoing' is undoubtedly central to Beckett's poetics, such layers of 'adding and redoing', whether suggested or implemented, must be acknowledged if we are to fully understand the political dynamics of his work (Van Hulle and Weller 2018: 243).

Analysing Beckett's late plays, Erik Tonning argues that Beckett's technique of 'abstraction' is very often 'at the service of a new concretion', that is, a specific kind of effect that Beckett is aiming at (2007: 118). While, as argued above, Beckett is not simply an 'undoer', it seems closer to the dominant process of Beckett's working practice to use the phrase of Theodor Adorno in the notes he took in preparation for a planned but unwritten essay on *The Unnamable*: 'Not abstraction but subtraction' (2010: 178; see also Rabaté 2010: 101). In the 'la Roquette' example, subtraction and addition work against one another in bilingual versions of the same work. Beckett's productions of *Godot* would follow increasingly formalized parameters, resulting in detailed stage diagrams which look like broken down versions of his later mime *Quad* (1984). For instance, when directing the 1975 production in Berlin, he sketched out the 'inspection place[s]' where his characters stop and examine the world around them (see Figure 2).

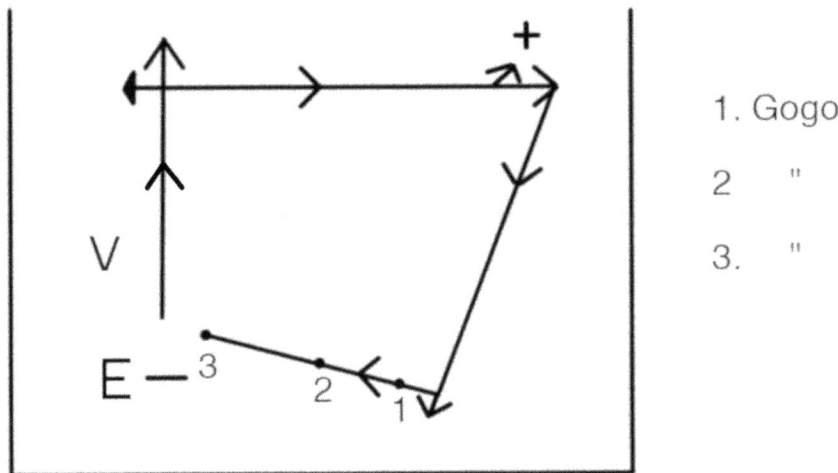

Figure 2 Beckett's stage diagram for his 1975 Berlin production of *Warten auf Godot* (*TN* I: 321).

Written out on Beckett's favoured graph paper, these sketches may seem on first glance to be mathematical exercises. However, the Beckettian stage is never the 'empty abstraction' which Lefebvre associates with the modern geometricization of space (1991: 338). Rather, as my examples of carceral pentimenti demonstrate, Beckett produces his stage spaces in self-conscious engagement with his sociopolitical context, frequently returning to institutions of confinement at important moments in this process of aesthetic spatial production.

'He'd punish us'

God's early appearance in the French text – albeit an appearance already under erasure as part of the phrase '[à] l'école *sans* Dieu' – was cut during *Godot's* translation into English, but the overhanging threat of punishment is important throughout the play. Pozzo punishes Lucky by pulling on the rope around his neck. At the start of the play, Estragon mentions having been beaten by a group (*CDW*: 11). In Act II, Vladimir suggests that the beatings – which Estragon has suffered again between the acts – are a form of punishment for 'whatever it was you were doing' (*CDW*: 55). When the boy first arrives, Estragon wants to punish him for lying about his place of origin (*CDW*: 48). The boy himself reports that Godot beats his brother, presumably as a form of punishment related to the work they do on his farm (*CDW*: 49). When Estragon suggests reneging on their engagement with Godot, Vladimir rejects this out of hand: 'He'd punish us' (*CDW*: 87). Remarkably, the notion of punishment was even more prevalent in an earlier draft, where a deleted passage demonstrates the play's connection with one of the best-known convicts in Western culture.

In Act II, just before Didi and Gogo roundly insult one another, there is a curious 'textual scar' which draws our attention to the play's drafts (Van Hulle 2014). '*Turning simultaneously*' towards one another, they start a question at the same time: 'Do you – ' (*CDW*: 70). But the question never gets finished. In the first draft, this question was spread over no less than seven pages of dialogue. Having decided to speak out the question word-by-word in unison, Didi and Gogo eventually manage to ask one another: 'Est-ce – que – [...] C'est.. la.. peine[?]' [Do you think it's worthwhile?] (BnF MS MY 440: 115r, *BDMP* VI). As Van Hulle and Verhulst argue, in a play where the characters repeatedly talk about hanging themselves, there are clear existentialist resonances to this passage (2017a: 237–45), particularly given the intertextual links between Beckett's question and Albert Camus's famous claim: 'Judging whether life is or is not worth living ["que la vie vaut ou ne vaut pas la peine d'être vécue"] amounts to answering the fundamental question of philosophy' (1979: 11; 1942: 15). While Beckett seems to have been influenced by Camus's portrait of social alienation in *L'Étranger* while writing his postwar prose, the above example shows that he considered having one of the central questions of Camus's philosophical work play a major role in a play from the same period. However, Beckett's interest in punishment went beyond that meted out to Sisyphus by the gods, who 'thought with some reason that there is no more dreadful punishment than futile and hopeless labor' ['qu'il n'est pas de punition plus terrible que le travail inutile et sans espoir'] (Camus 1942: 107; 1942: 161).[11] Beckett closes *Proust* with Schopenhauer's concept, as outlined in 'Additional Remarks on the Doctrine of the Suffering of the World', of 'the life of the body on earth as a pensum' (*PTD*: 93) or 'task to be worked off' (Schopenhauer 2000: 300). In 1979–80, Beckett re-read Schopenhauer's essay and noted 'life penal colony' in reference to the German philosopher's view of the world 'as a place of penance and hence a penal colony' (UoR MS 2901: 12v, qtd in Pothast 2008: 15; Schopenhauer 2000: 302). Didi and Gogo too see life as 'a place of penance':

VLADIMIR. Suppose we repented.
ESTRAGON. Repented what?
VLADIMIR. Oh ... [*He reflects.*] We wouldn't have to go into the details.
ESTRAGON. Our being born? (*CDW*: 13)

With this 'philosophical image' of life itself as a place of punishment, we are far from the specificity of Beckett's reference to 'la Roquette'. Indeed, one could argue that the notion of punishment becomes so vague here as to preclude any kind of political action. If the world is nothing but a punitive carceral institution, then, to quote Beckett in a very different context, 'we might as well go home and lie down', as the prospect for any kind of meaningful political action is dead.[12] Pozzo uses just such an argument when trying to deflect Didi's protest (the most vehement such moment in the entire play) that his treatment of Lucky is 'a scandal!': 'POZZO: [*To* VLADIMIR.] Are you alluding to anything in particular?'(*CDW*: 28). If, as Pozzo's comment suggests, the prospect of a just society is irrevocably doomed, politics becomes a meaningless matter of rearranging the deckchairs on board the *Titanic*.

---

[11] For more on Beckett's use of the figure of Sisyphus, see Verhulst (2019).
[12] Beckett used this phrase when rejecting permission for a stage adaptation of *All That Fall* and a film adaptation of *Act without Words I* (*Acte sans paroles I*, 1957) (SB to Barney Rosset, 27 August 1957, *LSB* III: 64).

The attempt to marry wide-reaching existential concerns in *Waiting for Godot* with the particularity of performance space has led to problematic interpretations of the play's relation to specific instances of carceral punishment. In his introduction to *The Theatre of the Absurd*, Martin Esslin, in one of the most influential interpretations of postwar theatre, connected what he identified as the existentialist absurdity of *Godot* to a production of the play in San Quentin Prison. Esslin's analysis is founded on the identification of a common human condition between the prisoners in the audience and the characters they see onstage – brilliantly summing up the heterotopic spatial dynamic of the play, one of the prisoners defines Godot as 'the outside' (qtd in Esslin 1983: 20). But Esslin's own argument is highly problematic, taking as its presupposition the 'unsophisticated' nature of the audience of convicts at San Quentin, who come to the theatre 'without any preconceived notions and ready-made expectations' (1983: 21). For Esslin, this is the noble savage behind bars, possessed of a keen insight which the 'highly sophisticated audiences in Western Europe' have lost (1983: 19). Esslin's book promises to restore that interpretative instinct to readers of the work of Beckett and his contemporaries, 'so that their relevance and force can emerge as clearly to the reader as *Waiting for Godot* did to the convicts of San Quentin' (1983: 28). While Beckett's plays did inspire the inmates of San Quentin to set up their own theatre company, these prisoners' interpretations of Beckett's work should be judged on their own merits, not in terms of their supposed unsophistication.

'Mon cher Prisonnier'

An examination of Beckett's correspondence with German prisoner Karl-Franz Lembke, exchanged between the writing of *Godot* and *Endgame*, can provide a much better idea of the politics of confinement in his work. In 1953, Lembke translated, cast, rehearsed and acted in a prisoners' production of *Godot* in Lüttringhausen Prison. In a letter of 1 October 1954, he told Beckett what an impact the play had had on his fellow prisoners, reporting that many critics had come to see them 'not act but live your play' ['pas jouer mais vivre votre pièce'] (qtd in Tophoven 2015: 12). Beckett was clearly moved, as can be seen in his response (of which only a draft survives):

> My dear Prisoner
> I read and re-read your letter. [...] For a long time now, more or less aware of this extraordinary Lüttringhausen affair, I've thought often of the man who, in his cage, read, translated, put on my play. In all my life as man and writer, nothing

like this has ever happened to me. To someone moved as I am, phrases come easily. But I can say calmly to you that I am no longer the same, and will never again be able to be the same, after what you have done, all of you. In the place where I have always found myself, where I will always find myself, turning round and round, falling over, getting up again, it is no longer wholly dark nor wholly silent. (on or after 14 October 1954, TCD MS 4662: 13v, *BDMP* VII)[13]

In this letter, Beckett sets up a parallel between the 'cage' of the prison cell and the 'dark', 'silent' and – importantly – unnamed space in which he exists but does not draw a direct equivalence between the two. This gap between the experience of confinement and its perception from without, already outlined in the failure of communication between protagonist and inmate in *Murphy*, is central to the politics of Beckett's writing for the stage.

Though Beckett never took up Lembke's invitation to come and visit Lüttringhausen, he was keen to help the German prisoner, as he told Patrick Bowles on 10 November 1955. Lembke, soon to be released, planned to tour *Godot* in the German provinces. After speaking of the financial difficulties Lembke would face, Beckett said: 'It would be a good idea [...], I would like to do it, to write a play for him alone, and give it to him. And say, here you are, you need not worry about the rights' (Bowles 1994: 28). Beckett did indeed send Lembke money through his German agents Fischer Verlag and made sure they authorized Lembke's production of *Godot* (SB to Helmut Castagne, 14 July 1956, *LSB* II: 636). He also asked Limes Verlag that Lembke be given 'a few easy poems' ['quelques poèmes faciles'] to translate for their multilingual edition of his poetry; this plan was quickly called off when it emerged that Lembke had embezzled the funds of the *Godot* performances, demonstrating another kind of gap, this time between the poetry of Beckett and Lembke's correspondence and the grim reality of the German's criminal life (SB to Max Niedermayer, 21 July 1956, *LSB* II: 638, 637).

Another of Beckett's draft letters raises once more the possibility of writing a play specifically for Lembke: 'As for the new play, I think we will see Godot first ["j'ai l'impression que nous verrons Godot avant"]. If it is ever completed, and if you stage it, I will come and see you as agreed' (TCD MS 4662: 30r, *BDMP* VII).[14] Between finishing *Godot* and starting his drafts of *Endgame*, Beckett had a number of false starts, one of which features strongly the

[13] Trans. in *LSB* II: 506, modified based on transcription in Van Hulle and Weller (2018: 51).
[14] Though this draft letter is unaddressed and undated, it is highly probable that Beckett wrote it for Lembke (Van Hulle and Weller 2018: 53).

theme of institutional confinement which underpins his correspondence
with the German prisoner. 'Louis & Blanc', an eight-page sketch featuring
two characters engaged in dialogue strongly reminiscent of *Godot*, is set in an
institution where the inmates are allowed out for fresh air at a rate of two per
day. In response to Blanc's claims that, because these 'airings' ['mises à l'air']
do not take place according to a regular pattern, there is 'no justice here' ['pas
de justice ici'], Louis contends that it is not the manner ['la manière'] of their
being temporarily allowed outside that counts – claiming that he personally
can be put 'under the snow for three weeks and then ten years under the belljar
["la cloche"] without for a second thinking of crying foul' ['crier à l'injustice'] –
and spends the rest of the dialogue calculating and giving examples to try and
convince Blanc of this fact (HTC MS THR 70/3: 6r, 1r, 7r, *BDMP* VII; trans.
based on Van Hulle and Weller 2018: 143–6). The *Godot*-like dialogue, the
lack of stage machinery and the all-male cast point to something that could
be easily staged in a male prison. Strengthening the hypothesis that this is a
prison play in the making, a 'guard' ['gardien', which also translates as 'prison
warden'] pops his head in to check on the two men (HTC MS THR 70/3: 2r,
BDMP VII). However, the piece remained unfinished and in spite of his close
affinity with prison inmates, Beckett would never realize the carceral space of
a jail in a published play.

While the space of the prison did not make it into *Fin de partie*, key political
concepts associated with the experience of incarceration were important to its
creation. Lembke foregrounded '[l]iberté' in his letter to Beckett of 1 October 1954
(qtd in Tophoven 2015: 11), a theme which Beckett also explored in his reply.
'Louis & Blanc', for its part, is a reflection on the absurdity of quantifying justice
by measuring a sentence in terms of weeks, months and years. Justice is also the
major theme of another piece written in 1952, between *Godot* and *Endgame*.
'Espace souterrain / Coups de gong' features a series of figures sinking into a
hole who are replaced by others who arrive from the flies, searching for the one
who has just disappeared. In the typescript version, 'L'Anonyme' describes this
system, by which one hole fills while a second empties, with the simple phrase:
'C'est justice' [That's justice] (UoR MS 2932: 1r, *BDMP* VII). As in *Molloy* and
the novellas, justice is here again an unexplained system, to be acknowledged if
not accepted.

Key political themes are again mentioned in the drafts of Hamm's final
monologue in *Fin de partie*. At one stage in the drafting process, as Hamm
takes off his hat and glasses, Beckett added to the declaration 'Egalité' one of
its corresponding terms from the motto of the French Revolution: 'Fraternité'

(TCD MS 4663: 39v, *BDMP* VII).[15] 'Fraternité' was later removed. But at no stage in the monologue's genesis does Hamm articulate the theme of Beckett's letters to Lembke – 'liberté'. Doing so would have been too celebratory and explicit for a writer whose favourite figure of freedom was the 'sadly rejoicing slave' of Dante's crew as imagined in *Molloy*, free only to crawl eastwards along the deck of a boat bound for the Pillars of Hercules (*Mo*: 50; see also *U*: 50). *Fin de partie* follows on from *Godot*'s allusions to the 'peine' of criminal punishment, but it does so through a more restricted spatial scenario. In one sense, this brings the play closer to the punishment of actual penal incarceration; in another sense, it brings it further away, in that Beckett clearly contemplated creating a prison play while composing the piece, but chose not to. Having experimented with a prison scenario in 'Louis & Blanc', Beckett stayed away from such spaces in his published plays, even when creating one whose characters he described as 'living in confinement' (SB to AS, 10 January 1958, *LSB* III: 94).

Endgame: 'Living in confinement'

When US director Alan Schneider suggested that *Godot* could be performed in the round, Beckett expressed his preference for a 'very closed box', referring to the rectangular space of a proscenium stage (SB to AS, 15 October 1956, *LSB* II: 659).[16] Beckett elaborated to Schneider that his preference for the proscenium was based on the fact that it made the audience feel that the characters were 'all trapped' (qtd in McMillan and Fehsenfeld 1988: 80). As well as developing further the theme of punishment, which Clov mentions in both his opening and closing monologues (*CDW*: 93, 132), *Endgame* intensifies the oppressive interpersonal dynamics of *Godot* by trapping its characters in a shared living space which is even more of a closed box than the outdoor setting of its dramatic predecessor. 'There must be maximum aggression between them [Hamm and Clov] from the first exchange of words onwards', Beckett told Michael Haerdter, his production assistant for the 1967 production of *Endspiel* in the Schiller Theater. 'Their war is the nucleus of the play' (qtd in McMillan and Fehsenfeld 1988: 205). In order to stage Hamm and Clov's 'war', Beckett favoured a particular form of closed space.

---

[15] In another draft, Hamm echoes Marie Antoinette when speaking of his 'paupers' (*CDW*: 96): 'When it wasn't bread they wanted it was cake' (HRC SB MS 3/5: 62r, *BDMP* VII).

[16] In spite of his reservations, Beckett did give Schneider permission to perform *Godot* in the round.

Beckett's letters show that he cared deeply about the size of *Endgame*'s living area. When, following the British and French premieres of *Fin de partie* in 1957, he was contacted about the possibility of another French-language production in Dublin, Beckett enquired about the 'stage dimensions' of the theatre (SB to Sebastian Ryan, 11 November 1957, *LSB* III: 70). As we can tell from Beckett's early reactions to stagings of *Fin de partie*, 'less [was] more' in this regard.[17] Having premiered in the Royal Court in April 1957, the production was brought to Paris and the Studio des Champs-Élysées, 'the smallness and intimacy' of which helped the play, according to its author (SB to A. J. Leventhal, 28 April 1957, *LSB* III: 45): 'The production has greatly improved since London and Blin gives now a very fine performance. The smaller theatre also helps' (SB to Donald McWhinnie, 7 May 1957, *LSB* III: 46). While working on the French typescript drafts of *Fin de partie*, Beckett described in a now famous phrase to Schneider that his new play depended on 'the power of the text to claw' (SB to AS, 21 June 1956, *NABS*: 11). Later on, he told Schneider that this visceral contact between text and audience was aided by the tight dimensions of the second staging: 'In the little Studio des Champs-Elysées the hooks went in', suggesting a political dimension to the onstage aggression (SB to AS, 12 August 1957, *NABS*: 15). Elsa Baroghel has analysed 'the centrality of subjection and power dynamics in *Endgame*'s paired relationships', labelling the interdependence between Hamm and Clov as that of a 'sadistic pseudocouple' (2010: 127). In a social art form such as the theatre, the confined space of performance makes the audience complicit in these claustrophobic power dynamics. If we recall Lefebvre's proposition that '([s]ocial) space is a (social) product', then we can better understand Beckett's insistence on a particular form of confined space for *Endgame*.

A/non-A

Though it is a central part of his aesthetics, Beckett does not have a monopoly on theatrical confinement. According to Anne Ubersfeld, '[a]ll theatre space is by its nature closed to the extent to which it opposes itself against that which it is not, closed off from the world, from the city' ['à la "cité"'] (Ubersfeld 1996: 81). Beckett emphasized this enclosure in his own productions, cutting his initial

---

[17] Beckett cited the phrase 'less is more', which he may have known from Robert Browning's dramatic monologue 'Andrea Del Sarto' and which later became the motto of minimalist architect Ludwig Mies van der Rohe, in his drafts for *That Time* (UoR MS 1639: 1r, qtd in Bell 2011: 35).

references to the audience and to Clov gathering sand from the seashore (McMillan and Fehsenfeld 1988: 193). As Anthony Uhlmann points out, 'Beckett wanted his actors to imagine a fourth wall in *Endgame*, at the proscenium arch: he was not using this so much as the standard theatrical device, but because he wanted his actors to be aware of their confinement, the limitations of their world' (2013: 180). In doing so, Beckett refashioned a spatial set-up seemingly far removed from the theatrical *avant-garde* with which he has so often been associated.

Beckett's redefinition of stage space came about through his use of the picture-frame proscenium stage – the 'closed box' he favoured for *Godot* – for which Ubersfeld provides a valuable model. According to her, in a realist play, the boundaries of the performance space suggest a familiar, imagined world beyond what is seen: 'the bourgeois salon opens onto another, imagined room, or onto the garden, and behind the garden is the street, the 16th arrondissement, Paris, the rest of the world' (1996: 55). Ubersfeld has in mind here the so-called '*théâtre de boulevard*', a popular form of drama with formulaic plots which is usually performed in an Italianate theatre with a proscenium stage.

In realist theatre, Ubersfeld's model involves the audience's imagined extension of the visible onstage world into the unseen offstage space. Equating the difference between what she calls the 'theatrical space within' and the 'theatrical space without' with the Lefebvrian concepts of 'perceived' and 'conceived space', Hanna Scolnicov observes that 'the theatrical space within is perceived directly and sensuously, and the theatrical spaces outside can be conceived as extrapolations of the concrete visible space on stage' (1987: 14).[18] Ubersfeld calls this the dynamic between 'an A zone and a non-A zone, such that at any moment, non-A is defined by its relation with A' (1999: 115; see Figure 3). Thus, in Ibsen's *Doll's House*, a foundational play in the realist representation of middle-class domestic life, the visible space of the Helmers' living room leads on to the invisible rooms such as the study, the entrance hall and the other rooms within the flat. But crucially, this space is nested within, and gets its meaning from, what is beyond the walls of the Helmers' flat: the other apartments in the house, the street, the town, the rest of the world. It is this spatial dynamic Beckett would subvert and challenge in *Godot* and *Endgame*.

---

[18] Scolnicov distinguishes between '*theatre space*', '[t]he physical space in which a performance takes place', and '*theatrical space*, which, in a theatre, might be confined to the stage alone or appropriate the aisles and balconies or even extend to encompass the audience sitting in the auditorium' (1987: 11).

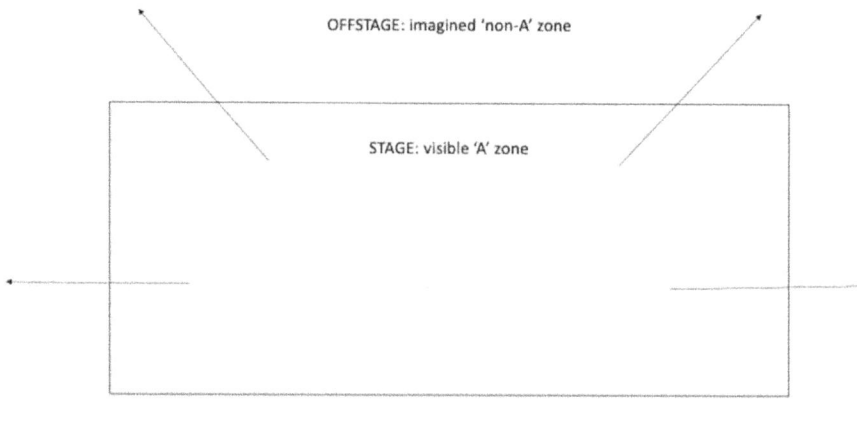

Figure 3 Diagram of proscenium stage space, based on Morash and Richards (2016: 38).

Before writing *Godot* and *Endgame,* Beckett had already constructed a much more blatant attack on the spatial dynamic of theatrical realism. As the sketch of a proscenium stage in the manuscript of his first completed play *Eleutheria* clearly demonstrates, this was written to be set in the 'closed box' favoured by writers as different in their aesthetic strategies as Ibsen and Beckett (see Figure 4). Instead of this stage sketch, the posthumously published text of the play begins with a long note on the piece's spatial set-up, detailing the 'dualist space' ['espace dualiste'] of two simultaneously presented 'A zones': a well-furnished middle-class salon occupied by the Krap family and the bare, sordid, rented room of their son Victor, a dropout whose rejection of the socialization involved in middle-class life – particularly his freezing-out of his fiancée – recalls that of his predecessor in prose Belacqua Shuah (Beckett 1996: 5, 2008: 14). The action switches between the two zones, with Act I taking place in the Krap salon and Act II in Victor's room. The silent presence of the characters in the unused room of each act renders this less a standard 'A zone' than an 'A-minus zone', missing as it is the dramatic dialogue standard in theatrical realism. By the third act, Victor's room has taken over the stage completely, with his family's bourgeois living space '*swallowed up by the orchestra pit*', reduced to a non-A space the prospective audience can now only imagine (Beckett 1996: 118).

There is a clear sense in which *Eleutheria*'s rejection of 'the conformity of middle-class life' goes hand-in-hand with its assault on 'the representational norms of the conventionally well-made play', including the literal marginalization of the realist domestic stage (Grene 2014: 127). Victor also represents an

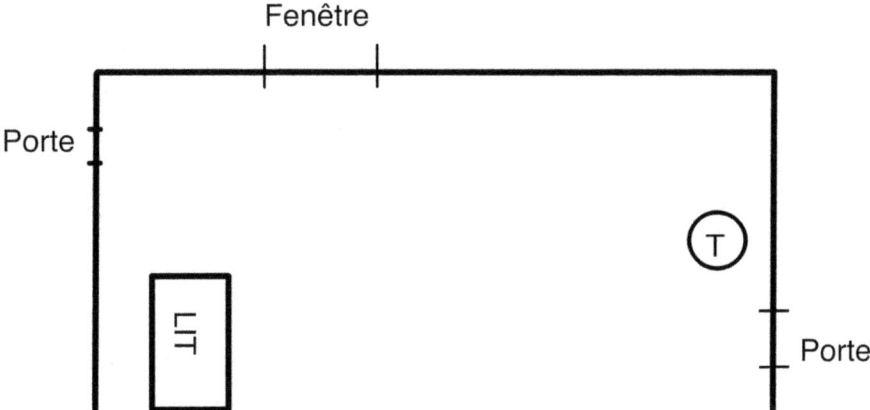

Figure 4 Beckett's sketch of a proscenium stage on the first page of the *Eleutheria* manuscript notebook (HRC SB MS 3/2: 1r).

authorial self-critique, insofar as the figures of self-confinement so crucial to Victor's attempts at self-definition echo both Belacqua's 'wombtomb' and Beckett's own correspondence of the 1930s. Like Belacqua and the later Murphy, Victor is a young man ill at ease with the world – significantly, he shares Murphy's address in the French translation of that novel.[19] Following on from Belacqua's encounters with inmates in 'Dante and the Lobster' and 'Fingal' as well as Murphy's idealization of Mr Endon, Victor, in a key passage, defines himself in relation to the insane and prisoners. Though Victor does at certain points distinguish between his own form of self-alienation and that of those behind bars, the fact that he reaches for incarceration as a source for his images is significant in the development of Beckett's stage politics.

Firstly, Victor accuses society of not accepting the gap between him and the world as they do with the mad: 'In the case of the madman ["du fou"], you accept it. But in my case, you don't. Why not? Unless I too am mad. But you don't dare hope for that.' He then goes on to describe his self-alienation in terms which recall the self-confinement of earlier protagonists: 'At first I was a prisoner ["prisonnier"] of other people. So I left them. Then I was a prisoner of myself. That was worse' (Beckett 1996: 147; 2008: 146). However, as rightly argued by the Spectator – who breaks the fourth wall and climbs on stage in Act III in order to make Victor explain himself – these attempts at self-definition are nothing

---

[19] In a trick of bi-location, Beckett added the Parisian street 'l'impasse de l'Enfant-Jésus' to Murphy's London address in translation (2013d: 9). This is the same street on which Victor's room is found in the Paris-based play (Beckett 1996: 18).

more than 'an avalanche of absurdities about *our* life and the life of the insane' ['aliénés'] (Beckett 1996: 146; emphasis in original; Beckett 2008: 145). There is nothing in the play which would lead us to believe that Victor has ever left his room in the impasse de l'Enfant-Jésus to visit those suffering in the adjacent Hôpital Necker or the nearby Santé Prison. Though the latter would become a point of intense interest for Beckett himself in later life, the development of his poetics would lead the politics of his work away from Victor's cringeworthy comparisons.

Nicholas Grene argues that *Eleutheria* constitutes a clearing of the stage before the pared-back minimalism of *Godot* and *Endgame*, with the latter in particular developing Beckett's assault on the domestic scenarios that populated (and still populate) the proscenium stages in Paris, London and Berlin where he directed his work (2014: 132). From the point of view of Beckett's politics, this play marks his final depiction of a young male character's self-alienation conceptualized in terms of the incarceration of others. In comparing his treatment at the hands of society to that meted out to the insane, Victor claims that his life is 'essentially other than yours' ['essentiellement autre que la vôtre'] (Beckett 1995b: 161; 2008: 145), describing those who interrogate him as 'strangers' ['étrangers'] (Beckett 1996: 144; 2008: 143). This estranged otherness would no more be granted to snotty-nosed rebels in Beckett's work, obsessed, as Victor is, with achieving freedom from the constraints of bourgeois family life. Instead, Beckett would construct his confined, heterotopic proscenium stages around an acknowledged gap between incarceration and its representation.

Hamm's home

The figure of Godot played a crucial part in constructing a vaguely defined, punitive 'non-A zone' in Beckett's debut play. *Endgame* goes further than this. By cutting references to the outer world in his own productions, Beckett intensified the sense of enclosure on which the play thrives. 'Beyond is the … other hell', says Hamm (*CDW*: 104). But it is essential that we as an audience do not identify the 'non-A zone' that Hamm speaks of, which would in turn help us to positively identify the 'hell' we see in front of us. In his lectures on Racine, Beckett emphasized that the French dramatist used background '[a]ll to create atmosphere, not explicating background of Balzac.' He went on to explain Racine's psychological portraits using a musical metaphor: 'Depth of character as overtone is to note' (TCD MIC 60/69, qtd in Le Juez 2008: 61). As a keen amateur musician, Beckett would have known that an overtone is not fully heard by the listener. Beckett's reactions to other productions of his plays show that he was determined to keep the political pentimenti of his plays functioning below the level of explicit statement in the visible 'A zone' of performance as well as avoiding any suggestion of an explicatory 'non-A zone'.

Beckett's drafting and subsequent abandonment of the 'Louis & Blanc' draft demonstrate the role institutional confinement played as a pentimento beneath the surface of the published text. But having discarded this paradigm himself, Beckett did not want to see others institutionalize the play's living space. In 1973, Beckett was contacted by German dramaturge Peter Kleinschmidt who, working with director Rolf-Harold Kiefer, proposed to set a production of *Endspiel* in a different space of institutional confinement, replacing Nagg and Nell's dustbins with nursing home beds. By doing so, Kleinschmidt and Kiefer emphasized what recently published manuscripts show to be the medical pentimento in *Endgame*, which could be termed one of Beckett's 'painkiller plays'. Beckett used a schedule of medicinal doses as a structural device in two of his unpublished dramatic pieces, 'Mime du rêveur A' [Mime of Dreamer A] (written 1956) and the 'Petit Odéon' fragments. Aside from May's offer to inject her mother in *Footfalls* (1976), however, he avoided making such features central parts of his published work (*CDW*: 400). In the radio play *Embers* (1959), when we hear the story of Holloway, a doctor, suggesting to Bolton that he give him an injection to ease his suffering, it still remains unclear as to whether this treatment is the motivation for Bolton's sending for him (*CDW*: 263–4). In the published text of *Endgame*, the motivation behind Hamm's request for his medication is clear but the medicine itself is absent. It is present, though unused, in an early draft entitled 'Avant *Fin de partie*' in which X (an early version of Hamm) gets F (an early version of Clov) to bring him a syringe filled with morphine, cocaine, cannabis and cyanide (UoR MS 1227/7/16/7: 8r, *BDMP* VII). In the published text, Hamm instead begs unsuccessfully on six different occasions for his 'calmant' (Beckett 2013b: 19, 24, 38, 50, 65, 91):[20]

HAMM: Is it not time for my pain-killer?
CLOV: Yes.
HAMM: Ah! At last! Give it to me! Quick!
    [*Pause.*]

---

[20] Though Beckett named one of his short stories 'The Calmative', it is 'The End' in which his protagonist takes this form of medicine (*CSP*: 99).

CLOV: There's no more pain-killer.
    [*Pause.*]
HAMM: [*Appalled.*] Good…! [*Pause.*] No more pain-killer!
CLOV: No more pain-killer. You'll never get any more pain-killer.
    [*Pause.*]
HAMM: But the little round box. It was full!
CLOV: Yes. But now it's empty. (*CDW*: 127)

If the second member of *Endgame*'s 'sadistic pseudocouple' frequently 'is […] deployed as a palliative device in order to distract the subject from his own existential sufferings without curing their cause' (Baroghel 2010: 128), here Clov is the opposite of such a human painkiller, bringing Hamm's attention to his own suffering in a cruel twist to the motif of dwindling supplies found throughout the play.

Having this suffering explained through medical props visible in the 'A zone' was anathema to Beckett. This explains his ferocious response to Kleinschmidt and Kiefer's institutional proposal:

> I am totally opposed to your idea of bringing <u>Endgame</u> up to date in an Altersheim [old people's home] or other fashionable hell. This play can only function if performed strictly as written and in accordance with its stage instructions, nothing added and nothing removed. The director's job is to ensure this, not to invent improvements. If and where such an approach is deemed incompatible with prevailing needs the play should be left in peace. There is no lack of others to fit the bill. (SB to Kleinschmidt, 24 August 1973, qtd in Stadelmaier 2014)

In spite of his objections, the production went ahead and placed what Hamm sardonically calls, when speaking of his parents Nagg and Nell, '[t]he old folks at home' into a representation of an actual old folks home (*CDW*: 96). The stage space of *Endgame*, with its offstage kitchen, servant–master relationship and familial drama, evolved, as another pentimento in the drafts shows, from a recognizable – if highly unusual – domestic situation, 'composed of a living room […] and a box room hallway converted to a kitchen'.[21] One late typescript contains clear identifications of Nell, Hamm and Clov in terms of their relation to Nagg: 'sa femme' [his wife], 'leur fils' [their son] and 'le factotum'

---

[21] 'Votre habitation, édifiée sur la falaise, comporte un living-room (X le présente, d'un large geste circulaire) et un ~~réduit~~ ^{couloir} transformé en cuisine' (UoR MS 1227/7/16/7: 14r, *BDMP* VII).

(TCD MS 11316: dp, *BDMP* VII).[22] These identifications are absent from the published text, where Hamm nevertheless speaks about the confined living space functioning as a 'home' for Clov (*CDW*: 110). By setting their production within an institutional version of the home, Kleinschmidt and Kiefer framed this residual domesticity with a context which the play's author could not accept, having already tried and abandoned his own setting of institutional confinement in the 'Louis & Blanc' draft.

The A.R.T. of confinement

Jonathan Kalb sees Kleinschmidt and Kiefer's production as part of a deliberate reaction in Germany against Beckett's own highly formalized 1967 production of *Endspiel* in the Schiller Theater Werkstatt (1991: 77). 'We have to retrench everything even further', Beckett told his German cast in 1967, 'it's got to become simple, just a few small precise motions' (qtd in Gontarski 1992: xvi). The 1984 American Repertory Theater (A.R.T.) production of *Endgame* directed by JoAnne Akalaitis, set 'in and around a subway carriage', followed a very different spatial aesthetic to Beckett's stage minimalism (Addyman 2010b: 306):

> A wrecked subway car rests on its rusted shocks. Glaring light bulbs dangle from an unseen height. Seven oil drums are off to one side. The pitted cement floor is awash. Fixed ladders lead up steep walls. A plastic sheet hides a mound of debris center stage.[23]

Natka Bianchini makes the point that, due to the death of Alan Schneider in a car accident earlier in 1984, Beckett had recently lost half of a two-man team who had monitored productions of his plays in the United States since 1957, setting the scene for a poorly managed confrontation. This took place mainly between the A.R.T. and Barney Rosset, Beckett's US publisher, who alerted his author to the production (Bianchini 2007: 139).[24] However, Rosset, like Beckett, never actually went to see the production himself.[25] With Beckett reportedly fuming in Paris, Akalaitis's fellow Mabou Mines member Frederick

---

[22] An almost identical list appears in handwriting on the earlier typescript OSU MS 29/5: 1r, *BDMP* VII.

[23] Kevin Kelly, '*Endgame* Takes Its Course', *The Boston Globe* (13 December 1984), sec. D:68, qtd in Bianchini (2007: 132).

[24] According to one newspaper article, the A.R.T.'s refusal to remove their dedication to Schneider was a sticking point in negotiations (McLaughlin 1984: 2r).

[25] Tickets were given to Grove Press Vice President Fred Jordan and Jack Garfein, who was himself producing *Endgame* in New York at the time (Bianchini 2007: 133).

Neumann acted as a go-between in the dispute. According to Neumann, Beckett focused his objections on what he had heard about the dimensions of the Loeb Drama Center's main stage, which is an expansive 28.65 metres wide and 9.75 metres deep ('Data Sheet'):

> Beckett said, 'It was meant for a small, tightly confined space.' That was the biggest thing he objected to, this enormous space. You never had the sense of Clov's enslavement or confinement. Beckett was not going to deny this claustrophobic tightness of space. [...] He just talked about it being a room, a small place where everybody was confined. [...] He said that with JoAnne's set there was no confinement. (qtd in Oppenheim 2000: 37)[26]

Almost three decades after its first staging, Beckett stresses here again the central function of confinement to *Endgame*. Why was this so important to him? For Grene '[t]he challenge of the play is [...] the way in which it imprisons an audience in that place, that world, without the let-out of symbolism or allegory' (2014: 130). By setting *Endgame* in a post-apocalyptic subway, Akalaitis gave her audience an escape from this confined 'A zone' by suggesting a 'non-A zone' prompted by the wrecked subway car visible onstage, presumably extending in the audience's imagination to include something analogous to New York's famous underground network. It is this escape from the hermeneutic confinement of the enclosed 'A zone' which ended up restricting its meaning. As versions of the play which experimented much more radically with the stage space caused no such reaction from its author, I contend that it was this literalist let-out in addition to the increased stage space that provoked Beckett's objections.[27] This would be in line with his own minimalist practice as a director as well as his protest against the earlier setting of the play in a nursing home.

Conclusion

'I open the door of the cell and go' (*CDW*: 132). Clov's carceral metaphor as he envisages his departure from the refuge is not the last such image in Beckett's canon, but it does stand as a clear move away from the representations of institutions of confinement in his earlier prose. Beckett also removed another

---

[26] Rosset described the production as having a large set (Rosset to Brustein, 10 December 1984, JBL SB MS 38/6: 2r).

[27] For examples of experimental productions of *Endgame* in the 1970s and early 1980s, see Kalb (1991: 77–8).

figure of confinement when translating the play, deleting Clov's song, '[j]oli oiseau, quitte ta cage' [pretty bird, leave your cage] (Beckett 2013b: 105; *TN* II: 266). As we have seen, Beckett developed his stage aesthetic in such a way that punitive carceral spaces are kept beneath the top layer of his palimpsestic texts, or offstage, in the 'non-A zone'. This is why the only mention of an institution of confinement within the text of *Endgame* emphatically lacks the certainty of a referent in the world outside the refuge:

> HAMM: I once knew a madman who thought the end of the world had come. He was a painter – and engraver. I had a great fondness for him. I used to go and see him, in the asylum. I'd take him by the hand and drag him to the window. Look! There! All that rising corn! And there! Look! The sails of the herring fleet! All that loveliness! [*Pause.*] He'd snatch away his hand and go back into his corner. Appalled. All he had seen was ashes. (*CDW*: 113)

In Beckett's two-act draft of the play, it is A (an early version of Hamm), who recalls receiving a visit in his 'cellule', making this another instance in which confinement was 'undone' by being displaced onto another character, in another time (UoR MS 1660: 50r, *BDMP* VII). In the passage as published, the asylum as trace of confinement retains the ethical imperative in Beckett's correspondence with Lembke – prompted by *Godot*; influential in the composition of *Endgame* – as Hamm literally reaches out to make contact with the madman, who is figured in Romantic terms as a seer. Beckett's letters to Lembke show how ethical questions connected to the politics of confinement are central to the genesis of these two major early theatre works. However, given the representation of carceral space at the level of pentimenti, Beckett's use of 'heterotopias of deviation' in the heterotopic space of the theatre is best described in terms of 'anethics', a concept to which I will return in Chapter 9. As it is not possible to analyse the politics of Beckett's 'fiction of 2 places' on the stage without taking into account 'that of 2 people' on the page, I turn now to the dismantling of confined space in *The Unnamable*, which is key to Beckett's process of learning to say 'not I'.

6

Learning to Say 'Not I'

The Unnamable

As Beckett's stage spaces became more confined between the country road of *Godot* and the refuge of *Endgame*, a novel written between these two plays subjected closed space to a thorough disintegration. In 1950, while struggling to have his early dramatic work staged in the theatre, Beckett began work on the first manuscript notebook of *The Unnamable* (*L'Innommable*, 1953), in which the narrator asks himself two questions: 'Où maintenant?' [Where now?] and '[q]ui maintenant?' [Who now?] (HRC SB MS 3/10: front fly leaf v, *BDMP* II).[1] As in the novellas, this narrator's persistent inability to identify the place from which he is speaking is intimately related to the disintegration of self. This self-fragmentation can be traced back to the fragment at the end of the second *Malone meurt* notebook, whose tone and subject matter suggest that it may be an early version of *The Unnamable* (Van Hulle and Verhulst 2017b: 253). Like the published *Unnamable*, the fragment opens by trying to 'say I', but Beckett erased this first attempt (*U*: 1): 'je suis, à chaque instant' [I am, at each instant]. The narrator then tries the conditional: 'Si je pouvais me définir à un n'importe quel moment donné je pouvais me définir totalement' ['If, at any given moment, I could define myself completely'] but completely fails to do so in the paragraphs which follow (HRC SB MS 7/4: 111r, *BDMP* V; Van Hulle and Verhulst 2017b: 306). Just as this failure foreshadows Beckett's 'fiction of 2 people', as in the struggles of the Unnamable to cohere with a first-person pronoun over the course of his narrative, so too does 'the fiction of 2 places' play an important role in a novel

---

[1] As Van Hulle and Weller point out, the incipit composed of questions 'is not in fact how the first manuscript version commences' (2014: 97). In their view, '[t]he text on this flyleaf is an addition to the text on the facing recto, which was probably written earlier' (2014: 98). 'Quand maintenant' was added to a later draft (UoR MS 1227/7/9/1: 1r, *BDMP* II).

which opens with the question '[w]here now?' (*U*: 1) and decomposes multiple narrative spaces in trying to answer it.

The opening questions of *The Unnamable* are reminiscent of the genesis of *Watt*, whose drafts begin with a list of questions from which Beckett derived his initial protagonist: 'who, what, where, by what means, why, in what way, when' (HRC SB MS 6/5/3, qtd in Ackerley 2005: 228).[2] This interrogative compositional strategy eventually resulted in a novel in which key narrative questions remain unanswered. The gaps in information regarding narrative location which are so crucial to *Watt*, 'The End' and 'The Expelled' become overwhelmingly large in the first-person narrative of *The Unnamable*, producing an epistemological dark zone which Beckett would later transpose onto his stage spaces in plays such as *Not I*. Unlike *Watt*, in which the introduction of first-person narration in Part III exercises an important gravitational shift in the narrative dynamic, *The Unnamable* never provides a narrative turn or a trail of intertextual clues from which we can deduce that the narrator is (or has been) in an asylum or prison. Though spaces of confinement are central to this destabilization of narrative in *The Unnamable*, its own multiplicity of confined spaces is far removed from the institutional heterotopias which were so important to Beckett's previous prose.

As a figure who declares himself to be 'in words, made of words, others' words' (*U*: 104), it is unsurprising that accounts of the crisis experienced by the Unnamable have often focused on his problematic relationship with language.[3] But Addyman has rightly contested 'the widespread assumption that Beckett's works move towards placelessness or pure displacement in the groundlessness of language', an assumption which is a consequence of an insufficiently nuanced critical model of Beckett's spatial 'undoing'. One of Addyman's main targets is what he calls 'the tendency to reduce everything to language' in poststructuralist critiques of Beckett's work (2010a: 113–14). In one of the scholarly works Addyman critiques, Steven Connor puts forward the argument that Beckett's move from the 'abundance of narrative detail' in *More Pricks than Kicks* to what he terms 'the last extremity of solitude' in *The Unnamable* – a 'solitude' paradoxically 'thronged with revenants' – carries with it a strengthened political charge (2007: 56–7). The power structures that result, he argues, 'may not be

---

[2] This in turn echoes Willoughby Kelly's desire to know 'the who, what, where, by what means, why, in what way and when' of his granddaughter Celia's relationship with Murphy (*Mu*: 13).

[3] See Brown (2011); Katz (1999: 95–124); Moorjani (1990); Moorjani (2008); Mathieu (2013); Kiely (2014); Mooney (2011: 119–60); Slote (2011).

exact or paradigmatic reflections of structures of power in the social world, but they are not wholly separate from them either' (2007: 188). So how, precisely, are the power dynamics of the novel structured? What kinds of politics are left when Beckett destabilizes both the 'who' and 'where' of narration?

This chapter will argue that the politics of *The Unnamable* are based on the resistance to interpretation of the novel's closed spaces within a fixed political paradigm due to the disintegration of space and self in the novel. To analyse Beckett's process of 'learning to say "not I"', I will focus on a feature of *The Unnamable* that previous commentators seem to have missed – its use of non-reflexive object pronouns in statements of self-expression (such as 'I'll find *me*' rather than the standard 'I'll find *myself*').[4] First we must track Beckett's use of this unusual grammatical feature back to his poetic work of the 1930s and 1940s, during which period Beckett learned to say 'I'.

'From self estranged': Learning to say 'I'

As is the case with Beckett's decision to write in French, his move from the predominantly third-person narratives of the prewar prose to the first-person narrators of the postwar prose is not a clear-cut shift but more 'a series of blurry zigzags' (Slote 2015: 114). In other words, Beckett's use of the first-person pronoun needs to be understood in terms of a gradual learning process during the 1930s and 1940s: a process which included experiments with the first person in prose work such as 'Ding-Dong' and *Watt*, poems such as the collection *Echo's Bones and Other Precipitates* (1935), the 'Petit Sot' poems (written 1938–9) and 'Match Nul ou L'Amour Paisible' (written 1938) as well as in his diaries, letters and essays. Before discussing an early example, in 'Serena I', of a pronominal form which plays an important role in *The Unnamable*'s later denarration of the first-person narrative voice, I will focus on a selection of Beckett's poetry, paying particular attention to the use of the first person in the 'Petit Sot' collection, the pronominal idiosyncrasies of his translations of Guillaume Apollinaire's 'Zone' (1912; Beckett's translation 1950) and the differing valences of translated pronouns in Beckett's 'they come' (1946).

---

[4] Even Daniel Katz, who puts *The Unnamable* at the centre of his excellent study into 'how Beckett disrupts the traditional function of the first-person pronoun as mark of the source of utterance', does not explore the function of such pronouns (1999: 8).

The so-called 'Petit Sot' collection is a series of remarkably unusual efforts to say 'I'.[5] There is one long poem entitled 'les joues rouges', which Beckett described as one of two 'straightforward descriptive poems (in French), of episodes in the life of a child' (SB to TM, 18 April 1939, *LSB* I: 657).[6] While 'les joues rouges' describes the hatred felt by the 'Petit Sot' [little fool] from a third-person perspective (qtd in Atik 2001: 10), there are also twenty-one shorter poems which are written from this figure's own point of view. Sixteen start with the first-person pronoun and four – very unusually for Beckett's poetry – open with the phrase 'je suis' [I am] (UoR MS 5479: 258–63).[7] These shorter poems are declarative rather than purely descriptive, with the figure of the 'Petit Sot' a crucial, shifting lens through which the rest of the world is imagined. As Beckett's use of the image of the 'wombtomb' in his prose of the 1930s demonstrates, images of confinement are central to the self-estrangement of his early protagonists. Confinement is also found in his poetry. Recalling Belacqua's self-made judas hole in *Dream*, the speaker of 'Le Grenier' stays close in his attic to a 'hublot' [deadlight], retreating into a space where '[p]ersonne ne me trouvera' [no one will find me] (UoR MS 5479: 261).[8] This use of an aperture of minimal size also recalls Beckett's attempt to create 'light in the monad' in *Murphy*, but in 'Le Grenier' the perspective has shifted and, in this first-person description of '2 places', light comes from without to the speaker confined within his hiding place.

This shift towards a homodiegetic first-person narrative in a confined space was also central to the composition of *Watt* during the wartime years. However, the effort to say 'I' in Beckett's poetry did not last for long after the war. Following 'Six Poèmes', composed, according to their author, between 1947 and 1949, the first-person pronoun disappeared completely from his poetic work.[9] Another key index of Beckett's shift away from the first-person pronoun is that none of his fifty-nine *mirlitonnades* (composed between 1976 and 1980; first published 1978) contain 'I', 'je', 'me' or 'moi'. Nor do any of the other poems composed between 1974 and 1989. While, as is clear in the case of 'Serena I', the poems of Beckett's first published collection *Echo's Bones* often register their self-

---

[5]   The authorship of these poems has been contested. They were initially included in an appendix to *CPSB* which the editors were then obliged to omit before the book went to press (see Pilling 2015: 198–209 and Van Hulle and Verhulst 2017c).

[6]   The other long poem has not been located.

[7]   The only other poem authored by Beckett which starts with 'je suis' is 'je suis ce cours de sable qui glisse' (1948), translated by Beckett as 'my way is in the sand flowing' (*CPSB*: 118).

[8]   Beckett translates 'hublot' as 'deadlight' in 'what would I do without this world' ('que ferais-je sans ce monde', 1948), through which the confined speaker looks for company (*CPSB*: 119).

[9]   'Six Poèmes' were first published together in 1959.

estrangement in terms of the gap between first-person speaker and environment, the later poetry is 'from self estranged' in a more literal sense, lacking as it does the pronouns associated with self-expression following Beckett's move away from saying 'I'.[10] As we shall see, *The Unnamable* follows a different approach to 'undoing' the first-person pronoun.

Saying 'I' in translation

While Beckett's own late poetry is 'not-I' writing, some of his postwar translations of others' poems do carry first-person pronouns over into English, notably his translation of Guillaume Apollinaire's 'Zone'. 'Zone' is a self-reflexive description of the physical and imaginative wanderings of a central male figure who refers to himself with both the first- and second-person pronoun, a pronominal disjunction which is central to the self-alienation in the poem.[11] Emphasizing Apollinaire's experience of institutional confinement, Beckett included a reference to the line '[q]ue lentement passent les heures' from the French poet's prison sequence 'À la Santé' in 'les joues rouges', suggesting a link between the Petit Sot's self-confinement in hatred and the involuntary carceral confinement of Apollinaire.[12] In Beckett's translation of 'Zone', closely following a rhyming couplet which invokes Apollinaire's period in prison on false charges of stealing the *Mona Lisa* in 1911 (during which time he wrote 'À la Santé') there is a line which Beckett translated in *Transition* (1950) as '[y]ou dare not look at your hands tears haunt your eyes' (Apollinaire 1950: 130). When this translation was republished for a 1972 deluxe edition, the final possessive pronoun was changed so that the line instead ended 'my eyes' (Apollinaire 1972: 19). Apollinaire himself had altered the subject pronoun of the same line when revising the poem at draft stage: 'Je n'ose plus regarder' became '[t]u n'oses plus regarder' (Apollinaire 1956: 43, 1033). In these changes, we can see both poets trying to pin down a set of pronominal forms that will best refer to a self estranged from itself. Later on in life, by which time he was living so close to the Santé Prison in

---

[10] Francisco de Terrazas, 'Sonnet', trans. Samuel Beckett (1958) (*CPSB*: 152). See also SB to TM, 18 October 1956: 'It is not easy to get through the ages from self so estranged and one overdoes the lair' (*LSB* II: 663). On 11 October 1956, Beckett had received a letter from the publishers of the *Anthology of Mexican Poetry* (1958), in which his translation of 'Sonnet' was to be published, which is no doubt why this phrase was on his mind at the time (Edith Greenburg to SB, *LSB* II: 666 n. 1).

[11] Apollinaire's speaker uses both 'je' and 'tu', the latter the informal form of second-person address (1993: 122).

[12] See Atik (2001: 10); Apollinaire (1993: 112).

which Apollinaire had been incarcerated that he was able to communicate with its prisoners from his window, Beckett quoted parts of this sequence in letters and recited it with his friend Anne Atik while walking outside the jail.[13] But it was Apollinaire's depiction of the mutable confines of a poetic voice, not the writer's time in a prison cell, which attracted Beckett's attention as a translator, providing yet another testing ground for a poetics of '2 people'.

In Beckett's postwar prose, learning to say 'I' also involved learning to say 'they', the first word of 'The End'. Examining the translation of Beckett's prewar poem 'they come' can provide insight into his sensitivity towards the different valences of this third-person plural pronoun between English and French as well as another notable exception to his general process of 'vaguening'. Beckett said the poem 'dictated itself' to him on 25 January 1938, three days after being discharged from the Hôpital Broussais in Paris where he was recovering from a near-fatal stabbing (SB to TM, 27 January 1938, *LSB* I: 596):

> they come
> different and the same
> with each it is different and the same
> with each the absence of love is different
> with each the absence of love is the same (*CPSB*: 91)

Judging by the dominant critical readings of this poem, the 'they' of 'they come' would appear to be far removed from the ominous 'they' of the postwar novellas. The poem is predominantly read in the context of Beckett's 'exceptionally tangled' romantic involvements, which involved three separate women at the time: the American heiress Peggy Guggenheim; a Dublin antique-shop owner Adrienne Bethel; and the French music graduate Suzanne Deschevaux-Dumesnil (*CPSB*: 375; see also Knowlson 1997: 284–6). In light of the long list of visitors in Beckett's letter to MacGreevy of 27 January 1938, which contains the earliest known draft of the poem, it would also be perfectly valid to interpret the referent of 'they' as the constant stream of well-wishers who had sprung to Beckett's aid while convalescing. Indeed, these two readings are not mutually exclusive, given that this group included his then lover Peggy and his future wife Suzanne. However, the most important aspect of this poem is the openness of 'they' beyond the confines of such biographical readings. Not only are Beckett's friends and girlfriends of 1938 'different and the same' but, by implication, the

---

[13] See SB to Kay Boyle, 7 January 1983 and 1 February 1983, qtd in Van Hulle and Nixon (2013: 233–4 n. 78); SB to BB, 11 September 1981, TCD MS 10948/1/665; Atik (2001: 119). For an account of Beckett's communication with the prisoners of the Santé Prison, see Knowlson (1997: 642).

absence of love from any relationship is both different (as the context within which one is lacking love from a particular individual changes) and the same (as lack of love itself is not substantive and therefore cannot be contrasted to other similar absences). In this light, 'they come' provides evidence of Beckett moving towards the substantially anonymized social structures of his postwar writing.

In translation, the pronominal plot thickens. With the French version, first published in 1968, sameness itself is rendered different, with the adjective 'pareil' appearing in feminine plural ('pareilles'), masculine singular ('pareil') and feminine singular ('pareille') forms:

> elles viennent
> autres et pareilles
> avec chacune c'est autre et c'est pareil
> avec chacune l'absence d'amour est autre
> avec chacune l'absence d'amour est pareille (*CPSB*: 91)

Even more so than the opening '[t]hey' of 'The End', the initial pronoun of 'they come' offers a broad range of interpretative options to its readers. But Beckett also used his poetic pronouns to create other kinds of effects. The contemporaneous poem 'Ooftish' (1938) uses an anonymized 'we' to attack a more specific target, protesting against particular medical, religious and social discourses surrounding acute physical suffering, what its speakers call 'the whole misery diagnosed undiagnosed misdiagnosed'. Having started with the imperative 'offer it up plank it down', the anonymous group demands: 'get your friends to do the same we'll make use of it / we'll make sense of it we'll put it in the pot with the rest', anticipating the virulence of the much less readily identifiable groups of speakers in later works like *The Unnamable* (*CPSB*: 59). 'Ooftish' specifically references the tuberculosis that had killed Beckett's uncle 'Boss' Sinclair shortly before the poem was written, whereas 'they come' is analogous to the writing Beckett did during and after his time working for the French Resistance: it is composed in the wake of an important life event from which it is unmoored by the hermeneutic and, in this case, grammatical, openness of the work in translation (Pilling 2006: 67). Though this is a rather peaceful autographical unmooring compared to the chaos which governs *The Unnamable*, it is an important instance of Beckett's sharp awareness as a translator of the different weight of pronominal expression between English and French.

Beckett himself was keen to downplay the sexual overtones of 'they come' but recognized this all-too-obvious reading would make it difficult to get the poem published in his prudish and censorious country of birth:

I sent 'they come' (translated by Péron as '<u>ils</u> viennent'!!) to <u>Ireland To-day</u>, where
the great purity of mind & charity of thought will no doubt see orgasms where
nothing so innocent or easy is intended, and reject the poem in consequence.
(SB to TM, 11 February 1938, *LSB* I: 597 n. 11)

Whoever 'they' might be, they certainly are not, according to Beckett's letter,
a group containing one or more men, as Alfred Péron's 'ils' indicated.[14] When
Beckett himself came to translate the poem into French in 1946, the first line was
'unvaguened' to 'elles viennent', specifying that the group referred to by 'they' is all
female. This translation of 'they come' shows Beckett working with the gendered
particularities of the third-person plural pronoun as it shifts between languages.
As we shall see, the first-person pronoun is also subject to the sociopolitical
dynamics of (mis-)translation in *The Unnamable*.

Deliberate mistranslation is central to Beckett's playful contributor's note in
Transition (1948), which has the author 'confess[ing] in a strong or rather weak
Dublin accent' with an 'original syntactical usage of his adopted tongue' that he
was writing in French '[*p*]*our faire remarquer moi*' (qtd in Slote 2015: 119). While,
as Sam Slote points out, this note, with its misplaced and incorrect pronoun – the
correct version would be '[p]our me faire remarquer' [to draw attention to myself]
(Slote 2015: 119) – draws attention to Beckett as a writer, the very particular uses of
pronouns in his translation of 'Zone' and 'they come' draw our attention towards
his extreme sensitivity towards the role of these pronouns in his writing. The same
is true of his poetry written in English which Beckett did not translate. Because of
the long and complex process of Beckett learning to say 'not I', it is necessary to
study one such poem, composed eighteen years before *The Unnamable*, in order to
understand the relationship between speaking self and confined space in the novel.

Finding 'me' in 'Serena I'

Written in 1932, 'Serena I' contains a pronominal idiosyncrasy that Beckett
would draw on over two decades later when translating *The Unnamable* into
English. While Lawrence Harvey identifies 'the substitution of the non-reflexive
"me", as direct object of the verb, for the reflexive "myself"' as 'a distinctive

---

[14] Péron helped Beckett revise the proofs of *Murphy* while he was in hospital and suggested that he
translate the novel into French (see Pilling 2006: 73 and SB to TM, 21 January 1938, *LSB* I: 589). It
has been persuasively suggested that Beckett's dissatisfaction with Péron as a translator of his poetry
led him to compose poems directly in French himself (Stacey 2015). I would like to thank Stephen
Stacey for sharing the script of this paper with me.

and significant stylistic trait' of 'Serena I', the implications of this pronominal disjunction for the politics of Beckett's work have yet to be explored (1970: 91). As the editors of Beckett's *Collected Poems* point out, the first instance of this pronominal anomaly in 'Serena I' can be read as 'a literal, if disorientating, translation of the French idiom "je me trouve"' (*CPSB*: 286). This is then echoed in standard, interrogative form three lines later:

> I find me taking the Crystal Palace
> for the Blessed Isles from Primrose Hill
> alas I must be that kind of person
> hence in Ken Wood who shall find me
> my breath held in the midst of thickets
> none but the most quarried lovers (*CPSB*: 16)

In the penultimate line of the earliest extant version of this stanza, sent with the rest of the poem in a letter to MacGreevy on 8 October 1932, Beckett makes a direct reference to the 'quiet breath' of Keats's 'Ode to a Nightingale' (Keats 1982: 281): 'my quiet breath in the midst of thickets' (*LSB* I: 131). Two other Keats poems also use the non-standard pronominal form – notably, they use it with the same verb as Beckett. In Book III of 'Endymion', when relating his enchantment and bondage by Circe, Glaucus states: 'Enforced, at the last by ocean's foam / I found me; by my fresh, my native home' (1982: 127).[15] The knight of 'La Belle Dame sans Merci' uses this form again, having likewise been seduced by an otherworldly female: 'And I awoke and found me here' (1982: 271). As in 'Serena I', there is a possible Francophone residue to the English used in 'La Belle Dame', particularly given the chivalric troubadour tradition's roots in France. However, as we will see below, it is specifically as an Anglophone grammatical feature that Beckett uses this pronominal disjunction to help further disintegrate the speaking self in *The Unnamable*.

More pragmatically, in terms of poetic metre, 'me', rather than the standard 'myself', keeps the tetrametric line of 'La Belle Dame' from slipping over into an ill-fitting pentameter, or a tripping anapaest. Unlike Keats's work, 'Serena I' was written in free verse, but it does fall into occasional rhythmic regularity, most notably in the six iambic tetrameters of the above stanza, which centres on Hampstead Heath where Keats once lived (Roe 2013: 155–6, 283–4). In doing so, it mirrors the dominant metre of 'La Belle Dame'. Keats's second residence on the Heath, Wentworth Place, which is situated between Primrose Hill and Kenwood

---

[15] Beckett refers to 'Endymion' in *Molloy* (*Mo*: 172).

House, was opened to the public in the decade before Beckett wrote his poem.[16] It is from Primrose Hill that the speaker of 'Serena I' has an unclear view of the Crystal Palace on the other side of the city. Beckett studied philosophy in the nearby 'grand old British Museum' – mentioned in the first line of 'Serena I' (*CPSB*: 16) – during the summer of 1932 and spent some time walking in the parks, including Hampstead Heath (Knowlson 1997: 161). Though it has not been possible to find any evidence of Beckett visiting Wentworth Place, it would not be surprising if he paid Keats's house a visit, especially given his professed admiration for the Romantic poet:[17]

> I like that crouching brooding quality in Keats – squatting on the moss, crushing a petal, licking his lips & rubbing his hands, 'counting the last oozings, hours by hours.' I like him the best of them all, because he doesn't beat his fists on the table. I like that awful sweetness and thick soft damp green [? richness]. And weariness: 'Take into the air my quiet breath.' (SB to TM, undated [April/ May 1930], TCD MS 10402/6, qtd in *LSB* I: 21)[18]

Beckett here shears Keats's line, lopping off the 'to' which subordinates it to preceding events in 'Ode to a Nightingale':

> Darkling I listen; and, for many a time
> I have been half in love with easeful Death,
> Call'd him soft names in many a mused rhyme,
> To take into the air my quiet breath (Keats 1982: 281)

Beckett does the same prepositional pruning when the line is used at the climax of 'Dante and the Lobster', making it appear again as an injunction to the self rather than a description of terminal poetic production (*MPTK*: 14).[19] As Nixon notes, Beckett 'used and adapted' this line as well as the poem's association of 'death' and 'breath' in *Dream, Murphy* and *Watt*, demonstrating the deep influence Keats had on Beckett's work while he was learning to say 'I' (2007: 70). Crucially

---

[16] The house was opened to the public in 1925. In 1931, a new building was erected beside the house in order to display a collection of books and other material relating to Keats ('History of the House'). This would have made the house an attractive prospect for Beckett to visit in 1932.

[17] Though there is no record of Beckett having signed the visitor's book, the records for the early 1930s contain very few signatures, suggesting that it is not a comprehensive record of visits made (Kenneth Page, Interpretation Officer, Keats House, email to the author, 27 January 2017). I would like to thank Kenneth Page for his help in this regard and Martina Pranić for her research assistance in London.

[18] Beckett's admiration for Keats continued on his deathbed, on which he recited lines by the Romantic poet (Pilling 2006: 230). For an alternative reading of the word marked uncertain in my transcription of the letter, see Nixon (2007: 71).

[19] As Christopher Ricks points out, the Keats line is in quotation marks in the first published version of the story (1993: 53 n. 8). See Beckett (1932: 236).

for my analysis, Beckett's framing of his admiration of Keats in opposition to the table-thumping of other Romantics in his letter to MacGreevy foreshadows the self-focused political dissent of *The Unnamable*, while the two quotations he uses in the letter – the first adapted from the personification of nature in 'To Autumn' (1982: 360) – emphasize the interdependence between such fictional selves and the spaces they inhabit.

Given the setting of 'Serena I' and its explicit reference to 'Ode to a Nightingale', I contend that Keats was the source of both the tetrametric metre of the third stanza and Beckett's use of the non-reflexive 'me' as a direct object pronoun. The three subsequent examples – 'I surprise me moved by the many a funnel hinged', 'then I hug me below among the canaille' as well as 'and afar off at all speed screw me up Wren's giant bully' – occur in a long stanza so metrically diverse that the saved syllables are all but irrelevant (*CBSB*: 16–17). However, in the short penultimate stanza, the focus reverts to the Heath and the iambic pattern with which it has earlier been associated: 'but in Ken Wood / who shall find me' (*CPSB*: 17). Such metrical constraint must be taken into account when considering the function of such pronouns in Beckett's poem. The text of *The Unnamable*, rhythmic as it is, has no such constraint, making the function of its non-object pronouns more overtly political.

According to Anne Atik (2001: 70–1), Beckett was fascinated by Keats's concept of '*Negative Capability*', which he famously outlined in a letter to his brothers of December 1817 in the following terms: 'when man is capable of being in uncertainties, Mysteries, doubts, without any irritable reaching after fact and reason' (2005: 60). This is in line with Beckett's own pronouncements regarding a poetics based on 'impotence, ignorance' rather than 'omniscience and omnipotence' (qtd in Shenker 1956: 3). Fittingly, the Unnamable rails against knowledge, from the reference to Ancient Greek scepticism in his (very learned) use of 'ephectic' on the novel's opening page to the repeated use of 'don't know' on the last page, culminating in the declaration 'I don't know, I'll never know, in the silence you don't know' (*U*: 1, 134). As this shows, Keats's influence on the novel precipitates not a placid, or even 'capable' acceptance of uncertainty, but an aggressive disintegration of self, which goes hand in hand with the spatial uncertainty of the text.[20] Specifically, this influence can be seen

---

[20] As well as noting other allusions to Keats in Beckett's work, C. J. Ackerley and S. E. Gontarski point out that *The Unnamable*'s line regarding windows which 'opened on the sea' (*U*: 117) is reminiscent of Keats's 'magic casements, opening on the foam' in 'Ode to a Nightingale' (2004: 297; Keats 1982: 281).

in *The Unnamable*'s adoption of the non-reflexive pronouns of 'Serena I', as Beckett turns from saying 'I' to 'not I'.

An assault on the pronouns: Finding 'me' in *The Unnamable*

Based on the settings of Beckett's previous fiction, *The Unnamable*'s first readers may have justifiably expected an institution of coercive confinement to emerge as the narrative's answer to the opening question 'where now?'. But while the political dynamics of confined space are central to *The Unnamable*, the novel remains resistant to such carceral interpretations. Why is this so?

Like Beckett's previous prose, *The Unnamable* is a text abounding in bounded space. Over the course of his futile attempt to fix his location, the narrator tells stories of himself in an urn (*U*: 39–46, 54–9) and an enclosed yard at the centre of which is a windowless rotunda (*U*: 29). He also imagines Worm, one of his 'vice-exister[s]', confined inside a windowless inspection place with holes through which his tormentors peep, shine lights and grab him – a kind of negative panopticon (*U*: 26, 70–3). Elsewhere, the narrator tells us that he is 'in a head' (*U*: 65, 88), a 'dungeon' (*U*: 85) and a prison (*U*: 109, 128–9). But due to persistent 'denarration', defined by Brian Richardson as 'a kind of narrative negation in which a narrator denies significant aspects of his or her narrative that had earlier been presented as given', the possibility of any of these spaces emerging as a stable narrative locale is undermined (2006: 87). The enclosure, the inspection place and the prison are all described as 'vast' (*U*: 29, 73, 129) and, in spite of the many depictions of confinement, there is no certainty that the space from which the narrator speaks is a restricted one: 'as I have said, the place may well be vast, as it may well measure twelve feet in diameter' (*U*: 5). Each confined space is undermined by a first-person narrative style which has left far behind the meticulous topography of third-person narration in *Murphy*. As the narrator puts it, 'I'm where I always was, wherever that is' (*U*: 102).

According to the narrator, both this topographical crisis and the existential crisis which it entails are 'the fault of the pronouns, there is no name for me, no pronoun for me, all the trouble comes from that' (*U*: 123). Elsewhere in the text, he pointedly attacks his own narrative 'I': 'But enough of this cursed first person, it is really too red a herring, I'll get out of my depth if I'm not careful' (*U*: 56). In a draft version of this sentence, there is a list of different grammatical forms of the pronoun he wants to get rid of: 'Et puis assez de moi aussi, assez de moi, de je, de me' [Anyway enough also of me, enough of me, of I, of myself] (HRC SB MS 3/10:

inside back cover, *BDMP* II). This draft sentence undoes its own 'undoing' of
the self by adding further versions of the first-person pronoun to a sentence
which sets out to repudiate that pronoun, one of the paradoxical consequences
of trying to create what Beckett famously described in his 1937 letter to Kaun as
a 'literature of the non-word' ['Literatur des Unworts'] by adding more language
to what went before (*LSB* I: 520, 515). In order to create such a literature, Beckett
recommended to Kaun the practice of '[w]ord-storming' ['Wörterstürmerei']
(*LSB* I: 520, 515). The original German compound has also been translated as
'[a]n assault against words' (*Dis*: 173). In the narrative voice of *The Unnamable*,
confined to saying 'I' though not to any single carceral space, Beckett's pronouns
were the primary targets of this attack. While Beckett simply eliminated the first-
person pronoun from the poems which followed 'Six Poèmes', *The Unnamable*
demonstrates the narrative self-division and spatial disintegration that occurs
as 'I' is being undone. Translating 'Literatur des Unworts' as 'literature of the
unword', Van Hulle and Weller have described Beckett's poetics in terms of
'unwording' (2014: 162). This 'unwording' process is closely linked to Beckett's
denarration of confined space.

Having tried for more than one hundred pages, the narrator is no closer to
locating himself as his narrative draws to a finish: 'first the place, then I'll find me
in it', directly echoing the pronominal idiosyncrasy of 'Serena I' (*U*: 118). As well
as calling to mind Beckett's debt to Keats, this statement neatly dispenses with
the theological and metaphysical baggage of the more standard phrase: 'I'll find
myself.' Just as Beckett considered, but then rejected, the woolly sounding title
'<u>Beyond Words</u>' when composing his novel, it is hard to imagine the Unnamable
ever using the verb 'to find' to express his own self-fulfilment in this reflexive
manner, beloved of self-help gurus (HRC SB MS 5/9/2: front cover, *BDMP* II).
The title Beckett ultimately chose points instead to the narrating subject as the
locus of his poetics of 'unwording'. The text's assault on the reflexive first-person
pronoun is key to these poetics: the most common use of a non-reflexive direct
object pronoun in *The Unnamable* is in conjunction with a verb of self-expression.
From very early on, the narrator expresses doubts about his ability to 'utter me'
(*U*: 10). In spite of this, he declares early on his intention to 'speak of me' all the
same (*U*: 14) – this phrase is repeated throughout the novel. He also imagines
himself 'referring to me' and 'talking to me about me' before wondering, at the
end of his narrative: 'perhaps they have said me already' (*U*: 68, 112, 134).

Such self-expression cannot get by without a 'they'. As the narrator's fractious
relationship with this 'they' demonstrates, Beckett's grammatical assault is also
deeply political, reflecting Beckett's philosophical interests in the language

scepticism of Fritz Mauthner. The idea that language is a system of communication which is something 'between people' (qtd and trans. in Weiler 1970: 55), and therefore fundamentally sociopolitical, is marked in Beckett's copy of Mauthner's *Beiträge zu einer Kritik der Sprache* ['Contributions to a Critique of Language'], a text which Beckett read intensively prior to writing *The Unnamable* (BDL; Van Hulle and Weller 2014: 21).[21] Van Hulle and Weller see *The Unnamable* as a 'Mauthnerian' novel due to 'the positing and then the rejection of a series of metaphors' which form such an important part of Beckett's text (2014: 190). In their view, the novel shares with Mauthner's philosophy the idea that the 'gates of truth' lead 'beyond the world and beyond thought into emptiness' (Mauthner qtd and trans. in Van Hulle and Weller 2014: 190). As Beckett does with his draft title 'Beyond Words', Mauthner here conceptualizes the limit of language in explicitly spatial terms. Beckett seems to have realized that such spatial images – such as the veil he had used in his letter to Kaun and the 'wombtomb' of his early prose – themselves needed to be decomposed in order to prevent them becoming yet further metaphors for the self, such as the 'skullscape' of the narrator's mind.[22] This is why *The Unnamable*'s closed spaces are subject to a repeated and radical denarration, making confinement one of the necessary conditions for Beckett's (de-)composition of the narrative self, along with language.

With regard to politics, it is the Mauthnerian idea that 'I have no language but theirs' which the narrator is so keen to reject (*U*: 38):

> Not to be able to open my mouth without proclaiming them, and our fellowship, that's what they imagine they'll have me reduced to. It's a poor trick that consists in ramming a set of words down your gullet on the principle that you can't bring them up without being branded as belonging to their breed. But I'll fix their gibberish for them. (*U*: 37)

The narrator's second declaration of intent to 'utter me' occurs in a passage which begins with the denarration of a story he has just told of his family's death by poisoning and, more particularly, of the space associated with that story: 'I was never anywhere but here, no one ever got me out of here.' He then describes his oppression by lamenting the fact that his voice is imposed on him by an

---

[21] There is no guarantee this mark is Beckett's own and dating precisely his reading of Mauthner has proven problematic for scholars (Van Hulle and Nixon 2013: 158–63). However, it is certain that he read Mauthner's *Beiträge* before writing *The Unnamable*.

[22] For a critique of the concept of the 'skullscape' in Beckett criticism, see Beloborodova, who uses a postcognitivist paradigm to argue that *The Unnamable* 'deals a serious blow to the ubiquitous all-internal Cartesian mind' (2018: 216). I am grateful to Olga Beloborodova for sharing her unpublished research on this topic with me.

anonymous group of others: 'What I speak of, what I speak with, all comes from them' (*U*: 36). Self-expression in words which have been given to him by these others might be possible, the narrator contends, through a private language which is for his ears only, rather than those of the oppressive 'they' who force him to speak:

> Do they consider me so plastered with their rubbish that I can never extricate myself, never make a gesture but their cast must come to life? But within, motionless, I can live, and utter me, for no ears but my own. (*U*: 37)

However, the peculiar grammatical structure of the declaration to 'utter me' in the English version of the text points to a dichotomy involved in this attempt to speak of oneself to oneself. The irony of a fictional narrator telling us that what he is narrating is for no one else to hear – or, presumably, to read – brings into sharp focus the contradiction inherent in his attempt at inward escape. The oppression that the first-person narrator of *The Unnamable* suffers is due directly to his being bound up in a discursive system from which he feels alienated. Yet it is clear that he must use this discourse if he is to express his sense of alienation. This is important evidence of how Beckett's move to first-person narration 'involves only superficially a break with questions of power' (Connor 2007: 188).

As can be seen in Beckett's drafts, the French 'me déclarer' which appears in the published version of the above passage – '[m]ais là-dedans, sans bouger, je pourrai vivre, et me déclarer, seul à m'entendre' (1987: 64) – was first translated as the reflexive 'give utterance to myself' (HRC SB MS 5/9/1: 42r, *BDMP* II). In the first typescript of the English translation, this was changed: 'But ~~inside my shell~~ within, motionless, I can live, and ~~give utterance~~ utter me, ~~to myself,~~ for no ears but my own' (HRC SB MS 5/10: 42r, *BDMP* II). Beckett had, from the very start of his translation process, used non-reflexive object pronouns in both his notebooks and typescripts, so this edit was a grafting of a grammatical feature already employed previously. Moreover, given Beckett's use of such pronouns over two decades earlier in 'Serena I' as well as his sensitivity towards the dynamics of pronominal translation in Apollinaire's 'Zone' and his own 'they come', it seems clear that this non-standard pronominal form was part of Beckett's attempt to further destabilize the narrating subject of the novel, thus intensifying the uncertainty which governs this narrator's place of being. Another consequence of the change is to give a different dynamic to the 'textual construction of subjectivity' in the English version of the text (Katz 1999: 19): while the Francophone narrator can achieve some form of self-reflexive expression, the Anglophone narrator can only 'utter me'. Moreover, he can only do so confined 'motionless' from 'within' a place which cannot be identified. Otherwise the process of denarrating space would have to begin all over again.

In spite of this distance between the self that speaks and the self that is spoken in *The Unnamable*, the narrator is never quite able to prise these two selves apart in order to create a 'fiction of 2 people', distinctly defined from one another. Rather, just as it uses many kinds of confined space, this is also a first-person fiction which creates narrative tension by using multiple narrative voices. At certain points, it seems that Worm and Mahood are telling the Unnamable's story; at other stages it appears that a group of 'delegates' have taken it over (*U*: 7). Despite the insistence on the first-person voice as *The Unnamable* approaches its end, the novel never quite manages to put back together a speaking self that has been emptied out from the first page of the first draft: 'Moi qui ~~suis~~ semble souvent le sujet des propositions que voici, je ne le suis jamais. Je n'en suis pas davantage l'objet. J'en suis absent' (HRC SB MS 3/10: 1r, *BDMP* II). [I, who ~~am~~ seem often to be the subject of these propositions, I am never that. I am not the object either. I am absent from them.] While this early version calls to mind the initial title of *Malone Dies*, 'L'ABSENT', pointing to the self-alienation of Beckett's previous characters, the version that appears in the published text also introduces the first self-negation of the narrative (HRC SB MS 7/2: front cover, HRC SB MS 7/4: front cover, *BDMP* V). No sooner has the narrator given himself an injunction to 'say I' than he begins to say 'not I': 'I seem to speak, it is not I, about me, it is not about me' (*U*: 1). The 'pronominal vertigo' which results from Beckett's assault on the first-person pronoun means that, in spite of this pronoun's insistent, repeated return at the end of the text, the narrator never quite manages to reclaim his narrative (Genette 1983: 246).

If *L'Innommable* is constructed using a 'non-self-coincidental voice' (Trezise 1990: 107, 138), then, because of its paradoxical pronouns, the speaking self of *The Unnamable* is even further away from itself. Given the pressure the Unnamable is under from an indistinct 'they' to tell his story, this further self-division in translation has implications for the politics of the text.

Beckett's resistance

The textual resistance of *The Unnamable*, in which key grounds for interpretation (narrative self and narrated space) are consistently undermined, lies at the heart of the novel's political effects. For Slote, 'Beckettian resistance is such that it resists being made into a tool of resistance' (2019: 143). While Beckett frequently was instrumental in particular political causes – most notably the French Resistance during the Second World War – the denarration of self and confined space in *The Unnamable* demonstrates a resistance to the confinement of textual interpretation within a given sociopolitical paradigm. The political charge of Beckett's writing emerges not solely from the subject matter he chose to represent – figures of dereliction, often found in spaces of confinement – but also in the 'resistance [...] to representation' of these key elements in his compositional repertoire (Lloyd 2016: 226). To clarify this point, it is worth examining Beckett's knowledge of a contemporary whose work also charts a relentless assault on the first-person pronoun. Though he told Rosemary Pountney in a letter of January 1978 that he was 'unaware of any influence from [the French theatre practitioner and writer Antonin] Artaud' (qtd in Pountney 1988: 182), Beckett confirmed in a questionnaire sent to James Knowlson six years earlier that he had indeed read Artaud 'for the odd blaze' prior to writing *Waiting for Godot* (UoR JEK A/1/2/4).[23]

Like the first-person narrators of many of Artaud's texts, the narrative 'I' of *The Unnamable* feels oppressed by a threatening and frequently sadistic 'they', recalling the social dynamics of the postwar novellas. The narrator of *The Unnamable* even quotes the opening line of 'The End': 'They clothed me and gave me money' (*U*: 23; *CSP*: 78). Later, this charity takes a sinister turn: 'You've been sufficiently assassinated, sufficiently suicided, to be able now to stand on your own feet, like a big boy' (*U*: 46). Whereas the English version is passive, the French contains 'the paradoxical grammatical construction "[i]ls t'ont [...] assez suicidé"' [they have suicided you enough] (Van Hulle and Weller 2014: 142; Beckett 1987: 77). The idea of an artist's suicide being effected by social norms, enforced by the discipline of psychiatry, is the central subject of Artaud's *Van Gogh le suicidé de la société*. More specifically, Artaud's book was written as a critique of 'the text-book attitude' towards asylum patients (*Mu*: 111), with Artaud furious at the diagnosis of Van Gogh as 'déséquilibré' [unstable] by a psychiatrist writing in *Arts* magazine (qtd in Artaud 2016: 1436). This article was published to coincide with a 1947 exhibition of Van Gogh's work at the Musée de l'Orangerie in Paris, which both Artaud and Beckett had occasion to visit.

Though the publication of Artaud's book on Van Gogh would have put the substantive term 'suicidé' in the air of postwar discourse, this was not the first time he had used the unusual verbal form. It had already appeared in his 1925 article in *La Révolution surréaliste* on the question of suicide:

---

[23] Beckett's quotation on Artaud is taken from the University of Reading archival finding aid, http://www.reading.ac.uk/adlib/Details/archiveSpecial/110246027.

I suffer hideously from life. There is no state that I can attain. And it is certain that
I have been dead for a long time, I have already committed suicide. They have
suicided me, so to speak ['ON m'a suicidé, c'est-à-dire']. (1976: 103; 2016: 124)

Writing over two decades later, Artaud had many more reasons for a focused
attack on the normative social institutions represented by this 'they', having spent
over eight years in confinement, suffering fifty-eight electroshock treatments
during his nineteen months in an asylum at Rodez (Shafer 2016: 165). Released
to more humane conditions at a nursing home in Ivry, Artaud gave an infamous
performance at the Théâtre du Vieux-Colombier on 13 January 1947, within
walking distance of Beckett's apartment on the rue des Favorites. Beckett would
have been able to follow the fallout from this performance in *Combat* (see
Artaud 2016: 1190–1), which he regularly read in the 1940s (Morin 2017: 25).
When Artaud passed away in 1948, Beckett linked his confinement to that of
Lucia Joyce, whom Beckett had visited regularly in the same nursing home
before the war: 'Artaud died the other day in Lucia's home at Ivry' (SB to
TM, 18 March 1948, *LSB* II: 75). It is highly likely, therefore, that Artaud was
not far from Beckett's mind as he started drafting *L'Innommable* in January 1950.

According to Artaud's book on Van Gogh, 'one does not commit suicide
by oneself [...], there must be an army of evil beings ["mauvais êtres"] to
cause the body to make the gesture against nature, that of taking its own life'
(1976: 511; 2016: 1462). The unusual grammatical construction 'suicidé'
reinforces the fact that for the Unnamable, self-constitution (and its opposite,
self-destruction) is still intimately connected to the 'dirty pack of fake maniacs'
to whom he opposes himself (*U*: 84). This resistance to socialization is an
intensification of the relationship between the narrators of the novellas and
their ominous 'they', though without the institutions of confinement with
which this earlier 'they' is associated. Instead, *The Unnamable*'s echo of Artaud's
idiosyncratic pronominal form is part of a more aggressively dissonant form of
resistance against social interaction.

The fiercely anti-institutional thrust of Artaud's book on Van Gogh, borne
out of his own mistreatment in confinement, was part of a wider wave of postwar
writing which would in succeeding decades forcefully challenge the discipline of
psychiatry (see Porter 2003: 2–5). Where should we situate Beckett's postwar
writing in this context? And what can it tell us about the political dynamics of his
writing on confinement? In *Van Gogh*, Artaud identifies himself as an 'authentic
madman' ['aliéné authentique'] 'who preferred to become mad, in the socially
accepted sense of the word, rather than forfeit a certain superior idea of human

honor' (1976: 485; 2016: 1441). For readers of Beckett, such heroism in madness brings *Murphy*'s Mr Endon to mind – or, rather, Murphy's opinion of Mr Endon as a hero who refuses to bow to social norms. Our greater narrative proximity to the disintegrating self in *The Unnamable*, as well as the undermining of any fixed or reliable space of narration, leads to a shift of political effect when Beckett echoes Artaud's polemical text on Van Gogh. For Van Hulle and Weller, '[a]n entire history of institutionalization, mental instability, victimization and artistic resistance is captured in that one, Artaudian word "suicidé" (suicided)' (2014: 143). Yet the speaking self who utters this word is no longer embedded in the world of those institutions to the same degree as Murphy, Belacqua or Malone's Macmann. This makes the form of resistance in *The Unnamable* different. Beckett's depictions of asylums in *Murphy* and *Malone Dies* share with Artaud's work a sharply critical perspective on structures of 'hierarchy and power in institutional environments' (Baroghel 2016) but, due to the undermining of confined space in the novel, the single Artaudian echo in *The Unnamable* resists being interpreted as a sustained attack on these institutions. Instead, the politics of *The Unnamable* are based on the resistance to interpretation of a disintegrating 'I', who struggles to find 'me', continually positing and denarrating spaces of confinement which fail to definitively 'shut me up' (*U*: 85).

7

Redoing *Not I* in 'Non-A'

It is hard to 'go on' when one is stuck in a mound. In developing his theatre of confinement through the spatial restriction of the mound-bound figure of Winnie in *Happy Days* (1961), Beckett duly expressed concern as to 'whether this is really a dramatic text or a complete aberration and whether there is justification for trying to push further this kind of theatre' (SB to AS, 15 September 1961, *LSB* III: 435). He would express similar concerns regarding *Not I*.[1] All Beckett's plays written prior to *Happy Days* feature locomotion, however constrained, of their central protagonists. Six of his next nine works composed for theatre – *Play* (1964), *Not I* (1973), *That Time* (1976), *A Piece of Monologue* (1979), *Rockaby* (1981) and *Ohio Impromptu* (1981) – fix their principal actors in place, be it in urns, chairs or under spotlights. In order to reshape the limits of theatre practice after *Godot* and *Endgame*, Beckett constricted the spatial limits of performance.

Beckett was not the only theatre practitioner trying to redefine stage space in the postwar period. Though there is very little in Beckett's library that could have served as a practical training manual as he began his career as a director, he did own the 1958 English translation of Artaud's *Theatre and Its Double*, which has been hugely influential as a manifesto for a post-proscenium theatre space (Alston 2016: 6; Brook 1996: 58). Artaud famously sought a model for this radically new performance space in the Balinese theatre which he saw at the Paris Colonial Exposition in 1931 (Shafer 2016: 98). For Artaud, this form of theatre avoided the Occidental fault of privileging words over other forms of theatrical communication (such as bodily movement). It could therefore 'address not only the mind but the senses', something Artaud wished to emulate in his creation of a new kind of stage voice, as emphasized throughout *The Theatre and Its Double* (1958: 119). Beckett's well-known description of the stage voice of *Not I*

---

[1] 'Hope to work on Not I in London next month and find out ᵗʰᵉⁿ if it's theatre or not' (SB to Barney Rosset, 3 November 1972, SU Grove Press Records, box 85, qtd in Gontarski 2018: 165).

draws on the same concepts: 'I hear it breathless, urgent, feverish, rhythmic, panting along, without undue concern with intelligibility. Addressed less to the understanding than to the nerves of the audience which should in a sense *share her bewilderment*' (SB to AS, 16 October 1972, *NABS*: 283; emphasis in original). Beckett repeated this wish to undo the perceived hierarchy between mind and senses in a conversation with Jessica Tandy, the first actor to play Mouth: 'I am not unduly concerned with intelligibility [...]. I hope the piece may work on the nerves of the audience, not its intellect' (qtd in Brater 1987: 23). Though both Artaud's and Beckett's statements reflect a Romantic privileging of 'Sensations rather than of Thoughts' (Keats to Benjamin Bailey, 22 November 1817, Keats 2005: 54), we are clearly far from the 'quiet melancholy' which Beckett so admired in Keats (Nixon 2011: 143). Rather, as in *The Unnamable*, there is an aggressive disintegration of subject and object which occurs on the stage of *Not I*.

Beckett's above comments on *Not I* concern its vocal delivery. What of the spatial arrangement that allowed this piece to 'work on the nerves of the audience'? While Beckett's monologue on a largely dark stage clearly 'privileges speech' to a certain extent, this chapter will argue that the playing space of *Not I* is not 'a stage subjugated to the power of speech and text', as Derrida reformulates Artaud's polemic against Occidental theatre (2005: 307, 301). Indeed, as against the false dichotomy drawn by William Gruber between 'verbal construction' and 'direct sensory experience', one of Beckett's aims in *Not I* was to present onstage speech as a direct experience for the audience's senses (2010: 6, 21). As part of this, Beckett's use of the heterotopic spatial dynamic of the proscenium demands to be taken into account if we want to understand how the play produces political meanings.

Like Beckett, Artaud sought to create a 'new notion of space' in the theatre (1958: 124). But unlike Beckett, he also sought to do away with the proscenium stage which has dominated modern Western performance practice. In seeking to 'leave no portion of the stage space unutilized', Artaud wanted to break down the division between stage and audience which the proscenium stage enforces (1958: 54). Beckett, by contrast, was one of those theatre practitioners who created a new kind of performance space through 'a subversion or an overstatement of the principles of the proscenium-arch theatre', overstating it by foregrounding the fourth wall in earlier work such as *Endgame*, subverting it in the darkened stages of his later plays (Pavis 1998: 134). As we have seen, one of these principles is that the proscenium space is always divided into a visible 'A zone' and an invisible 'non-A zone', giving it a specific dynamic in how it functions as a mode of theatre heterotopia. Though we might follow Kevin Hetherington in describing Artaud's (largely imagined) theatre as 'heterotopic' in that its assault on the senses lends itself to a kind of 'limit experience' (2003: 45–6), Beckett's theatre is heterotopic in a more literal sense, depending as it does on the division of theatre space into 'A' and 'non-A zones'.

Because it is a play which depends so much on what is unseen, it is useful to think of *Not I* in terms of what Andrew Sofer calls 'dark matter', 'the invisible dimension of theater that escapes visual detection, even though its effects are felt everywhere in performance' (2013: 3). Mouth is of course not invisible, but the protagonist of the story she tells (and the spaces mentioned in that story) can be considered 'dark matter', in that her presence is inferred by effects on the visible matter onstage. What are the political effects produced by this dark matter? Like her predecessor Watt, the marginalized figure of whom Mouth speaks is not just unseen but appears to be without a voice in the police order of her community, as when she is put on trial: 'that time in court … what had she to say for herself … guilty or not guilty … stand up woman … speak up woman … stood there staring into space … mouth half open as usual … waiting to be led away' (*CDW*: 381). Beckett stages this 'unseeing' of a subject that would seem to be beyond the field of the sensible, 'locating a subject in what cannot be reproduced within the ideology of the visible' (Phelan 2005: 1). But of course, we do have a reproduction of Mouth herself, night after night in the auditorium, suggesting that for Beckett, in addition to resisting instrumentalization, 'resistance does not lie in denying the power of the visible, but rather in co-opting it' (Reinelt 1994: 105). Beckett's subversion of the proscenium stage is crucial to this. Analysing Beckett's creation of a 'new room space' in the manuscripts of *Not I* shows that his refashioning of 'les coordonnées du représentable' [the coordinates of the representable] depended upon subverting the A/non-A binary of realist theatre (Rancière 2008: 72).

Producing *Not I*'s 'non-A zone'

For Artaud, the manipulation of space was a vital part of the creative process in the theatre: 'In my view no one has the right to call himself author, that is to say creator, except the person who controls the direct handling of the stage' (1958: 117). As 'performance is first and foremost a spatial event', Beckett's construction of space in *Not I*, on both the page and stage, has a particularly rich dynamic which, while resulting in similar kinds of challenges for topographical interpretation, differs from the process of establishing and subsequently denarrating confined locales in *The Unnamable*.[2] In spite of these differences between the construction of the spaces of Beckett's prose and those of his dramatic work, some basic interpretative questions remain, echoing those outlined on the first manuscript page of *Watt* and in the opening of *The Unnamable*: Who is the speaker? Where is she speaking from? 'I no more know where she is or why thus than she does. All I know is in the text. "She" is purely a stage entity, part of a stage image and purveyor of a stage text. The rest is Ibsen' (SB to AS, 16 October 1972, *NABS*: 283). Beckett's response to Alan Schneider's efforts to locate Mouth is usually read as a dismissal of the attempt to root the play in a realistic backstory (see Gontarski 2015a: 138). However, while trying to naturalize the image of a woman's mouth suspended in the dark on the model of 'natural' narratology would impoverish rather than enrich the interpretative process (Fludernik 2005), it is the very possibility of such a backstory that makes the play function. In Beckett's construction of his theatrical image, the bodies onstage, particularly those only partially visible, encourage such hermeneutic endeavour, even while resisting interpretative closure. Beckett himself acknowledges this in a letter to German director Carlheinz Caspari, following the author's disavowal of the suggestion that *Godot* was 'a symbolist play': 'That at any moment Symbols, Ideas, Forms might show up ["se profilent"], this is for me secondary – is there anything they do not show up behind? In any event there is nothing to be gained by giving them clear form' (SB to Caspari, 25 July 1953, *LSB* II: 391, 389). Beckett here accepts the inevitability of interpretative frames being imposed on his dramatic work as part of the hermeneutic process but warns against overtly explicative directorial work on his playtexts. As Erik Tonning points out, Beckett's letter to Schneider 'will not prevent any audience […] from reconstructing what they can' of Mouth's story (Tonning 2007: 117). What we can interpret is based very much on what we can make of the spaces evoked by Mouth in her monologue on a darkened stage.

Not I, as well as rejecting its first-person pronoun, seems to invert the dynamic between onstage reality and offstage imaginary that Ubersfeld identifies as central to the production of theatre space. However, the 'non-A zone' of *Not I* is not one of those easily identifiable 'unenclosed places', such as 'the street or the open mountains'.[3] For Ubersfeld, 'the enclosure with regard to the wings

---

2   '[L]a représentation est d'abord un événement spatial' (Ubersfeld 1996: 19).

3   'Sont […] non-A les lieux non clos' [non-A are those unenclosed places]; '[le] cadre naturel [du héros B] est la rue ou les libres montagnes' [The natural surroundings for the hero of B is the street or the open mountains] (Ubersfeld 1974: 409, 410). In this work, Ubersfeld uses 'B' and 'non-A' interchangeably (see 408).

[...] [has] as its corollary [...] the opening of the stage space onto an imaginary elsewhere'.[4] By putting Mouth eight feet above the stage in darkness and having her create the storyworld of the play diegetically, Beckett creates onstage an image of that very 'elsewhere', the 'non-A zone' suggested by the onstage world of theatrical realism with which Ibsen is associated. If Mouth was an Ibsen character, we would get a detailed backstory explaining what has led her to this abnormal state, like we do with the character of Irene in Ibsen's *When We Dead Awaken*, who has become a psychotic murderer because she gave the sculptor Rubek her 'living soul' by letting him use her as a model for his art (1978: 1055). But Beckett's postwar protagonists do not have such explanatory backstories, and his onstage 'non-A zones' never provide the 'explicating background of Balzac' (TCD MIC 60/69, qtd in Le Juez 2008: 61). Yet the stage image that remains means '[t]he offstage gobbling up the stage in its entirety [is] never really actualized' (Chattopadhyay 2015: 243). If Mouth was staged on the '*country road*' of her theatrical predecessors in *Godot* (*CDW*: 11), interpretation would be easy. If she was not visible on the stage, we could imagine her voice coming out of whatever space we liked. But instead of a direct inversion of realist spatial dynamics in an outdoor 'non-A zone', or disconnecting Mouth from the space of visible representation altogether by having a dark stage with no actor in sight, the space of *Not I* is more like the in-between space described in Beckett's short prose piece 'neither' (1977), in which a lone figure, having moved in vain from 'self' to 'unself' 'halt[s] for good': 'gently light unfading on that unheeded neither / unspeakable home' (*CSP*: 258). In her mention of 'the other waifs' she grew up with, Mouth alludes to an institutional home (an orphanage) that takes the place of the family 'home' she never had (*CDW*: 377, 376). But the place from which she tells her story lacks the positive qualities of any kind of living space – domestic or institutional. Rather, it is describable only in tenuous relation to such narrated locations, a relation made even more fragile by her refusal to identify with the figure she describes in her story.

In order to fully understand how the play functions spatially, we must examine the pronominal conflict which structures the text, a narratological conflict initially figured in the compositional manuscripts as an opposition between voices as sound objects. This will also involve examining the performance history of *Play* and *Cascando* (1963), two works which had a significant influence on the voice of *Not I*.

---

[4] '[L]a clôture par rapport aux coulisses [...] ayant pour corollaire [...] l'ouverture de l'espace scénique sur un ailleurs imaginaire' (Ubersfeld 1991: 93–4).

Undoing 'Kilcool'

Beckett's work on *Not I* started with a manuscript which uses multiple place-names and ended up producing a monologue in the dark shorn of toponymic references, making it a key text in the critical model of Beckett's poetics of 'undoing' (Gontarski 1985: 131–49). As I have been arguing, this model, helpful as it is in understanding Beckett's working process, needs to be re-evaluated in the light of closer analysis of the development of his work as well as the instances in which he introduced, not just removed, detail from his texts. Many of Beckett's epigenetic changes took place in the rehearsal room. With this in mind, the French term for a theatrical rehearsal – 'répétition' – points to the fact that an important part of Beckett's working process of 'undoing' involved the repetitious 'redoing' of his work in performance (Gontarski 2006: 153; Van Hulle 2013: 221; Weller 2005: 135–6), during which elements were added as well as subtracted.[5]

Beckett gave various answers when asked about the sources of *Not I*: Enoch Brater was told by actors Jessica Tandy and Hume Cronyn that Beckett picked up the image of the Auditor from watching a woman in a djellaba in Tunisia; Beckett told Deirdre Bair 'and others' that Mouth's monologue was that of a derelict old Irish woman; and, as well as pointing to *The Unnamable* as the source of Mouth's monologue, he told James Knowlson that inspiration for the piece came from Caravaggio's *Beheading of St John the Baptist* (Brater 1975: 50; Knowlson 1997: 590; SB to Knowlson, 29 April 1973, *LSB* IV: 332).[6] Like his remark that the wall in *Film* was based on that of the Santé Prison in Paris, such comments tell us a lot about Beckett's view of his own sources, particularly that institutions of coercive confinement continued to be sources of creative inspiration for him long after he stopped giving recognizable depictions of them in his writing (Beckett in conversation with Damian Pettigrew, qtd in Tucker 2015). However, they tell us little about how space functions in his work. In order to analyse Beckett's use of confinement in *Not I*, we must examine the work of this creative process in the manuscripts and performance history of the play, studying what Beckett did as well as what he said.

---

[5]　See also Finn Fordham's *I Do I Undo I Redo: The Textual Genesis of Modernist Selves in Hopkins, Yeats, Conrad, Forster, Joyce, and Woolf* (2010). While Fordham is interested in the redoing of the authorial self through writing, my focus here is on the redoing of the text in performance.

[6]　Bair's account is doubtful as she reports Beckett telling the same story, using exactly the same words, to multiple people: 'Alan Schneider, Billie Whitelaw, A. J. Leventhal and others' (Bair 1990: 748 n. 59). For more on Beckett's admiration of Caravaggio's painting in Malta and its influence on *Not I*, see SB to Avigdor Arikha and Anne Atik, 25 October 1971, *LSB* IV: 271; SB to Edith Kern, 15 March 1986, *LSB* IV: 671.

On 25 August 1963, Beckett mentioned to Alan Schneider that he had started work on a 'face play' they had previously discussed (*NABS*: 139). The 'Kilcool' manuscript, containing various attempts at getting the composition of such a play underway, consists of eleven pages.[7] Pountney identifies three separate 'fragment[s]' and, like Gontarski, only studies seven of the pages (Pountney 1988: 92). Gontarski discounts the draft beginning on folio 17r as belonging to a 'different play, with three or four characters' and disregards the subsequent monologue on 18r–19r (1985: 141).[8] Certainly, elements in this monologue also point to other late dramatic works: the lover who turns up at night both prefigures the situation narrated in … *but the clouds* … (1977) and echoes the title of Beckett's short prose piece 'Horn Came Always at Night' ('Horn venait la nuit', 1973); the relationship between the main female protagonist described in the monologue and the older Mrs Frost prefigures that between Amy and her mother Mrs Winter in the story recounted in *Footfalls*.[9] However, features which relate the monologue to preceding material – the interruption of speech by 'tears', the presence of a 'lover', and mention of 'age' and the 'voice', all of which are elements listed in an early outline – suggest that it too should be seen as a draft towards *Not I*, even if, as seems most likely, this fourth draft is a compositional dead end (TCD MS 4664: 18r–19r, 11v, qtd in Gontarski 1985: 136). The three earlier drafts contain more direct links with the published play, the most important of which concern the relationship between space and voice. In a list of notes on the first page of the draft material, there are already the elements which will form the basis for *Not I*, such as a single face lit against a dark background ('Woman's face alone in constant light […] Nothing but fixed lit face & speech') (TCD MS 4664: 10r, qtd in Gontarski 1985: 135) and speech which begins before the houselights are fully up: 'When theatre lights down [? ~~curtain~~] before curtain up, light on face and speech already. […] Opening: [? 4]–5 lines [? ~~text xxx~~] muffled [? ~~text~~] ^speech^, curtain up, conclusion of this speech' (TCD MS 4664: 10r).

Both the voices of 'Kilcool' as well as its spatial features have similarities with Beckett's other dramatic work of the early 1960s. Three months after starting the first draft, he told director Alan Schneider: 'The best background [for *Play*] is

---

[7]   The manuscript is dated [? 24] August and 23 and 29 December 1963 (TCD MS 4664: 10r, 12r, 15r).

[8]   I follow Peter Shillingsburg's definition of a draft as being 'a preliminary form of a version' which is in turn 'one specific form of the work', which is 'conceptually that which is implied by authoritative texts' (1999: 45, 44, 1; 2013).

[9]   The composition date of 'Horn venait la nuit' is uncertain. Beckett told John Calder he composed it circa 1960 (Nixon 2010: xvii).

that which best suggests empty unlit space' (SB to AS, 26 November 1963, *LSB* III: 584). This stage darkness, a central part of Beckett's late theatrical style, is mentioned in a later version of the stage directions in 'Kilcool': '<u>Old woman's face, 4 ft. above stage level, slightly off centre, lit by strong steady light. Body not visible. Stage in darkness. Nothing visible but face</u>' (TCD MS 4664: 14r, qtd in Gontarski 1985: 139).[10] This would become a crucial part of the text as performed in the theatre.

The early list of notes in the manuscript which contains some of the basic concepts for *Not I* also includes a statement which would eventually give the published play its title and its structure: the unnamed central protagonist, we are told, '[t]alks of herself in 3rd person' (TCD MS 4664: 10r, qtd in Gontarski 1985: 135). A later note continues this aversion towards the first-person pronoun: '"I" "me" etc. never spoken outside assumed voice' (TCD MS 4664: 11r, qtd in Gontarski 1985: 136). This note demonstrates the importance of the status of the voice as sound object in shaping the narratological structure of the play, a structure based on the opposition between an 'assumed' and 'normal' voice of the same speaker. The rule that the first-person pronoun should only be spoken by this 'assumed' voice is broken in a later passage which revisits the images of intrauterine confinement found in Beckett's Psychology Notes and early prose: 'Someone in me, trying to get out, saying let me out, [...] someone there, wanting out, into the light, poor creature' (TCD MS 4664: 16r, qtd in Gontarski 1985: 140). The stage directions then indicate a switch to the assumed voice: 'Let me out! Let me out!'; then the normal voice resumes: 'Was I in someone once, and where is she now, if I was in her once, and she let me out' (TCD MS 4664: 16r, qtd in Pountney 1988: 98). As the assumed voice is given to the figure trapped inside the main speaker who needs to 'get out' in order to go on, the lines preceding her appeal, which include both 'me' and 'I', must be attributed to the '[n]ormal voice' of the speaker. By the fourth draft of 'Kilcool', Beckett had cut the explicit conflict between voices, leaving one voice recounting a story on her own and notes such as '[y]ou speak what you hear etc' echoing the novel *How It Is* (*Comment c'est*, 1961) in which, as the narrator repeatedly puts it, 'I say it as I hear it' (TCD MS 4664: 18v; Beckett 2009a).

In the first and second drafts in the 'Kilcool' manuscript, Beckett specified that the assumed voice should be '<u>low, fast, breathless</u>' (TCD MS 4664: 10v, 13r, qtd in Gontarski 1985: 139). In other stage directions, the assumed voice is described as '<u>panting</u>' (TCD MS 4664: 10v, 13r). Such stage directions show direct similarities

---

[10] All writing on this recto is erased with a diagonal line.

with the Voice of *Cascando*, a recording of which Beckett had attended in Paris earlier in 1963. In this recording, the Voice was rendered much faster than that of the later BBC version, the recording sessions for which Beckett did not attend (Verhulst 2015). Drafts of *Cascando* have 'débit rapide, haletant' [rapid delivery, panting] (HL MS Thr 70/1: 6r; HL MS Thr 70/4: 1r, qtd in Sánchez 2016: 36) and, even when this was changed to 'bas, haletant' [low, panting] in one of the later drafts, the timings which Beckett jotted in the manuscript margin indicate that he still had a rapid tempo in mind (HL MS Thr 70/5: 1r, qtd in Sánchez 2016: 36). As Pim Verhulst points out, in French, 'débit' 'has the connotation of a flow or an outpouring, reminiscent of logorrhea', a description which also evokes the delivery of Mouth's monologue in *Not I* (qtd in Sánchez 2016: 36). The stage direction '*panting*', which Beckett uses in his English translation of *Cascando*, is also noteworthy due to the relation it has with *How It Is*, in which the word 'panting' appears repeatedly (*CDW*: 297; Beckett 2009a).[11] Beckett started his translation of *How It Is* in early 1960, preparing part of its opening for Patrick Magee to read on the BBC. In a letter to the actor, he described the work as being 'separated by pauses during which panting cordially invited' (26 February 1960, *LSB* III: 306). Clearly, a rapid, panting voice was on Beckett's mind when composing both prose and dramatic work during the early 1960s.

While translating *How It Is*, Beckett also composed *Play*. This theatre piece, as well as sharing important vocal features with *Cascando*, was a crucial work in developing the confined stage image of *Not I*.[12] In winter 1963, during which period he was composing the 'Kilcool' drafts, Beckett rushed back from rehearsals of the world premiere of *Spiel* (*Play*) in Ulm, Germany, in order to attend the *Cascando* recording sessions in the Radiodiffusion-télévision française studios in Paris.[13] Like the French radio broadcast of *Cascando*, *Play* is delivered with a '[r]apid tempo throughout' (*CDW*: 307). While this tempo caused significant problems during rehearsals for the 1964 London premiere in the Old Vic, during which Beckett worked for the first time with Billie Whitelaw, the playwright was impressed enough by the speed of vocal delivery achieved to bring a tape of the rehearsal back to Paris to demonstrate to the actors playing *Comédie* (*Play*) just how fast he wanted the piece to be performed (Knowlson 1997: 517). As one actor from the Paris production noted, Beckett 'wanted it spoken with

[11] The French text most often uses the infinitive 'haleter' (Beckett 2015a).
[12] The spatial arrangement of *Play* is strongly foreshadowed in Beckett's suggestions for a staged reading of *All That Fall* featuring 'a stage in darkness with a spot picking out the faces as required' (SB to Alan Simpson, 28 January 1958, *LSB* III: 102).
[13] Pilling (2006: 162); 'Chronology 1963', *LSB* III: 523.

the speed of a machine gun' (Michael Lonsdale qtd and trans. in Ackerley and Gontarski 2004: 444). Unlike her co-stars in London, Whitelaw had no problems with this rapid speed of delivery so it is no surprise that Beckett requested that she play Mouth in the 1973 Royal Court production of *Not I* (Whitelaw 1996: 78; *NABS*: 287 n. 1).

In summary, the high vocal tempo that Beckett experimented with in the 'Kilcool' drafts, which is key to the distinction between the 'normal' and the 'assumed' voice in those drafts and which would eventually lead to the restrictive performance conditions of the play, must be seen as part of a broader move on Beckett's part in the 1960s to speed up the delivery of certain of his texts in performance. 'All I feel sure of is the text must go very fast', Beckett wrote to Schneider of *Not I* on 25 July 1972 (*NABS*: 273). In addition, it is evident from the mention of the speaking mouth being behind a 'curtain' in the 'Kilcool' drafts that Beckett conceived his play to be performed on a proscenium stage. Having 'overstated' the proscenium in *Endgame*, where better to stage the breakdown of subject and object than in the performance space where the concept of the modern subject was forged through the scenarios of realist drama?

Redoing *Not I*

In 1963, Beckett decided to put aside his work on the play that would eventually become *Not I*, returning to it early the following decade. Ruby Cohn recalls Beckett asking her in 1971: 'Can you stage a mouth? Just a moving mouth with the rest of the stage in darkness?' (Cohn 2008: 315). The central image of the play was still with him eight years after starting 'Kilcool', during which time he had worked closely on constructing similar images for productions of *Play*, including a 1966 French TV version in which the rapid-fire voices were constructed mechanically in post-production.[14] The technical challenges of staging voices in the dark were significant and Beckett's work with the new media of television and radio was important in developing the style of theatrical writing which produced *Not I*, a play in which the performer's body that produces a voice 'coming out of the dark' is often confined in that darkness.[15] Such darkness allowed for the presentation

---

[14] Director Marin Karmitz, working in collaboration with Beckett, used a machine called a *phonogène*, with which one can speed up voices without altering their tone (Sánchez 2016: 37–9). I would like to thank Luz María Sánchez for her help with my research into the 1966 TV production of *Comédie*.

[15] Beckett described his radio play *All That Fall* as 'coming out of the dark' in a letter refusing permission for a staging of it (SB to Barney Rosset, 27 August 1957, *LSB* III: 63).

of images and voices in Beckett's dramatic work which both call out for and resist interpretation.

The conflict between voices which is outlined explicitly in the four drafts of 'Kilcool' by having two different voices comprise an antiphonal narrative is framed differently in the manuscript of *Not I* itself, which Beckett started writing on 20 March 1972, as well as the subsequent typescripts (UoR MS 1227/7/12/1: 1r).[16] Here, as in the fourth draft of 'Kilcool', there is only one voice, which again begins speaking prior to the curtain going up. Rather than giving the speaker assumed and normal voices, Beckett has this voice aggressively attack the first-person pronoun each time it appears: 'what? ... I? ... no ... no! ... she ... ' (UoR MS 1227/7/12/1: 2r, qtd in Van Hulle 2008: 134). In TS 2, the 'I' is replaced: 'what? ... I? ^who?...what? ... no ... no ^NO! ... she ... ' (UoR MS 1227/7/12/3: 1r, qtd in Van Hulle 2008: 134). By TS 4, the first-person pronoun has been erased completely, only for it to appear again, for the first time, in the title of the play (UoR MS 1227/7/12/5: 1r).

On 12 November 1981, Beckett told André Bernold of his desire to create 'a voice that is a shadow. A white voice' (Bernold 2015: 77). However, as Beckett's characters' uses of 'a white voice' to make public pronouncements in *More Pricks than Kicks* demonstrate – such as the pedlar selling '[s]eats in heaven [...] tuppence apiece, four fer a tanner' – such voices are by no means devoid of social specificity (*MPTK*: 38, see also 39, 138). As when he drafted *Krapp's Last Tape* for the voice of Patrick Magee, Beckett frequently had very particular kinds of voices in mind for his dramatic work, a particularity which is at odds with William Worthen's account of the voice in Beckett's dramatic corpus as being '[e]mptied as a sign of the protagonist's expressive presence' (1992: 137).[17] In an early note on 'Kilcool', Beckett recorded the idea of giving a 'different voice quality' to each theme in his draft (TCD MS 4664: 11r). In a synopsis typed up while composing *Not I* almost a decade later, Beckett noted that Mouth recognizes her own voice because of its accent (UoR MS 1227/7/12/10: 1r). This is also made clear in the published text: 'then finally had to admit ... could be none other ... than her own ... certain vowel sounds ... she had never heard ... elsewhere' (*CDW*: 379).

Additions to typescripts of *Not I* suggest that Beckett considered having this voice which rejects the first-person pronoun come from an identifiable place. In TS 5, Beckett underlined by hand the word which describes the specific tonal

---

[16] I number the manuscripts and typescripts of *Not I / Pas moi* according to their listed order in Bryden, Garforth and Mills (1998: 65–8).

[17] The first draft of *Krapp* is entitled 'Magee Monologue' (UoR MS 1227/7/7/1: 11r, *BDMP* III).

quality of the voice that Mouth describes: 'certain <u>vowel</u> sounds'. He inserted 'vow-ell' in the left margin (UoR MS 1227/7/12/6: 3r). On the same typescript, Beckett developed a note which seems to indicate that Mouth has an Irish accent, a note which is included on Billie Whitelaw's rehearsal script for the Royal Court production of the play in early 1973:

> 'Any': pronounce 'anny'. (for example)
> baby"[pronounce] babby
> either"[pronounce] eether (UoR MS 1227/7/12/6: 6r; see also UoR BW A/2/1: 8)[18]

In the same letter which warns Schneider off trying to give Mouth a backstory in order to quell his actors, Beckett rejects the suggestion that a local context be read into such vocal instructions: 'Simply an example of the "certain vowel sounds". No Irishness intended' (SB to AS, 16 October 1972, *NABS*: 283).

As well as having queries about Mouth's place of origin, Schneider was also concerned regarding the space occupied by the performer playing Mouth, specifically the fact that for the play's premiere, this space was a thrust stage. He expressed these concerns to Beckett: 'I have enclosed floor plan of FORUM theatre, probably best small theatre in New York. Although you may be disturbed because it is not proscenium.' This production did go ahead and Schneider was presumably able to seat the audience at such an angle that they could see both Mouth and the Auditor. Later in the same letter, Schneider wrote: 'As you must surmise, there's no actual "curtain" at Forum.' Instead of *ad-libbing* behind the curtain before it rose to reveal a blacked-out picture frame, actor Jessica Tandy was 'roll[ed] on in dark' (AS to SB, 30 September 1972, *NABS*: 279–80). But when Beckett was involved himself at productions in Paris and London, the play returned to the picture-frame stage for which he had written it, first in the Royal Court, then in the Théâtre d'Orsay (Gontarski 2015a: 139).

As noted by Gontarski, Beckett started the 'Kilcool' drafts by using Irish indicators of place: the title of the manuscript itself is a misspelled version of the town adjacent to Greystones where Beckett's mother lived and there is reference made to 'Redford by the sea', the part of Greystones where both Beckett's parents are buried, as well as to the 'Slow & Easy' [Dublin and Southeastern] train which served the area (TCD MS 4664: 10r, 11r, qtd in Gontarski 1985: 136).[19] It is worth noting that these references only appear in the first draft of the play; none of the

---

[18] The first line of this note appears as a handwritten addition on UoR MS 1227/7/12/5: 5r.
[19] Beckett re-inserted the terminal 'e' in 'Kilcoole' when revising his first draft (TCD MS 4664: 10r).

other 'Kilcool' drafts have any Irish toponyms. Beckett's 'undoing' of space is thus best represented not by a smooth curve but rather, like his process of learning to say 'I', by zigzag lines. When Beckett deleted the South County Dublin place-name 'Croker's Acres' in translating the play from English to French, the translated text lost the last of its topographic markers of Beckett's homeland.[20] However, the reference to Croker's Acres itself was only added in the fourth *Not I* typescript (Verhulst 2008: 274), going against the received opinion that Beckett made his texts progressively less topographically grounded as he worked. While 'undoing' was a vital part of Beckett's working process, such instances demonstrate that his poetics was characterized by a balancing of topographic detail through addition and 'redoing' as well as the predominant process of subtraction.

Further complicating the idea of the creative process behind Beckett's plays being one of simply paring away specifics, Billie Whitelaw uses 'babby' in the BBC television production broadcast in 1976, slipping into a broad, North of England accent to include the piece of dialect (Wright 1898: 107).[21] In the bare, dark, 'non-A zone' of *Not I*, this dialectal inflection in the *après-texte*, which develops Beckett's note in the *avant-texte*, adds specific sociocultural nuance to Mouth's descriptions of vagrancy. The voice of Mouth, who recognizes herself because of her own accent, will necessarily be open to the 'redoing' of particular performers adding their own accents in performance. Such tiny shifts become even more important in the absence of the Auditor, whom Beckett had suggested cutting even prior to the world premiere in New York.[22] When it came to recording the play for the BBC, Beckett approved the removal of the Auditor, an omission he would retain for the Paris production starring Madelaine Renaud in 1975.[23] With so little visible onstage, the introduction of the smallest detail opens potential interpretative avenues, the politics of which can be examined by analysing contemporary productions, in which *Not I* continues to be 'redone'.

---

[20] It gained references in the margins to verses of the Bible, which Beckett matched to biblical allusions in the draft (*Pas moi* MS 2, UoR MS 1396/4/26: 6r–7r).

[21] It is too hard to say whether Whitelaw uses 'any' or 'anny' (*A Wake for Sam*: 3:27–3:30, 9:59–10:00; *CDW*: 376, 380). Her repetition 'any … any' uses standard pronunciation (*A Wake for Sam*: 7:20–7:21; *CDW*: 378). She uses RP pronunciation for 'either' (*A Wake for Sam*: 12:56–13:05; *CDW*: 382).

[22] 'The auditor? only answer worth giving: try it without him. The more he disturbs the better' (SB to AS, 5 November 1972, *NABS*: 287).

[23] The Auditor was restored for the production Beckett directed in Paris in 1978. 'At the end of this production of the play, Auditor covered his head with his hands in a gesture of increased helplessness and despair, as if unable to bear any longer the torrent of sound' (Knowlson and Pilling 1979: 198). According to Ruby Cohn, the Auditor's gestures in this production 'were still unsatisfactory to Beckett' (1980: 267).

Not I's politics of confinement

For Rancière, because they involve changing the conditions of thought, 'the "fictions" of art and politics are [...] heterotopias rather than utopias' (see Introduction). Rather than the 'no-place' suggested by the etymology of 'utopia', *Not I*'s politics arise out of the relations between the voice on a darkened proscenium stage space and the spaces created diegetically in Beckett's play, however distorted and disjunctive these relations may appear. As *Not I*'s politics continue to be reformulated in different performance contexts, it is important to examine these productions in order to understand the continuing political effects of confinement in Beckett's play.

In March 2016, Ireland's National Concert Hall staged versions of Beckett's *Not I* and *Footfalls* as part of an evening of performance which included theatre pieces by Bernard Shaw and Fintan O'Toole, music by Franz Schubert, John Field and Krzysztof Penderecki and a reading of T. S. Eliot's 'The Waste Land' by Fiona Shaw. Because of this diversity of performance styles and the size of the stage in the Concert Hall – backed by a choir balcony which was closed off for the evening – *Not I* was performed as never before by special permission of the Beckett Estate.[24] Instead of positioning actor Lisa Dwan behind what would have been an unmanageably large blackout screen (which also would have been extremely difficult to remove for the other performances) in order to create the play's central image of a mouth suspended '*about 8 feet above stage level*', she took her place behind a waist-high horizontal bar, which she gripped while delivering Mouth's rapid-fire monologue in full view of the audience (*CDW*: 376). Dwan's performed movements challenge the received image of Beckett's late dramatic writing as a theatre of stasis, emphasizing her need for physical confinement in other productions of the play, during which she is restrained behind the blackout screen by a head harness.[25]

Dwan's use of stage equipment in her regular performances of the play follows on explicitly from the working practice of actor Billie Whitelaw, with whom Beckett worked closely. Dwan met Whitelaw in 2006 and went on to rehearse and discuss the play with her in detail (Dwan 2016). Though not every performance of *Not I* has the actor's body constrained in such a severe fashion, confinement has had an important role in the development of the

---

[24] The stage in the main auditorium of the Concert Hall is 14.63 m wide and 10.36 m deep ('National Concert Hall').

[25] 'From *Play* onward Beckett's stage images would grow increasingly de-humanized, reified and metonymic, featuring dismembered or incorporeal creatures. It became a theater finally static and undramatic in any traditional sense' (Gontarski 1997: 93). See also Oppenheim (2009).

play in performance, most notably in the first production Beckett worked on in person.[26] This production starred Whitelaw as Mouth with Brian Miller as the Auditor and was staged in London's Royal Court in 1973.[27] Whitelaw's difficulty in balancing while performing Mouth's monologue in rehearsal led her to change from a standing to a sitting posture, replacing a raised rostrum with a chair, in front of which there was a bar which she gripped in order to release tension.[28] However, due to the rapid voice which Beckett had developed in his manuscripts, her head started to shake during performances, moving her mouth out of the small spot of light which made it visible. In order to rectify this, an improvised solution was developed by designer Jocelyn Herbert and stage manager Robbie Hendry by which her head was clamped and she was strapped into the chair (Whitelaw 1996: 124–5). In this example, we can see how the voice developed by Beckett led directly to the confinement of his actor onstage.

What are the politics of confining an actor in such a way? At a Beckett conference in 2015, four scholars presented their research on a panel entitled 'The Performing Body', which discussed the constraints placed on actors by Beckett's work, including those placed on Lisa Dwan in her 2014 Royal Court performance of *Not I*. Hannah Simpson's paper, subtitled 'The Actor's Physical Suffering in the Beckettian Production' (2015), compared the descriptions of suffering by actors performing Beckett's work to definitions of torture. While the language of torture is often used to describe Beckett productions – Whitelaw speaks of 'torture' and 'sensory deprivation'; Dwan adds the politically loaded and highly problematic term 'waterboarding' (qtd in Knowlson 1978: 86, 87; qtd in Nonemake 2016) – there are clear differences between the experience of an actor and that of, say, a tortured political prisoner. Because of the heightened speed at which the play is performed, all reports indicate that the actor playing Mouth must be willing to put herself through a rigorous training process of learning and reciting the lines. It is precisely the self-willed confrontation with the difficulty of the playtext which precludes us from viewing the performer simply as a victim of the play's author or director.[29] As Simpson put it during

---

[26] Jessica Tandy used a strap to keep her head in place while rehearsing for the New York premiere of the play, directed by Alan Schneider, but took it off due to discomfort (Knowlson 1997: 592). In a 2015 production, Bríd Ní Neachtain used a chair with a chin rest and two bars on either side to hold onto (Sarah Jane Scaife, email to the author, 22 January 2017).

[27] The Royal Court production was reprised in 1975 with Melvyn Hastings as the Auditor. Beckett was assistant to director Anthony Page at the 1973 production.

[28] Whitelaw used a similar bar to release tension when performing *Play* in 1964 (Whitelaw 1996: 81–2).

[29] This is not to deny that such abuses of power exist in the performance industry, but they need not be – and should not be – a constitutive part of the performance process.

her 2015 conference presentation, 'you can't bully someone into doing *Not I*'. While such a statement is of course falsifiable, it is a very useful reminder of the skill required for a role like Mouth's.

The compositional process and performance history of *Not I* is an excellent example of the work Beckett did to balance indicators of place in his work, creating a piece which is open to multiple interpretations by practitioners, spectators, viewers and readers. Through the improvised solution of restricting an actor's body in order to ensure both a high-speed vocal delivery and a stable image, confinement became a practical measure of ensuring the hermeneutic openness of the play during the Royal Court production in 1973.[30] Given that Beckett elsewhere suppressed details which would have allowed his work to speak on behalf of inmates of institutions of confinement, we should be wary of statements which use the language of torture to describe the performance process of a play such as *Not I*, especially given the privileged position the actor holds as being 'no longer a consumer, but a producer of the text' who can easily create interpretative frames for the work itself (Barthes 1987: 4). Just as a reader or viewer interprets a work of art, so too does an actor make crucial interpretative decisions in their rehearsal and performance of a dramatic role. Whitelaw's marked-up working copy of *Not I* testifies to such active, productive reading in rehearsal and performance (UoR BW A/2/4). By drawing so heavily on imagery of torture in interviews, performers risk appropriating an experience of dereliction and undermining an important aspect of the politics of Beckett's work: namely, the gap in his writing between the experience of the text's 'producer' (be they author or actor) and that of an institutional inmate. While most spectators will not confuse the description of a difficult rehearsal process with an interpretation of the work, such statements do risk filling in important interpretative gaps in the play, gaps which are crucial to the way in which *Not I* functions.

One of the ways in which Mouth gets her audience to fill in the visual and narrative gaps in her story is by repeatedly imploring us (and possibly herself) to 'imagine!' the scenes she describes (*CDW*: 377, 379, 380). In *Offstage Space, Narrative, and the Theatre of the Imagination*, William Gruber explores the ways in which 'unseen people and events [...] tap spectators' imaginations' (2010: 6), arguing that things which are offstage gain in representational power because

---

[30] Illustrating the idea of stage confinement as a practical measure, Alan Schneider told Beckett that lighting the face of the Protagonist in *Catastrophe* was 'more difficult than in the urns [of *Play*] or in NOT I, where the actor is held rigid or confined' (AS to SB, 24 June 1983, *NABS*: 450).

they are created in our imaginations. In *Not I*, Beckett brought onstage some of the power of the offstage 'elsewhere' usually associated with the proscenium's 'non-A zone', staging the sociopolitical invisibility of Mouth's protagonist. But this was not the only work in which the act of imagination within a closed space was made central by Beckett. He would also do so in two prose pieces started in 1964, just one year after the drafting of the fragments towards *Not I* in the 'Kilcool' Notebook.

8

'The Limits of Interpretation'

Imagination Dead Imagine, All Strange Away

This book has so far tracked Beckett's use of closed space from institutions of coercive confinement, recognizably drawn from particular local contexts, to confined spaces which are far more open to interpretation. When it comes to setting interpretative limits in these 'undone' closed spaces, 'who is to decide?' (Genette 1997: 374). For Umberto Eco, 'it is not true that everything goes' when interpreting a literary text (Eco et al. 2004: 144). In 1990, he critiqued 'many modern theories' (i.e. those associated with deconstruction), which 'are unable to recognize that symbols are paradigmatically open to infinite meanings but syntagmatically, that is, textually, open only to the indefinite, but by no means infinite, interpretations allowed by the context' (1994: 21). Jonathan Culler disagreed:

> I believe that Eco has been misled by his concern with limits or boundaries. He wants to say that texts give a great deal of scope to readers but that there are limits. Deconstruction, on the contrary, stresses that meaning is context bound – a function of relations within or between texts – but that context itself is boundless. (2004a: 120)

In spite of their polemics, Eco and Culler share a certain amount of common ground, with Eco agreeing that 'contextual pressure' forms an important part of meaning-making (1994: 21). The closed spaces of Beckett's postwar work create specific kinds of contextual pressure. As Ulrika Maude puts it with regard to bodily movement in Beckett's prose: 'The lack of contextual definition [...] functions in a manner which forces us to focus our attention on what *is* described in minute detail', increasing the interpretative weight of the elements that remain in Beckett's minimalist texts (2009a: 90; emphasis in original). However, in their various forms of 'undoing', Beckett's texts trouble what Rita Felski has called 'a fealty to the clarifying power of historical context' (2011: 574). With regard to closed space, establishing that Beckett wrote about institutions of confinement across his early oeuvre and remained interested in prisons and prisoners all his life does not explain the politics of confinement in his later work. There is more interpretative work to be done than simply reading these closed spaces as 'vaguened' forms of the earlier institutions.

Though confinement is a persistent concern across Beckett's oeuvre, the attempt central to his closed-space texts to narrate a body in a bare, enclosed space constitutes a new spatial approach – 'staying in' – to the aesthetic problem of 'going on' (see *NHO*: 101). These texts are generally seen as comprising *Imagination Dead Imagine* (*Imagination morte imaginez*, 1965), 'Closed Place' ('Se voir', 1973), 'Ping' (*Bing*, 1966), *Lessness* (*Sans*, 1969), *The Lost Ones* and *All Strange Away* (1976).[1] On a draft translation of 'Se voir', dated 8 February 1974, Beckett made an edit which points to a key feature of the hermeneutics of his closed spaces. Having translated the opening line '[e]ndroit clos' as '[c]losed space', he then put a line through 'space' and replaced it with 'place' (UoR MS 1550/19: 1r, qtd in Van Hulle 2010: 258). Beckett chose not to focus on the literal meaning of 'se voir' [to see oneself/each other] when translating the title into English. Instead, he favoured 'Closed Place'.[2] But when the story was first published in the UK, it was entitled 'Closed place' [*sic*] in the contents list only and 'Closed Space' in the text (Beckett 1976a: 5, 47).[3] According to Yi-Fu Tuan, '[p]lace is security, space is freedom: we are attached to the one and long for the other' (2001: 3). In light of this definition of 'place' as representing a fixity which opposes itself to the openness of 'space', Beckett could be said to have made the locale of the piece more confined in his work on the English translation. However, given the connotations of openness and expanse carried by the word 'space', the phrase 'closed space' encapsulates very well the seeming paradox of imagining an area of confinement which nonetheless suggests other spaces beyond. It is this relationship between confinement and what the stage directions of *Endgame* call '*the without*' that means while they are spatially closed, Beckett's works tend to be hermeneutically open (*CDW*: 106).

---

[1] For various groupings, see Cohn (2008: 289); Nixon (2010: xii–xvii); Van Hulle (2010: 255–8). I also consider the unfinished 'Long Observation of the Ray' to be part of this group (see below). *Bing* receives italics because, unlike its English translation 'Ping', it gives its title to an edition in which it was published.

[2] For evidence that Beckett favoured the title 'Closed Place' over 'Closed Space', see SB to Christopher Ricks, 4 November 1976, *LSB* IV: 440.

[3] *CSP* uses 'Closed place', and this title is retained in *TFN*.

Central to this hermeneutic openness is what lies beyond the closed space. Beckett described his reading of other writers in terms of being 'on the lookout for an elsewhere' ['à l'affût d'un ailleurs'] (SB to Hans Naumann, 17 February 1954, *LSB* II: 465, 462). In his closed-space works, a key part of the creation of an 'elsewhere' comes from his use of intertextual references. While recent scholarship on *Imagination Dead Imagine* and *All Strange Away* has focused on the connection between Beckettian and Coleridgean aesthetics (Rodriguez 2007 and Lawley 2007), Shakespeare's *Midsummer Night's Dream* is crucial to the spatial dynamics of the two pieces. Beckett studied Shakespeare's play as an undergraduate in Trinity College Dublin (in 1923–4) (Pilling 2006: 8). Just over four decades later, in 1964, he recalled from memory Theseus' statement on poetic imagination from Act V, Scene I, jotting it down in the 'Fancy ~~Dead~~ Dying' Notebook while drafting what would become *Imagination Dead Imagine* and *All Strange Away*:

> And as imagination bodies forth
> The forms of things unknown, the poet's pen
> Turns them to shapes + gives to airy nothing
> A local habitation + a name. ('FD': 11v, qtd in Van Hulle and Nixon 2013: 26)[4]

Nothing would seem to be further from the received idea of Beckett's own creative practice as one which shuns the specific by 'undoing' location than Theseus' evocation of poetic creation as giving particular names to abstract forms. Indeed, in making indeterminate the link between the bottled-up storyworld and the world in which we read the text, Beckett creates a politics of confinement very different to Theseus' expression of fear at the subversive power of poetry.

Naming places in closed spaces

While the theatres in which Beckett's work is performed can be seen as heterotopias due to their inversion of 'real sites' (see Introduction), the prose spaces created in *Imagination Dead Imagine* and *All Strange Away* have a different relationship to the world in which they were written. In Foucault's definition of heterotopias, he stresses the importance of them being 'real places – places that

---

[4] As Beckett's punctuation in the 'Fancy ~~Dead~~ Dying' Notebook varies from that in standard editions of Shakespeare's plays, I contend that he wrote the Theseus quotation from memory rather than transcribing it from either his 1957 reprint of the 1954 OUP edition of Shakespeare or his 'Universal' edition, published by Frederick Warne (see *BDL*; Shakespeare 1957: 214; 1896: 184).

do exist', as opposed to the imagined space of utopia (Foucault 1986: 24). The closed spaces of *Imagination Dead Imagine* and *All Strange Away* are too 'short of world' to fit this definition of a heterotopia (Connor 2014: 180).[5] In the last of the *Three Dialogues with Georges Duthuit*, Beckett compares Bram van Velde's work favourably to art which is 'short of the world, short of self', as van Velde's is 'without these esteemed commodities' (*PTD*: 122). But Beckett's own closed spaces are never without the world. Rather, they draw our attention to the world without.

In a reading of Beckett's postwar oeuvre as one that both draws on and breaks from the genre of utopian fiction, H. Porter Abbott contends that the politics of *Imagination Dead Imagine* and *All Strange Away* rest upon the fact that the relation between the world we live in and the storyworld – found, as he points out, in the very title of George Orwell's *1984* – is rendered 'terminally indeterminate' in Beckett's prose (Abbott 1996: 135). Indeterminate, certainly, but like the imagination in Beckett's prose piece, political interpretation is not dead. In the same way as 'the fundamentally unreal spaces' of utopia, the imagined spaces of Beckett's late prose also retain critical relations to the world in which they were created, however indeterminate these relations may be (Foucault 1986: 24). While what constitutes action in Beckett's closed spaces takes place in dystopic confinement, there is no clear relation between this space and the world beyond, not to mention the world in which we read the text.

The early versions of the 'confining space' of *Imagination Dead Imagine* and *All Strange Away* are described using a multitude of terms in the 'Fancy ~~Dead~~ Dying' Notebook (Fraser 1995: 518). The narrator describes it variously as '[m]on cabinet' [my cabinet/office] (2r), '[une] stalle' [a stall] (4r), 'l'asile' [the refuge/madhouse] (7r), '[un] refuge' [a refuge] (7r, 8r), 'un réduit' [a cubbyhole/box room] (9r), a 'wall cupboard' (9r), a 'kind of closet or cupboard' (10r), an 'apertureless space' (12r), a 'place' which is 'round' (28v) and, finally, a 'rotunda' (29r and elsewhere) which is compared to 'the Pantheon at Rome [xx] and certain beehive tombs' (29r).[6] Like much of Beckett's postwar writing, this list testifies to the problem of describing a physical constraint which echoes the political dynamics of institutional confinement without naming a particular kind of institution. When a term associated with institutional confinement did make an appearance, Beckett was quick to get rid of it. 'Asile', linked etymologically to

---

[5]   For a different conception of the relationship between literature and heterotopias, see Dennis (2017).
[6]   The narrator also compares the size of the space in which his protagonist is found to that of a closet/cupboard ('FD': 7r).

the English word 'asylum', is an archaic French term for a psychiatric hospital (*PR*), which was quickly struck out and replaced by 'refuge' when used in the notebook ('FD': 9r). Far from giving his 'local habitation' a name, Beckett here avoids suggesting an interpretation of his text in terms of institutional confinement. Though confinement links the spaces of the 'Fancy ~~Dead~~ Dying' Notebook to the institutions of earlier works, there is nothing in the drafts to suggest that the closed spaces are 'vaguened' forms of a previously conceived carceral space.

'In here': Stranger things

There can be no inside without some implied outside. While Beckett did not write *Imagination Dead Imagine* or *All Strange Away* as performance texts – referring to them specifically as prose works in a letter of 18 October 1964 to Richard Seaver (qtd in Nixon 2012: 6) – Ubersfeld's concepts of performance space can help us better understand the spatial dynamics of these works.[7] If the onstage space of *Not I* is established in relation to the 'A zone' evoked in Mouth's monologue, the equally strange settings of these prose pieces open up spatial alternatives beyond their walls through confinement in an enclosed space of some of the remainders of everyday life. Like Ubersfeld, Lefebvre sees two sides to every physical limit: 'walls, enclosures and façades serve to define both a *scene* (where something takes place) and an *obscene* area to which everything that cannot or may not happen on the scene is relegated' (Lefebvre 1991: 36). Along the same lines, Irit Degani-Raz references Sam's attraction in *Watt* to what she terms 'transparent' rather than 'opaque' physical limits. Quoting from *Watt*, she includes in the former category 'wire fences, [...] the ditch, the dyke, the barred window, the bog, the quicksand, the paling' and in the latter 'walls', 'palissades' [*sic*] and 'opacious hedges' (*W*: 135). Degani-Raz argues that the imperative phrase 'imagination dead imagine' suggests an opaque limit of thought by compelling us to imagine what is by definition unimaginable – namely, the death of the imagination (2012: 226–7). It is these very spatial limits, transparent or opaque, which compel the reader to imagine spaces other than and beyond the ones presented in Beckett's closed-space texts. At the end of *Imagination Dead Imagine*, the possibility of such alternative spaces is suggested before being

---

[7] I would like to thank Mark Nixon for sharing his script of this conference presentation with me. I follow the pagination on the script.

undermined: 'Leave them there, sweating and icy, there is better elsewhere. No, life ends and no, there is nothing elsewhere' (*TFN*: 89).

For Edward Casey, the paradox associated with the Pythagorean philosopher Archytas that '[w]e cannot imagine any limit anywhere without at the same time imagining that there is space beyond it' is central to the history of Western philosophy of space.[8] The earliest surviving record of the argument is Simplicius' sixth century CE account of Eudemus' version of Archytas' conundrum. Carl Huffman, pointing out that Simplicius' text is part of a commentary on Aristotle, argues that this account of Archytas' argument, which seems to have largely focused on the question of absolute space, is here heavily influenced by the separate Aristotelian concern as to whether or not an unlimited body exists. Huffman also argues that Aristotle used Archytas' argument as a basis for his position in the *Physics* that 'the imagination can always conceive a beyond' (2005: 545). Though Beckett noted Archytas' name in his notes on Pythagoreanism, there is no evidence of him having read classical accounts of the philosopher's argument on space.[9] But Beckett did encounter a version of this argument when reading James Jeans's *The Universe Around Us* in the early 1930s: 'hard though it may be to imagine space extending for ever, it is far harder to imagine a barrier of something different from space which could prevent our imaginations from passing into further space beyond' (1929: 70).[10] Written over three decades later, the closed-space texts are deeply engaged with the problem of being able to imagine a 'space beyond'.

This relationship between confined space and what lies beyond is illuminated by the lines adjacent to the Theseus quote Beckett recalled from *Midsummer Night's Dream*. In Hippolyta's lines which frame Theseus' speech, she twice emphasizes the 'strange' nature of the story she and her husband-to-be have heard from the lovers in the forest:

> 'Tis strange, my Theseus, that these lovers speak of.
> [Theseus' speech]
> But all the story of the night told over,
> And all their minds transfigur'd so together,
> More witnesseth than fancy's images,
> And grows to something of great constancy;
> But howsoever, strange and admirable. (V. 1. 1: 23–7)[11]

---

[8] This wording of Archytas' argument is from an essay by Isaac Newton, 'De gravitatione et aequipondio fluidorum', qtd in Casey (1998: 149).

[9] TCD MS 10967: 1r, 19r, 22v.

[10] Jeans goes on to refute the argument (1929: 70–1).

[11] References are to Shakespeare (2001) unless otherwise stated.

Hippolyta here uses 'strange' to signify that the stories are fantastic. But there is another sense in which the term operates in Shakespeare's play. When Hermia says that her elopement with Lysander means that they will 'seek new friends, and stranger companies', she evokes the etymological root of the word in the Latin '*extraneus*', which means 'external'. In this context, 'stranger' is an adjective denoting people, such as Hippolyta herself, who are foreign to Athens. As Tuan points out in his essay 'Strangers and Strangeness', 'foreigner' and 'forest' are etymologically linked: 'The basic idea is derived from the Latin *foranus*, which means situated on the outside' (1986: 11). Theseus' sovereign ownership of 'the palace wood' is recognized by the other characters, yet one of the reasons the forest can serve as a playground for fantastical events, clandestine meetings and amorous misadventures is its position beyond the political stronghold marked by the gates of Athens.[12] By contrast, the unusualness of the rotunda in *All Strange Away* comes from the narrator's attempt to only '[i]magine what needed' and to exclude foreign elements from the space (*TFN*: 73).

However, 'like the cat and the dog in *Film*', such elements keep sneaking back in (Van Hulle 2010: 256; see *CDW*: 332–3). Indeed, as the 'cobweb' on the wall in *All Strange Away* must have at some stage been produced by a spider, the space cannot be fully closed, nor is it a completely dead space (*TFN*: 73). In his first sustained attempt at a draft in English, Beckett tried out a narrative which included an outside space that would explain the provenance of strange images:

> On my return, scrupulous as always, I looked to satisfy my mind that all was as I had left it. [...] There was in me for a time what could not have got in here, friendly faces, one particularly, strips of burning sky. ('FD': 4r)

Those inanimate objects which do make it into the published text of *All Strange Away* have no such backstory. One is a 'small grey punctured rubber ball or small grey ordinary rubber bulb' which recalls the 'small, old, black, hard, solid rubber ball' in *Krapp* and the 'kind of ball' belonging to Dan Rooney in *All That Fall* (*TFN*: 81; *CDW*: 220, 198). Having described this ball/bulb being squeezed by Emma, the narrator voices what could serve as a minimalist manifesto: 'so little by little all strange away'. Whereas 'on earth', we are told, an object such as this would be 'attached to bottle of scent or suchlike', here it is 'alone', separated from its

---

[12] While, as Jeffrey Theis argues, no character has full authority over the sylvan space and 'Shakespeare's reciprocal construction of the forest as green plot and the stage as forest blurs the pastoral opposition of country and city' (2009: 119), Theseus still legally owns the forest, as Peter Quince indicates by calling it 'the palace wood' (I. 2. 95). Indeed, the blurring of oppositions depends on the two zones' initial spatial disjunction.

context (*TFN*: 81). It is denarrated in the closing lines: 'gone now and never were sprayer bulb or punctured rubber ball and nothing ever in that hand' (*TFN*: 84). In a case such as this one, 'definition is through negative proposition, through reference to what no longer exists', the space being continually constructed in the narrative through the subtraction of its physical objects (Dearlove 1982: 113).

'Not here': Palimpsests

While confinement in the bare rotunda automatically invokes spaces beyond it, another way of creating alternative spaces in Beckett's closed-space texts is through their relations to the works of other writers. There are various levels of intertextuality in *Imagination Dead Imagine* and *All Strange Away*, which together create what Genette terms a 'palimpsest of reading' through which 'one text can become superimposed upon another, which it does not quite conceal but allows to show through' ['qu'il laisse voir par transparence'] (1997: 374, 399; 1992: 556). While Gontarski uses the concept of the palimpsest to draw attention to 'realistic content' in early drafts of Beckett's plays, it can also be very useful in outlining how intertexts in closed space extend our limits of interpretation.

Intertextuality is given a physical form in the shape of the syntaxes of Jolly and Draeger which litter the confined space of *All Strange Away*, these being the only objects mentioned in the first two *Faux départs*, prose segments composed on the opening pages of the 'Fancy ~~Dead~~ Dying' Notebook which share lines and key themes with *Imagination Dead Imagine* and *All Strange Away*.[13] These syntaxes provide physical evidence of textual production beyond and their 'tattered' state – mentioned in the fourth *Faux départ* as well as *All Strange Away* itself – suggests sustained use (*TFN*: 70, 73). Later in *All Strange Away*, these texts are subject to the same process of denarration as the ball/bulb: 'Jolly and Draeger gone, never were' (*TFN*: 77). The existence of objects such as a book describing the grammatical rules of Latin in the rotunda of *All Strange Away* points to a corresponding linguistic and social structure; this remains true even if we do not know the precise relation between the confined body and the body politic beyond.

Other references are autotextual. The Theseus quotation discussed above faces a passage in the 'Fancy ~~Dead~~ Dying' Notebook which evokes a staple scenario of

---

[13] The *Faux départs* were published in a group of four in 1965. Ackerley and Gontarski identify the Draeger work as Dr A. Draeger's *Historische Syntax der lateinischen Sprache* (1874–8) (2004: 149).

Beckett's postwar prose: 'Out of the door and down the road in the old hat + coat like after the war, no, not that again' ('FD': 12r). Another self-reference is to an unpublished piece of writing – the Philosophy Notes Beckett took in the 1930s – with Emma uttering the names of 'ancient Greek philosophers ejaculated with place of origin when possible suggesting pursuit of knowledge at some period' (*TFN*: 78). When she does utter the name of a philosopher, the place of origin is frequently inaudible, 'leaving sometimes in some doubt such things as which Diogenes' (*TFN*: 79). Beckett mentions both Diogenes of Apollonia and Diogenes of Sinope in his Philosophy Notes (TCD MS 10967: 50r, 68r). In *All Strange Away*, the 'local habitation' which would identify the philosopher is hinted at, but omitted. Elsewhere she mentions a figure in an unnamed place: 'In a hammock in the sun and here the name of some bewitching site she lies sleeping' (*TFN*: 78). In such cases, not only is the figure in the rotunda, to use the protagonist's own words, 'not here', the place against which 'here' is defined is deliberately withheld.[14]

The intertextuality of *Imagination Dead Imagine* and *All Strange Away* is also signalled in the play between the title of the former and, in the latter, the repeated references to the protagonists in the rotunda murmuring that 'fancy is' 'his' or 'her' 'only hope' (*TFN*: 74, 76). Beckett would have come across a well-known distinction between fancy and imagination while reading Coleridge's *Biographia Literaria* 'without much pleasure' in 1962, two years before starting work on the 'Fancy ~~Dead~~ Dying' Notebook (SB to Mary Hutchinson, 11 June 1962, qtd in Van Hulle and Nixon 2013: 35). But here the Shakespearian context is again relevant; indeed, there is evidence that the *Biographia* may have been an intertextual gateway which led Beckett back to Shakespeare's play. If Beckett still read editorial footnotes with the same scholarly zeal in 1962 as he had done when reading Boswell and Windelband in the 1930s (see Addyman and Feldman 2011: 763), he would have come across a version of Theseus' statement in John Shawcross's editorial notes to Coleridge's *Biographia Literaria*, which are included in the 1907 edition of which Beckett owned a reprint (*BDL*).[15]

While Coleridge sees fancy and imagination as distinct faculties, Hippolyta's response to Theseus' speech in *Midsummer Night's Dream* – that the stories they

---

[14] 'He's not here' and 'She's not here' are two of the other common phrases spoken by the confined figure. They vary depending on whether the protagonist is described as being male or female (*TFN*: 74–8, 83).

[15] Shawcross cites Henry Crabb Robinson's diary, in which Robinson recalls Wordsworth reciting two lines from his poem 'To the Cuckoo', 'Shall I call thee bird / Or but a wandering voice?', as an example of the imagination 'giving local habitation to an abstraction' (Coleridge 1907: 228).

have heard from the lovers in the forest '[m]ore witnesseth than fancy's images' – posits fancy as synonymous with imagination, both words describing the creative faculty that Theseus believes unduly sways the reason of lovers, madmen and poets.[16] Pilling argues: 'Beckett [...] resuscitates the category of Fancy which the great Romantic poets considered decidedly inferior to Imagination, reminding us implicitly that he is a good deal less interested in the Sublime than they were' (Knowlson and Pilling 1979: 138).[17] However, there is a clear hierarchy in how the two terms are used in *All Strange Away*. While 'imagine' serves as the narrative impetus, prompting the reader to call up images, fancy is repeatedly referred to as being 'dead'. Moreover, while the phrase '[i]magination dead imagine', which opens *All Strange Away*, contains the paradoxical instruction to imagine the death of the imagination, the phrase 'fancy [...] dead', which ends it, is terminal (*TFN*: 73; 84). Apart from changing the title of his compositional notebook from 'Fancy ~~Dead~~ Dying' to the published title *Imagination morte imaginez* ('FD': front cover), Beckett never replaced one term with the other in composition, which again suggests they should be read as distinct concepts.[18]

While Beckett does not outline Coleridge's tripartite differentiation between primary and secondary imagination and fancy, the hierarchy between imagination and fancy in *Imagination Dead Imagine* and *All Strange Away* is a departure from the early modern equivalence between the two terms.[19] *Imagination Dead Imagine* is not simply a 'minimal, stark dramatization' of the quotation from *Midsummer Night's Dream*; rather, it challenges the spatial aesthetic expounded in Shakespeare's play (Van Hulle and Nixon 2013: 26). Whereas Theseus sees poetry as politically subversive because it gives a name to forms with no real existence, *Imagination Dead Imagine* and *All Strange Away* generate their spatial dynamic by both suggesting and withholding names from their confined habitations. In this sense, while not written for the theatre, the spatial dynamics of Beckett's prose works are closer to the spatial dynamic governing theatrical performance than what Theseus himself says onstage. As in his theatre, written for the proscenium stage, Beckett's closed-space pieces depend on invisible – or

---

[16] Such comparative definitions of fancy and imagination were more common in the early modern than in the Romantic period (Engell 2012: 668–73).

[17] In their co-authored book, Pilling deals with the prose; Knowlson with the drama (1979: ix).

[18] This downplaying of fancy is also found in 'Still 3', where the sound of a bell is dismissed as 'perhaps mere fancy' (*TFN*: 173).

[19] For Coleridge, the primary imagination underpins all perception by repeating 'in the finite mind [...] the eternal act of creation in the infinite I AM' and the secondary imagination 'struggles to idealize and to unify' impressions given to the mind. Fancy is a lower creative faculty which arranges 'fixities and definites' according to their associative qualities (1907: 202).

partially visible – elements which are both 'not there' yet also 'not not there' (Sofer 2013: 4).[20] It is these elements which his intertexts bring into focus.

If not those of Theseus' Platonic anti-mimeticism, what are the political dynamics created in Beckett's closed spaces? As in *Not I*, there is a redistribution of the field of the sensible, suggesting a confined dystopia – 'a planet in the shape of a prison cell' (Abbott 1996: 141) – while never providing the context necessary to settle this interpretation. On a thematic level, the spatial politics of *All Strange Away* are also discernible through an inversion of a phrase from William Henley's 'Invictus' (1888), which was included in W. B. Yeats's *Oxford Book of Modern Verse* (1936). Beckett owned a copy of this book and, according to Yeats's letter to Dorothy Wellesley of 19 May 1937, Beckett even wrote a review of it which the *Irish Times* refused to publish because it was too hostile (Yeats 1994; see Morin 2017: 76). So Beckett would have known the text quite well. However, as with *A Midsummer Night's Dream*, it is unlikely that he would have needed to consult the Yeats edition in order to use Henley's phrase (*BDL*).[21] Yeats famously excluded poems written by First World War combatants from his collection because, according to him, 'passive suffering is not a theme for poetry' (1952: xxxiv). In 'Invictus', Henley's speaker expresses a stoic attitude to suffering:

> In the fell clutch of circumstance
> I have not winced nor cried aloud.
> Under the bludgeonings of chance
> My head is bloody, but unbowed (Yeats 1952: 25)

Beckett's inversion of the phrase in *All Strange Away* gives a purposefully undramatic description of the beaten-down situation of his protagonist: 'back of head touching the ceiling, gaze on ground, lifetime of unbloody bowed unseeing glaring' (*TFN*: 75). While the '*bowed*' heads of the Protagonist in *Catastrophe* and the interrogated figures in *What Where* signal their oppression by a dominant antagonist, that in *All Strange Away*, brought about by 'a lifetime of walking bowed and full height when brought to a stand', has more in common with the crouched figures of 'He Is Barehead' ('Il est tête nue', 1972) and 'Mongrel Mime', who are 'bowed' because of the restricted space in which they move (*CDW*: 457, 470;

---

[20] Sofer here draws on Richard Schechner's model of the performer as being both 'not me' and 'not not me' (qtd in Sofer 2013: 149 n. 14).

[21] As it still is now, 'Invictus' was extremely popular in the middle part of the twentieth century. For instance, Churchill used it in one of his wartime speeches to the House of Commons on 9 September 1941 (1981: 769).

TFN: 73; *CSP*: 224). This attempt at movement stymied by the spatial restriction of an imagined location is not quite as passive as the crouched indolence of Dante's Belacqua, itself referenced in the supine postures of *Imagination Dead Imagine* and *All Strange Away*.[22] On the other hand, we are nowhere near the protest of the Protagonist raising his bowed head at the end of *Catastrophe*. If, for Tuan, '[t]he standing posture is assertive, solemn, and aloof' and '[t]he prone position is submissive' the crouched, standing posture of the figure in *All Strange Away* is set between passivity and protest (Tuan 2001: 37). With regard to Beckett's TV play *Quad*, Amanda Dennis argues persuasively that Beckett 'troubles the rigid dichotomy between active and passive', thereby creating 'alternatives to ready-made meaning' (2018: 15). For Dennis, this troubling of the line between passivity and action 'is not without political significance' (2018: 16). While the meaning-making activity of interpretation has often been thought of in opposition to political action, the 'active passivity' (Dennis 2018: 15) of the 'unbloody bowed' head of *All Strange Away*'s protagonist forces us to think anew the political relationships between the body and the spaces it inhabits.

In 'A Thanksgiving', one of two textual precursors to 'Invictus', Henley's speaker declares himself impervious to fear of the vast unknown: 'I front unfeared the threat of Space' (qtd in Cohen 1974: 194). For Beckett's closed-space protagonists, the prospect of open, expansive space is something which is generally beyond reach. But its possibility does exist and, significantly, this possibility depends on competing interpretations. In the enclosed cylinder of *The Lost Ones*, these interpretations are created intertextually, through the 'words of the poet'. Regarding this outside space, we are told, there are two prevailing opinions: one group of inhabitants believes that there is a secret passage in the tunnels which would take one out of the cylinder to 'nature's sanctuaries'; another thinks that there is a trapdoor in the ceiling, beyond which 'the sun and other stars would still be shining' (*TFN*: 105). As Daniela Caselli points out, the latter phrase is a translation of the last words of Dante's *Paradiso* (2005: 195).[23] The former allusion is less straightforward: some scholars attribute the phrase 'nature's sanctuaries' ['asiles de la nature' (Beckett 2013a: 16)] to Alphonse de Lamartine's poem 'Le Vallon' ('The Valley'), in which the speaker asks a valley

---

[22] 'And even sit, knees drawn up, trunk best bowed, head between knees, arms round knees to hold all together' (*TFN*: 75). Across Beckett's oeuvre, this crouched posture is repeatedly linked to Dante's Belacqua, explicitly so in *The Lost Ones*: 'those who do not search or non-searchers sitting for the most part against the wall in the attitude which wrung from Dante one of his rare wan smiles' (*TFN*: 103; see Caselli 2005: 190).

[23] '[T]he Love that moves the sun and all the other stars' (Dante, *Paradiso* canto XXXIII, line 145).

known since childhood for 'Un asile d'un jour pour attendre la mort' ['A day's asylum to wait for death'] (de Lamartine 1993: 50–1).[24] It is equally possible that the phrase is an allusion to Jean-Jacques Rousseau's third letter to his supporter Chrétien-Guillaume de Lamoignon de Malesherbes. Having told Malesherbes in an earlier letter that his retreat to Montmorency outside Paris was caused by an innate love of solitude, Rousseau wrote on 26 January 1762 about going to an 'asile' [sanctuary/refuge] in the heart of a nearby forest, whose beautiful flora is devoid of any evidence of human contact.[25] It is here that his imagination starts to go to work in a process similar to the narrative acts of creation in *Imagination Dead Imagine* and *All Strange Away*:

> My imagination did not leave the earth, adorned this way, deserted for very long. I soon peopled it with beings in accordance with my heart, and driving opinion, prejudices, all factitious passions very far away, into these refuges of nature ['asiles de la nature'] I transported men worthy of inhabiting them. (2007: 155; 1824: 248)

Whatever Beckett's source was, '[t]he words of the poet', which lead to the interpretative actions of the protagonists, are key to the possibility of imagining a space outside the cylinder of *The Lost Ones*. Rousseau's contemporary James Boswell is also part of this intertextual palimpsest, albeit only in the pre-publication drafts. The description of the cavities in the upper part of the wall in an early French draft as 'galeries' [galleries/tunnels] recalls Boswell's description of Bethlem Asylum in his *Life of Johnson* (UoR MS 1536/3: 3r). The development of one instance of this term into 'alvéoles' in the published text – the latter term also used to describe the rooms of the nondescript institution in 'L'Expulsé' – calls to mind the earlier, more overtly institutional spaces in Beckett's prose, marking the road not taken in the genesis of the cylinder's space (2013a: 10). But the field of intertextual resonances these terms create is still relevant. As shown in Chapter 2, Boswell's *Life* is a key text in the creation of institutional space in *Murphy*, while Lamartine and Rousseau are referenced before the trip to Portrane Asylum in 'Fingal', where they serve as indices for Belacqua's bloated intelligence. In the two earlier works, sanctuary denotes both the safety of a sought-out mental refuge (Murphy being 'obliged [...] to call sanctuary what the psychiatrists called exile') and the confinement of enforced enclosure, in Belacqua's labelling the carceral landscape of Portrane 'a land of sanctuary [...] where much has been

---

[24] Caselli follows Sebastien Neumeister in doing so (Caselli 2005: 197 n. 7).
[25] Beckett called Rousseau 'a champion of the right to be alone' (SB to TM, 16 September 1934, *LSB* I: 228).

suffered in secret, especially by women' (*Mu*: 111–12; *MPTK*: 18). The gendering of 'sanctuary' comes forcefully to the fore again in *All Strange Away*. In order to explore the gendered politics of confinement in this text, it is first necessary to examine the role of the body in producing Beckett's closed spaces.

'Say a body'

If '[s]ocial relations are always spatial', the converse is also true (Harvey 1996: 112). That is, one cannot study closed space without an awareness of the ways in which it acts upon, and is produced through, the bodies which inhabit it. John Cage described his form of minimalism as a 'new music [in which] nothing takes place but sounds' (2011: 7). But it would be a mistake to say that nothing takes place but unembodied space in Beckett's minimalist prose. As the narrator of *Worstward Ho* puts it, it is necessary to '[s]ay a body' in order to create Beckett's closed spaces, mirroring Lefebvre's concept that 'the whole of (social) space proceeds from the body' (*NHO*: 101; Lefebvre 1991: 405). In the closed-space texts, the primary evidence of a world outside the closed space is the body, as when the 'scars' born by the figure confined in the white room of 'Ping' suggest acts of violence originating beyond (*CSP*: 195).

For Tuan, '[e]nclosed and humanized space is place', meaning that the spaces humans inhabit through lived routine become homely and domesticated (Tuan 2001: 54). While the rotundas of *Imagination Dead Imagine* and *All Strange Away* are certainly enclosed, the extent to which they are humanized in Tuan's sense is certainly open to question. In imagining the bodies as being alive, the narrator of *Imagination Dead Imagine* also raises the possibility that they might be something other than human:

> Sweat and mirror notwithstanding they might well pass for inanimate but for the left eyes which at incalculable intervals suddenly open wide and gaze in unblinking exposure long beyond what is humanly possible. (*TFN*: 89)

The figures in *Imagination Dead Imagine* and *All Strange Away* occupy dehumanized spaces, with the narrator of *All Strange Away* even suggesting that the rotunda may be in an extraterrestrial location, comparing the passage of time there to 'years of time on earth', a 'minute on earth', 'hours of time on earth', 'thirty seconds on earth' and 'five seconds on earth' – the implication being that we are not on earth (*TFN*: 74, 76, 77, 82). The question therefore arises as to whether or not we are dealing with the human race.

In a thought experiment regarding the possibility of human thought living on beyond a solar apocalypse, Jean-François Lyotard asks: 'Can Thought go on without a Body?' (1991: 8–23). Adapting Lyotard's question to Beckett's texts, we might ask if his fictional spaces can go on being produced without a human body. That the one extant closed-space piece which does not contain a body, 'Long Observation of the Ray' (written 1975–6), was never completed would suggest that they cannot (see Connor 1992; Davies 2019). But in order to answer this question, we need to look beyond the closed-space texts to Beckett's polemical critical writing on the topic of 'the human'.

'Speak of the "human"'

In two pieces written at the end of the Second World War, at a time when such issues had been thrown into doubt by the barbarism of war, Beckett explicitly addresses the question of what it means to define something as human. Beckett starts 'La peinture des van Velde ou le monde et le pantalon' (1945) by suggesting 'parlons d'autre chose' [let's speak of something else] and goes on to satirize contemporary systems of aesthetic evaluation for works of fine art, as apprehended and evaluated by 'bipèdes sans plumes' [non-feathered bipeds] (Dis: 118, 119). Having then discussed the painting of the van Veldes, he begins his conclusion by repeating his opening: 'parlons d'autre chose'. Beckett then immediately turns his attention to 'the "human"' ['parlons de l'"humain"'] warning of the danger of the term (Dis: 131):

> Here is a word, no doubt a concept too, that has to be reserved for times of huge slaughters. One needs the pestilence, Lisbon and a major religious butchery for people to think of loving one another, of leaving the neighboring gardener in peace, of being radically simple. This is a word that is being bandied around today with an unrivalled fury. Just like dum-dum bullets. (qtd and trans. in Rabaté 2016: 19)[26]

What is under attack here is not the concept of the human as such, but rather its being used only at times of crisis: the fact that we would need a religious war to remind us to love our neighbour should make us suspicious about the integrity

---

[26] 'C'est là un vocable, et sans doute un concept aussi, qu'on réserve pour les temps des grands massacres. Il faut la pestilence, Lisbonne et une boucherie religieuse majeure, pour que les êtres songent à s'aimer, à foutre la paix au jardinier d'à côté, à être simplissimes. C'est un mot qu'on se renvoie aujourd'hui avec une fureur jamais égalée. On dirait des dum-dum' (Dis: 131).

of humanist conceptions of love. Beckett then excoriates those who would judge a work of art by attributing to it a certain level of humanity, before going on to claim that real humanity is to be found in the 'peinture solitaire' [solitary painting] of the van Velde brothers:

> This painting's least particle contains more true humanity than all a procession toward their happiness of sacred sheep. I suppose it will be stoned.[27]

In 'The Capital of the Ruins' (written 1946; published 1986), a radio piece written for the Irish national broadcaster Raidió Éireann on his time as 'interpreter–storekeeper' for the Irish Red Cross in the bombed-out French town of Saint-Lô, Beckett returns to the category of the human (SB to Gwynedd Reavey, 21 June 1945, *LSB* II: 15). He writes of 'a time-honoured conception of humanity in ruins' which, he said, those working in the Red Cross Irish Hospital picked up during their experience in France 'and perhaps even an inkling of the terms in which our condition is to be thought again' (*CSP*: 278).[28] The phrase 'time-honoured' suggests continuity with a tradition of thought in which the human is a central figure, while it is made clear that this system of thought must be rethought in what Beckett calls this 'universe become provisional' (*CSP*: 278). At key rhetorical points in these pieces, when the conditions for any form of shared humanity seem to have been thoroughly undermined – in 'La peinture des van Velde' through the misuse of the term 'human' in the wake of the Second World War; in 'The Capital of the Ruins' through the levelling of urban society which gives the piece its backdrop – Beckett reclaims 'the human' as a valid, if substantially altered, concept. This is a refashioning of 'the human' with 'humanity at the limit' (Rabaté 2016: 195).

In a chapter of *The Inhuman* entitled 'God and the Puppet', Lyotard discusses death and aesthetic experience, two occasions on which, according to him, one can step out of the repetition and difference governed by time. It is in this context that he mentions the puppets described in Heinrich von Kleist's 1810 essay 'On the Marionette Theatre' (Von Kleist 1972), which recounts a conversation with a dancer who persuades Kleist of the grace of the dancing, inanimate figures, seemingly given life through their connection with a puppeteer. For Lyotard, these figures are able to approach the 'infinite divine grace' of a god who stands

---

[27] 'Cette peinture dont la moindre parcelle contient plus d'humanité vraie que toutes leurs processions vers un bonheur de mouton sacré. Je suppose qu'elle sera lapidée' (*Dis*: 132; first sentence trans. in Rabaté 2016: 20).

[28] Beckett takes the phrase 'humanity in ruins' and the title of his piece, 'The Capital of the Ruins', from the local name for the town, 'la Capitale des Ruines' (SB to TM, 19 August 1945, *LSB* II: 18).

outside of time (Lyotard 1991: 163). Beckett too was deeply interested in Kleist's essay, and his single annotation on his copy likewise notes the 'göttliche Anmut' [divine grace] of the marionettes (*BDL*). As James Knowlson reports, images from Kleist's text – particularly that of the unselfconscious bear who effortlessly parries a master fencer's blows – would go on to be important models for Beckett when he was directing his TV play *Ghost Trio*; he also quoted the essay when directing *Happy Days* (Knowlson and Pilling 1979: 279; Knowlson 1997: 584). For Knowlson, the 'severe restraint and economy of movement' in Beckett's late work brings him close to the automatized movement described by Kleist (Knowlson and Pilling 1979: 282). If the gap between subject and object was important for the development of Beckett's aesthetics in the 1930s, the distinction between human and non-human which is discussed in Kleist's work and the asymptotic tendency towards the latter in Beckett's late prose and drama is crucial to the production of closed space in these works. While Lyotard presents the possibility of thought continuing after the apocalypse, he notes also that a '[d]ehumanized' world, destroyed by nuclear war, 'still implies human' (1991: 10). Similarly, Beckett cannot dehumanize his spaces without humans, however inhuman they and the spaces they inhabit may appear.

All Strange Away's gendered genesis of space

Like *Watt*, the published text of *All Strange Away* produces what has, on the model of Roland Barthes's 'reality effect', been termed a 'manuscript effect', in which 'the text increasingly presents itself as a draft' (Van Hulle and Weller 2014: 162). This effect is created through the changing dimensions of the room in the published text, from a 5' × 5' × 6' to a 3' × 3' × 5' to a 3' × 3' × 3' cube, to a rotunda 'three foot diameter eighteen inches high', then 'three foot from ground to vertex' and finally 'two foot diameter and two from ground to vertex' (*TFN*: 73, 74, 76, 79, 80). The effect is further evident in the denarration of the postwar prose scenario which appears in the published texts of both *All Strange Away* and the third of the *Faux départs*: 'Out of the door and down the road in the old hat and coat like after the war, no, not that again' (*TFN*: 70, 73). The metafictional process of imaginative creation takes an important twist when the pronouns used to describe the single body confined in the rotunda change from male to female: 'No, no image, no fly here, no life or dying here but his, a speck of dirt. Or hers since sex not seen so far' (*TFN*: 76). When reading *Worstward Ho*, we have to take the narrator's word when told regarding the back of a body: 'Nothing to show a woman's and yet a woman's' (*NHO*: 120). In *All Strange Away*, the production of sexual difference, like the production of space, becomes part of the narration itself.

This shift of gender mid-composition, and, crucially, the choice to make this shift visible by publishing *All Strange Away* in 1976, over a decade after *Imagination Dead Imagine*, puts the manuscript production of body and space on display for Beckett's readers.[29] At the stage of composition when the cube changed to a rotunda, there are four verso pages filled with sketches and calculations in which Beckett tried to work out the measurements of the space and that of the body within it ('FD': 24v, 25v, 28v, 29v; see Figure 5). At the end of this series of sketches and calculations, there is an inaccurate calculation of the size of Emma's body:

> Emma knees to ft. 1"6
> arse to knees 1"6
> crown to arse 2"6
> 5 ft ('FD': 29v)

The mention of the '[w]aste [of] height' and 'waste [of] space' as well as the earlier phrase '[t]ighten it round him' in both manuscript and published text indicate a desire on the part of the narrator to keep Emma and Emmo in as confined a space as possible ('FD': 22r, 25r, 26r; *TFN*: 77, 74). This relation between the body and the space it occupies is noted early on in the published text: 'He says,

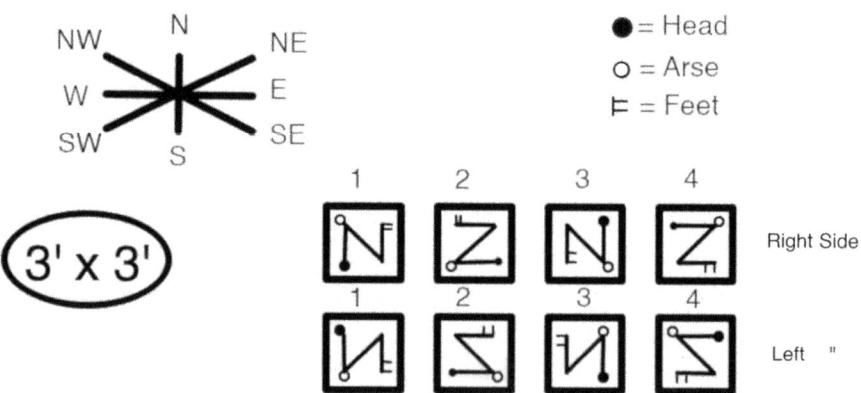

Figure 5 Body positions in a draft of *All Strange Away*, sketched on the back of a letter to Barbara Bray (SB to BB, 22 September 1964, *LSB* III: 628).

---

[29] *All Strange Away* was first published in a deluxe edition by Gotham Book Mart to raise money for Gloria MacGowran, the widow of one of Beckett's favourite actors Jack MacGowran (see SB to Andreas Brown, 27 June 1973, *LSB* IV: 336 n. 4).

no sound, The longer he lives and so the further goes the smaller they grow, the reasoning being the fuller he fills the space and so on, and the emptier, same reasoning' (*TFN*: 73). This line echoes the spatial theory of Albert Einstein as explained in Jeans's *Universe Around Us*, on which Beckett took the following notes in the 1930s: 'Dimensions of space determined by the amount of matter it contains. More matter, less space. No matter, infinite space' (*DN*: 150; see Jeans 1929: 73). It also recalls Hamm's lines on suffering in *Endgame*: 'the bigger a man is the fuller he is. [*Pause. Gloomily.*] And the emptier' (CDW: 93). In *All Strange Away*, the further Emmo develops and grows, the smaller (relatively speaking) the space he occupies becomes and therefore the more he suffers. In both the notebook drafts and the published text, Beckett produces the confined space of the rotunda by having his narrator fit it around the body in that space. In doing so, however, he designs an inhumane space, unfit for humans to inhabit.

As Graham Fraser points out, 'the place holds *more* obsessive interest than the "someone in it"' in *All Strange Away* (1995: 517; *TFN*: 73). Exemplifying the productive relation between body and space, when the narrator of *All Strange Away* does attempt to describe Emmo's figure, it is the space that ends up being described instead: 'Physique, flesh and fell, nail him to that while still tender, nothing clear, place again' (*TFN*: 74). Here, the description of the body itself calls up a carceral space through its reference to imprisonment in *King Lear*. As Lear is being marched off to prison with Cordelia, he comforts his daughter not to lose hope, that their jailers will die before this ever happens: 'The good years shall devour them, flesh and fell, / Ere they shall make us weep!' (V. 3. 24–5). In *Imagination Dead Imagine*, Beckett frames the impossibility of physical death, which parallels the unkillable imagination, by echoing Lear's raving later in the same scene as he carries his daughter's dead body.[30] The test of life – '[h]old a mirror to their lips, it mists' – is passed by the protagonists in the rotunda, whereas the signs of life on Cordelia's lips are the product of her father's grieving imagination: 'Lend me a looking-glass; / If that her breath will mist or stain the stone, / Why then she lives. [...] This feather stirs, she lives' (V. 3. 259–61, 263). Beckett's own stage work avoids presenting the moment at which life ebbs from the female body, opting instead for the hidden death of Nell in *Endgame*, mediated through the report of Clov, and the ambivalent disappearance of May at the end of *Footfalls*. Even *Rockaby* avoids being a straightforward description of onstage death through W's repetition of a few lines of her recorded voice,

---

[30] As the stage directions do not mention Cordelia dying onstage, we can presume she is dead on arrival.

suggesting that this, like the action of many of Beckett's late plays, may be taking place in the imagination of its characters. In *Imagination Dead Imagine*, the characters, like fancy, might be dying, but they are never quite dead. Hence, at the very end of the story, having stated 'life ends', the narrator can again wonder in his closing phrase about 'what they are doing' (*TFN*: 89). While there is a tendency towards death in Beckett's work, his characters nevertheless 'refuse to play dead' completely (Addyman 2009: 89). Having 'never properly been born', Beckett's characters are only (in the words of the Keats line Beckett liked to quote) '*half* in love with easeful death'.[31]

'Kissing, caressing, licking, sucking, fucking and buggering': Ending

In *Rhythmanalysis*, his study of the body's production of space in modern society, Lefebvre argues that we see ourselves 'almost [as] objects. Not completely, however' (2007: 10).[32] Working along similar conceptual lines, Mary Bryden calls the speaker in Beckett's late work an 'ob/subject', a term which points to the fact that the figures of this period are between being animate and inanimate (1993: 153). With this in mind, it is important to note that Emma's body in *All Strange Away* is objectified in a manner that is absent from the description of her male counterpart Emmo: 'Thence on to neck in health by nature blank chunk nearer to healthy natural neck with even hint of jugular and cords suggesting perhaps past her best and thence on down to other meat' (*TFN*: 81). Her body projected onto the walls gets dissected into parts – '[f]irst face alone, lovely beyond words, leave it at that, then deasil breasts alone, then thighs and cunt alone, then arse and hole alone' – and Emmo murmurs, '[i]magine him kissing, caressing, licking, sucking, fucking and buggering all this stuff' (*TFN*: 75). By contrast, Emmo's body, when thought of by Emma, is left to the reader's imagination: 'Emmo on the walls, first the face, handsome beyond words, then deasil details later' (*TFN*: 76). If the body produces space, the closed space of *All Strange Away* receives a literal imprint of sexual difference through the contrasting descriptions of projected corporeal images on its walls.

---

[31] Emphasis added. Beckett attended a lecture in London's Tavistock Clinic on 2 October 1935 at which Carl Gustav Jung spoke of girl who had 'never been born entirely'. Beckett used altered forms of this phrase throughout his work (see Melnyk 2005).

[32] '[N]*ous* sommes, corps et chair, pour nous, presque des objets. Pas tout à fait cependant' (Lefebvre 1992: 20; emphasis in original).

Just prior to the description of his body, the speck of dirt seen by Emmo is imagined as being a 'strand of Emma's motte' or pubic mound (*TFN*: 76). The word 'motte' is linked with the confinement of women in Beckett's work, particularly through the legend of Jonathan Swift's imprisonment of his 'motte' Stella, recounted to Winnie in 'Fingal' (see Chapter 2).[33] Swift's speaker dissects Celia into parts in his poem 'The Lady's Dressing Room', a practice Beckett follows at the opening of the second chapter of *Murphy*, where Murphy's girlfriend Celia is catalogued according to her various bodily measurements (1993: 129–33; *Mu*: 9). Such catalogues of female corporeality evoke Shakespeare's parody of the blazon in Sonnet 130, 'My Mistress's Eyes Are Nothing Like the Sun', in which the woman described cannot measure up to the elevated rhetoric of the genre. As Linda Hutcheon reminds us, the central paradox of parody is that 'its transgression is always authorized'; it both subverts and affirms the authority of the work parodied. Using Mikhail Bakhtin's idea of the 'carnivalesque', Hutcheon notes: 'The recognition of the inverted world still requires a knowledge of the order of the world which it inverts and, in a sense, incorporates' (1985: 26, 74). Hence, for instance, Shakespeare's highly critical, even self-critical, use of the blazon genre 'none the less remains embedded in the descriptive rhetoric it undercuts' (Vickers 2005: 111). The same is true of Beckett's parodic presentations of the female body. While Shakespeare's poem ends with a saving couplet which declares that the mistress of the poem is 'as rare / As any she belied with false compare', there is no such poetic mercy for Emma in *All Strange Away* (Sonnet 130, 13–14).

By 1964, when he started work in the 'Fancy ~~Dead~~ Dying' Notebook, Beckett had already fragmented the female body onstage, presenting it from the waist up in *Happy Days* and starting work on the lit female face of the 'Kilcool' manuscripts in 1963. While it is true that 'his early portraits of women in the fiction are far more stereotypic and scathing than any in the later drama' (Ben-Zvi 1992: xi), the description of an imagined Emma 'being all kissed, licked, sucked, fucked' in *All Strange Away* challenges any assumption that these portraits are made progressively milder over the course of Beckett's career (*TFN*: 76). The differences between the descriptions of Emmo and Emma also complicate what might otherwise be seen as 'a pendulum swing away from sexual hierarchisation' as Beckett's oeuvre progresses (Bryden 1993: 7). While the protagonist's gender in *Enough* was deliberately occluded by Beckett in the course of composition, it

---

[33] The standard Hiberno-English spelling is 'mot' (*OED*).

is not true to say that *All Strange Away* 'no longer proposes an objectified female referent' (Bryden 1993: 8).[34] While Bryden is right to point to a general 'softening of rigid gender delineations' in Beckett's drafts, this softening is reversed by his decision to publish the draft material which constitutes *All Strange Away* (1993: 3). Yet again, we have a clear exception to the received model of Beckett's poetics of 'vaguening', one which has an important impact on the political dynamics of the work.

Swift's gender politics in 'The Lady's Dressing Room' lend themselves to being analysed through a materialist lens by which the body becomes another series of objects in the world, evoking male disgust at the process behind the production of female beauty (Baudot 2009). By rendering its female protagonist more object than subject, *All Strange Away* invites a similar reading. The bodies in *All Strange Away* do not fit Bryden's presentation of Beckett's work as a move towards 'gender fluidity' (1993: 197). Nor are they part of a 'reduction to nothing of sexual difference' that Shane Weller identifies, valid as this may be for other works (2006: 180). Instead, they exemplify Maude's description of Beckett's hermeneutic set-ups, in which the lack of material context draws our attention to the signs of context that remain. The gender politics of *All Strange Away* arise not from a world in which sexual difference has been 'vaguened', but rather one in which the bodies on the wall quite literally produce the protagonists' closed space. When Beckett tried twice more to write plays for prisoners in the 1980s, it was again all-male carceral scenarios which gave him his creative impetus. My final chapter analyses the ways in which these stagings of confinement reframe the ethical questions posed in Beckett's early prose.

[34] Beckett changed a sentence in the first edition of the 1966 story *Assez* (*Enough*) from '[s]i je m'étais retourné je ne l'aurais pas vu' ['If I had looked back I would not have seen him' (*CSP*: 190)] to '[e]n me retournant je ne l'aurais pas vu' [in looking back I would not have seen him], thus 'vaguening' the protagonist's gender by avoiding the gendered past participle 'retourné' (qtd in Bryden 1993: 150; see Beckett 2013e: 41).

The 'Anethics' of Staging Confinement

'Mongrel Mime', *Catastrophe*

Responding on 29 October 1973 to Charles Juliet's suggestion 'that the artistic enterprise is inconceivable without rigorous ethical standards urgently held', Beckett considered the difficulty of making definitive value judgements about art:

> What you say is correct. But moral values are not accessible and not open to definition. To define them, you would have to make value judgements, and you can't do that. That's why I have never agreed with the idea of the theatre of the absurd. Because that implies making value judgements. (Juliet 1995: 148–9)

On 11 November 1977, Beckett returned to the same topic, addressing again the category of 'the absurd' with which his work has often been associated (see Esslin 1983): 'Negation is not possible. Nor affirmation. It is absurd to say that something is absurd. That's still a value judgement. It is impossible to protest, and equally impossible to assent' (Juliet 1995: 165). Beckett's statements to Juliet on morality closely resemble those made by Theodor Adorno when discussing the need for a dialectical definition of the will: 'There is no moral certainty. Its mere assumption would be immoral, would falsely relieve the individual of anything that might be called morality' (2004: 242–3). Both Adorno and Beckett question the possibility of an ethical system against which we can simply check off our actions, be they artistic or otherwise. In tactics recalling Beckett's critique of 'the human', there is a suggestion on the part of both writers that it is the rigorous questioning of ethical standards, rather than 'rigorous standards urgently held', which should be at the heart of any ethical project.

Beckett's oeuvre is not one in which affirmation is found at the heart of negation, as Alain Badiou argues in his adoption of the Beckettian phrase 'continuer' ['keep going'] as a central pillar of his own *Ethics* (2012; 2003a).

Rather, Beckett created an oeuvre that positions itself between affirmation and negation, as in the tension created by the closing lines of *The Unnamable*: 'you must go on, I can't go on, I'll go on' ['il faut continuer, je ne peux pas continuer, je vais continuer'] (*U*: 134; Beckett 1987: 213). In Beckett's letter to Thomas MacGreevy of 16 January 1936, he describes *Murphy* in a similar way: 'I suddenly see that <u>Murphy</u> is break down *between* his [Geulincx's] <u>ubi nihil vales ibi nihil velis</u> (positive) & Malraux's <u>Il est difficile à celui qui vit hors du monde de ne pas rechercher les siens</u> (negation)' (SB to TM, *LSB* I: 299; emphasis added). This chapter argues that we should conceptualize the ethics of Beckett's work in these terms, '*between*' affirmation and negation.

Shane Weller reads Beckett's work as being 'anethical', which he describes in terms of 'a kind of indecision that is not indifference', which 'is an occasion for invention, not of a new art or a new ethics, but rather of ways in which the experience of the disintegration of both art and ethics might be rendered visible – or audible – on a page or a stage' (2006: 194). For Weller, the prefix 'an-' encompasses both 'the Greek *an-*', indicating 'privation', and 'the Latin *an-*', meaning 'by way of' (2006: 56; emphasis in original). In terms of confinement, Beckett's political pentimenti point to both meanings of this prefix: he frequently produced his closed spaces 'by way of' the oppressive spaces of prisons and asylums, but there is also an important degree of 'privation' evident in his decision not to make these institutions the explicit subject of a published play. The strength of 'anethics' as a critical term is its ability to accommodate the openness of interpretation of Beckett's postwar work. From Sam and Watt's 'vaguened' asylum to Emmo and Emma's rotunda, Beckett's closed spaces lend themselves to acts of interpretation which neither close off meaning nor ignore the political resonances of confinement. Two very good examples of this are the late plays 'Mongrel Mime' (written 1983) and *Catastrophe* (1982), which show how freedom of interpretation as well as freedom of movement are crucial to the anethics of Beckett's theatre texts in composition and performance.

'Duly carceral': 'Mongrel Mime'

The politics of Beckett's theatre work are shaped by carceral 'pentimenti', such as the cell bars he considered projecting onstage in his 1975 production of *Godot* in Berlin. One of Beckett's assistants at this production was actor, playwright and founder of the San Quentin Drama Workshop Rick Cluchey. As well as going on to assist the former prisoner at the Workshop's productions of his plays, Beckett, in the year leading up to his death, read and gave feedback to drafts of Cluchey's memoirs, expressing admiration for his '[h]eroic struggle with conditions & self in Q. [San Quentin Prison]' (SB to RC, 6 July 1989, HRC CL MS 17/17). This was a theatre practitioner Beckett assisted on multiple occasions, both personally and professionally (Knowlson 1997: 611–14).

In late 1981, following a request that Beckett write something for Cluchey to perform at the Goodman Theatre, Chicago, Beckett tried to write a 'digestive – or appetizer' for Cluchey's production of *Krapp's Last Tape*, in place of what he called an 'impossible combination with *Endgame*' (SB to RC, 17 May 1981, UoR JEK A/2/57; SB to AS, 20 November 1981, *NABS*: 416). On holidays in Tangier in autumn 1981, he put his hand to a '[s]enile tandem' entitled 'Epilogue' (SB to BB, 1 October 1981, TCD MS 10948/1/666: 1r). The manuscript begins with a crossed-out passage of prose, containing a stage direction which indicates that the prose is being read aloud onstage: 'Raises head from book. ~~Remembers~~ [? ~~Stares~~] Gazes into space. Long pause. Resumes reading' (TCD MS 11286: 1r). Following this passage, two characters, A and B, play out various hapless attempts at communication, hampered by their bad hearing. Beckett linked 'Epilogue' clearly to the promise made to Cluchey in a series of letters to Barbara Bray (TCD MSS 10948/1/665–70). In one such letter, he even included the two figures from the piece:

> A. What's on after us?
> B. Krapp
> A. Good God. (1 October 1981, qtd in Maxwell 2013: 374)

In another letter to Bray, written early on during his stay in Tangier, Beckett followed his account of the struggle he was having writing something for Cluchey with a reference to another once incarcerated artist: 'Have stopped trying for Rick. Haven't looked at text begun at Ussy. Tried to remember Apollinaire's [? Comme] lentement passe l'heure. Can't get it right. Marvellous poem' (11 September 1981, TCD MS 10948/1/665, qtd in Van Hulle and Nixon 2013: 77).[1] By the end of his holiday, Beckett claimed to have 'stopped trying' to complete the Cluchey piece (SB to BB, [? 24/27] October 1981, TCD MS 10948/1/670).[2] He wrote to Billie Whitelaw when he was back in Paris: 'I have been trying to write a short piece for him [Rick] to eke out Krapp, without

---

[1] The line Beckett was trying to remember comes from Apollinaire's 'À la Santé' ('At the Santé'): 'Que lentement passent les heures / Comme passe un enterrement' ['As slowly as a burial / Hours pass'] (1956: 144; 1995: 151).
[2] Postmarked 28 October 1981.

success so far' (14 November 1981, UoR BW 1/16: 1r–1v, qtd in *LSB* IV: 566). He was still struggling to create something almost a year after giving up on 'Epilogue', telling Cluchey on 17 September 1982: 'My attempts to write a piece for you continue fruitless. Barren times from which I hope to emerge, but not surprising if I can't. I'll be in touch with you again about this before the end of the year' (UoR JEK A/2/57). Beckett's backup plan was to give Cluchey *Rough for Theatre I* to fill out his show (SB to RC, 25 November 1981, *LSB* IV: 564–5; SB to AS, 6 February 1982, *NABS*: 422). Beckett suggested in another letter to Schneider that 'the part of the Protagonist in *Catastrophe* is what he needs, his strong point being massive presence, his weak point speech' (19 September 1982, *NABS*: 435).[3] On 31 May 1983, Beckett told Cluchey how difficult it was proving to create something for him: 'hope we'll meet again before the curtain rattles down. And that, despite encircling gloom, I'll manage a piece for you before then, if only a piece of monologue, duly carceral' (UoR JEK A/2/57).[4] That same year, Beckett was working on what would have been his most explicitly carceral work for theatre, 'Mongrel Mime', which indeed requires 'massive presence' – and no 'speech' – from the sole actor onstage ('Mongrel Mime for one ᵒˡᵈ small (M)' TS, HRC CL MS 17/7: 1r).[5] The above evidence strongly suggests that 'Mongrel Mime' was written with Cluchey in mind, which appears to have quite literally shaped the size and carceral nature of the play's performance space.

'Mongrel Mime' is key to understanding the power dynamics at work in Beckett's use of stage space. In spite of this, it has received only cursory attention from scholars (Cohn 2008: 277; Connor 2007: 156; Maude 2009b: 90; McMullan 2010: 64; Nixon 2014: 299). Anna McMullan, following Ruby Cohn, dates its composition to 1963 (McMullan 2010: 153 n. 12). This dating may be due to two extremely flat '8's in Beckett's date on the manuscript and typescript (MS: 3r; TS: 1r).[6] Based on the epistolary evidence presented above, and having compared these '8's to others from Beckett's correspondence with Cluchey, I am confident it reads '1983'. Ruby Cohn suggests that the word 'mongrel' in the title probably refers 'to the inclusion of a voice' in the mime and the earlier, variant

---

[3] James Knowlson has confirmed this opinion of Beckett's, recalling the difficulty Beckett had in getting Cluchey to use a specific type of intonation for Hamm's lines 'Flora! Pomona! [...] Ceres!' during rehearsals for a San Quentin Drama Workshop production of *Endgame* (conversation with James Knowlson, University of Reading, October 2015; *CDW*: 111).

[4] '[C]arceral' is mistranscribed as 'careeral' on the UoR typed transcription of this letter.

[5] The 'Mongrel Mime' manuscript and typescript are cited hereafter as 'MS' and 'TS' respectively.

[6] The date 1983 on the manuscript is followed by a question mark but appears on the typescript without one. Despite the kind help of Richard Workman and Elizabeth Garver at the HRC and Linda Ashton, Literary Executor for the Estate of Carlton Lake, it has not been possible to pinpoint the HRC's acquisition date of 'Mongrel Mime'.

forms of the title confirm this (Cohn 2008: 277; MS: 1r). The draft material for the play – marked 'aborted' but featuring enough material for a full performance – comprises three manuscript pages and one typescript page (MS: 3r; TS: 1r). The first manuscript page contains two separate drafts which outline the stage space and a lone central figure (M). Both attempts are struck out with a large 'X'. The second manuscript page is a full-page draft of the same scenario; the typescript is an edited copy of this material.[7] The third manuscript page starts with a short, crossed-out paragraph describing M's onstage movements. The rest of the page details the injunctions of the Voice (V). Though the Voice and its imperative function are present from the earliest draft on the very first page, only the third manuscript page gives both the content of each injunction and M's reaction to them. V tells him to put down the gripsack he is carrying, then to shut, lock and bolt the door behind him after entering each room, deposit the key through a prison-like lattice – so there is no way of returning – rest for a moment, before going on and out of each room (MS: 2r–3r). In all drafts, the progressively waning volume of V corresponds with an increased gap between each injunction and its corresponding response, as well as a decrease in light and a darkening of colour as M progresses from room to room. The rooms also shrink in size as he moves cross-stage, making the section of stage space he occupies more and more enclosed. When he gets to the final room, there is no way out.

The aspect of the play with which Beckett seems to have had most difficulty is the relationship between M's movements and the stage space. While, in a key essay for advancing the importance of the body in modern spatial theory, Immanuel Kant used the 'incongruent counterparts' of left and right hands in his account of the relation between the human body and absolute space (1992: 370), Beckett's vacillation between M's use of his left and right hands for actions such as opening each door, dealing with the keys and holding a bag was part of his attempt to orient his protagonist's body within the specific, theatrical space he was trying to create.[8] Such vacillation, which recalls the multiple postural permutations in the sketches of the 'Fancy Dead Dying' Notebook, is most evident on the third page of manuscript, at the end of which there is a diagram of the stage and auditorium, containing the audience who would orient M's movements according to the layout of a proscenium stage (see Figure 6). This instance is another reminder

---

[7] There are minor changes made between MS: 2r and the typed content of TS: 1r. Beckett then made more extensive changes by hand on the typescript.

[8] For an account of the importance of Kant's essay for spatial theory, see Casey (1998: 188–9, 205–10).

that far from being 'an empty abstraction', Beckett's spaces of confinement are closely bound up with the bodies that produce them (Lefebvre 1991: 338).

In all the handwritten drafts, M enters audience left, as shown in the sketch, and makes his way across the stage. But Beckett was tinkering with the spatial configuration of 'Mongrel Mime' on the very first page of manuscript, changing the anticlockwise motion of the doors to clockwise (MS: 1r). On the typescript, he reversed the motion of the doors from clockwise back to anticlockwise and changed the orientation of the piece so that M enters audience right (TS: 1r). The effect of these changes is to have M hidden by each opening door, which instead displays its carceral features – key, bolt and lattice – to the audience. These features are emphasized throughout – the key and bolt are both big – and in the typescript, the door is white, giving the prospective audience a clear view of these black metallic objects (MS: 1r, 2r; TS: 1r).

The sound effects of 'Mongrel Mime' – such as the closing doors – are prompted by M's manipulation of the objects onstage. Yet these sounds are produced offstage by loudspeakers. Identified clearly in the manuscript as being unrealistic, these sounds are yet another instance of Beckett's undermining of realist stage space (TS: 1r). While the offstage sound effects create a relationship between onstage confinement and what lies beyond which corresponds with Pountney's model of a 'vaguened' space – in that it is not clear what kind of 'non-A zone' they might come from – one political pentimento shows that

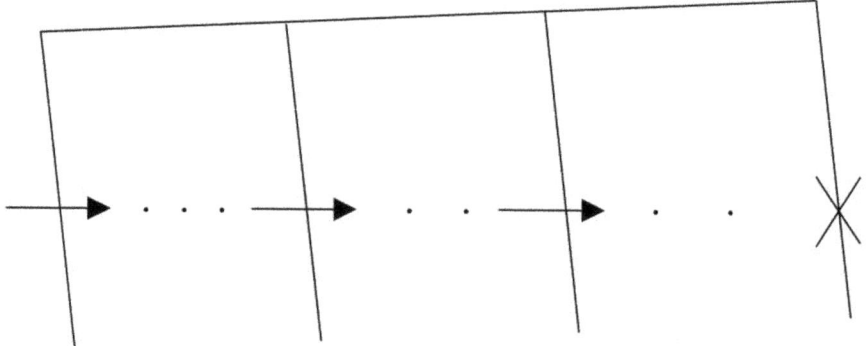

Audience

Figure 6 Beckett's sketch of the stage of 'Mongrel Mime' (MS: 3r).

Beckett considered making this spatial division explicit and making the 'non-A zone' recognizably institutional. In the same pen used to revise the main list of V's commands, which are written in the margin of the manuscript and also found in the body of the text, Beckett made a marginal addition denoting the clicking of a judas hole (MS: 3r). The 'shuttered judas' of *Murphy*, the first in a series of Beckett works starting with the letter 'm', breaks the monadic structure of the asylum cell and allows the warder to mount an assault on the 'little world' of the psychiatric patient. But Beckett kept such obviously carceral references out of his published writing for the stage, abandoning his only previous theatrical prison scenario 'Louis & Blanc'. Had it been used in performance, the click of a peephole would have made 'Mongrel Mime' Beckett's first staged play set inside an institution of confinement, making the audience complicit in the hierarchy of seeing and unseeing which the architecture of the M.M.M. is designed to enforce between nurse and patient in *Murphy*. However, in line with Beckett's aversion to explicitly political dramaturgy, the detail never made its way into the main body of text, and the text is yet to be published.

The extremely confined playing area of 'Mongrel Mime' would make it challenging to stage the play. In both the manuscript and typescript, the ceiling is 5' 6" high, with the actor's height specified at around 5' 9" in order to give him a crouched posture (MS: 2r; TS: 1r). These measurements support my hypothesis that Beckett wrote 'Mongrel Mime' to be performed by Rick Cluchey, whose driving licence recorded his height as 5' 8" (Nora Masterson, email to the author, 17 January 2017).[9] However, the spatial arrangement described would be very hard to present in a standard, raked auditorium without the ceiling of the rooms blocking the view of those seated at the back. In spite of having used multiple configurations of confinement across his theatrical oeuvre, this attempted combination of the movement of M's cross-stage journey within the closed spaces of the low-roofed rooms is one which would be difficult to present on any extant proscenium stage.[10] In writing 'Mongrel Mime', Beckett reached a dead end in his effort to outline a particular form of confinement within the spatial reality of the theatre. Based on the above evidence, as well as decisions Beckett made across his career to supress carceral detail as a writer and director, I contend that it was the explicitly carceral nature of the performance space, along with these spatial difficulties, that led to the abandonment of the play.

---

[9]   I would like to thank Nora Masterson and the late Rick Cluchey for their assistance with my research into 'Mongrel Mime'.

[10] One possibility would be to make the walls and ceiling transparent, but this would make it difficult to keep the lighting in each room distinct, as stipulated on the MS and TS.

Between a protest and *Catastrophe*

If 'Mongrel Mime' was abandoned due to its explicitly carceral nature, *Catastrophe*, Beckett's only play dedicated to a political prisoner, avoids direct political commentary by using the most explicitly realist stage scenario of Beckett's canon. This portrayal of a male Director and his female Assistant manipulating a Protagonist on an 18-inch block (40 cm in the French text) is an anomaly for Beckett, and not just because of its unusual dedicatee. As in other Beckett plays, one of the main figures is an authoritarian male bully, but he lacks the pathos, or indeed the eloquence, of Hamm or Pozzo and cannot as easily be played for laughs as the overblown Animator of *Rough for Radio II* (*Pochade radiophonique*, 1975). The atmosphere of oppression is also familiar, but instead of being set in the amorphous mud of *How It Is* or the dim light of *What Where*, the action takes place in an easily recognizable rehearsal space.

Catastrophe, like many other of Beckett's late works for theatre, was written on request, this time for AIDA (Association Internationale de Défense des Artistes), who were organizing a night of solidarity for the dissident Czech playwright Václav Havel at the 1982 Avignon Theatre Festival. The imprisoned writer, who was serving a sentence for '*subversive activities against the Socialist state*', had been closely associated with Beckett's drama in Czechoslovakia (prefatory note to Havel 1984b: 13). He had worked as unofficial dramaturge on the 1964 national premiere of *Godot* and cited Beckett in one of his prison letters as one of the playwrights 'who stimulated me to try to communicate everything I wanted to say through drama' (Pilný 2014: 214; Havel to Olga Havlová, 14 November 1981, Havel 1988: 248). Beckett's positive response was therefore both artistically and personally important to the future Czechoslovak president, as is evident in the letter Havel sent to Beckett soon after having been released:

> Dear Samuel Beckett,
> During the dark fifties when I was 16 or 18 of age, in a country where there were virtually no cultural or other contacts with the outside world, luckily I had the opportunity to read 'Waiting for Godot'. [...] It may be a foolish expression, but I am looking for a better one in vain: from the first you have been for me a deity in the heavens of spirit. I have been immensely influenced by you as a human being, and in a way as a writer, too. There can never disappear the memory of the adventurous search for, and finding of, spiritual values in the void around me. [...] I mention all this to make clearer to you the shock I experienced during my time in prison when on the occasion of one of her one-hour visits allowed four times a year, my wife told me in the presence of an obtuse warder that at Avignon

there took place a night of solidarity with me, and that you took the opportunity to write, and to make public for the first time, your play 'Catastrophe'. For a long time afterwards there accompanied me in the prison a great joy and emotion and helped to live on amidst all the dirt and baseness. (17 April 1983, VHL ID 5852: 1r–2r, qtd in Little 2015: 92–3)

The persistent concern with oppression in Beckett's postwar work has led to analysis of *Catastrophe* in terms of a power dynamics which 'extend[s] far beyond any specific political context' and constitutes a critique of the 'tyranny' inherent in representation itself (Abbott 1988; McMullan 2005: 26). It is my position that studying both the oppressive power dynamics of the play and the political context in which it was written will provide a better understanding of how the politics of Beckett's late work is related to the hermeneutic indeterminacy of his final stages of confinement. Rather than being subject to a unidirectional paring down of particulars in order to arrive at 'generic humanity' (Badiou 2003b: 3), Beckett's minimalist texts are unresolved sequences which suggest multiple possible resolutions. As composer Luciano Berio puts it, 'Beckett's writing [...] constantly prompts interpretation but, at the same time, it refuses to provide any meaningful or useful instrument' with which to do so (qtd in Bryden 1998: 189). It is through this hermeneutic openness that the anethics of Beckett's closed spaces emerge.

'Explicitation'

Responding to a suggestion made by his Assistant towards the end of *Catastrophe*, the Director emphasizes his desire to keep his own play ambiguous:

A: [*Timidly.*] What about a little ... a little ... gag?
D: For God's sake! This craze for explicitation! Every i dotted to death! Little gag! For God's sake!
A: Sure he won't utter?
D: Not a squeak. (*CDW*: 459)

'[E]xplicitation', which also appears in the corresponding passage in the original French text, is a word which is standard in that language (Beckett 1986: 77). Beckett would have found 'explicitation' in his edition of the *Larousse universel* dictionary, but not in his *OED* (*BDL*). In English, the word is a technical term used in translation studies to describe 'the process of rendering information which is only implicit in the source text explicit in the target text' (Frankenberg-Garcia 2004: 1). A good example of this is the addition of 'Londres' to the opening of the French translation of *Murphy*, contextual information which is left implicit in the English version (Beckett 2013d: 9).[11] Connor defines explicitation more broadly as a characteristic feature of modernism, by which one 'make[s] articulate principles of functioning that had previously been taken for granted' (2014: 9). In a letter of 23 July 1982 to Alan Schneider, Beckett underlined his own resistance to the explicitation brought about through theatrical overemphasis in his complaints about the effect of an additional stage prop at the Avignon premiere of *Catastrophe*: 'Saw a few depressing extracts on TV including a brief flash of the Protagonist all trussed up with screaming white bonds to facilitate comprehension' (*NABS*: 432). An even more explicative interpretation of Beckett's play was staged in New York a few months after his death, ending with the Czechoslovak national anthem ringing out triumphantly while the Protagonist raised his arms in victory (Elam 1994: 26 n. 20). Like the supplementary flag and anthem, the addition of white restraints in Avignon runs counter to what Beckett calls his '[p]rocess of elimination' in the production notebook for *Was Wo*, the 1985 German TV adaptation of *What Where* (first broadcast 1986) (*TN* IV: 431). Analysing Beckett's minimalist working process will help to illuminate the 'oblique relation' between *Catastrophe* and contemporary political events (Kennedy 2005: 22).

Beckett's protest

Dirk Van Hulle has made the point that '[t]o understand his [Beckett's] method of "stripping away", it is important to be aware of the particulars, without which there would be nothing to strip away in the first place' (2015: xix). The political and cultural details surrounding *Catastrophe*'s composition constitute such a rejected context, so they must be taken into account when analysing the politics of Beckett's writing. However, the way in which these details were rejected by Beckett goes against the received notion of the author as unidirectional 'undoer'. The most immediately relevant contextual factor is that, unlike most of Beckett's late drama, the play was composed in French, due to the fact that it was written for performance in Avignon. In the drafts, the overall trend is towards greater specificity: the definite article 'le' [the] preceding 'piédouche' [pedestal]

---

[11] In the English version, London is not mentioned by name until Chapter 3 (*Mu*: 19).

and 'chapeau' [hat] becomes the demonstrative pronoun 'ce' [this/that] (UoR MS 2456/3: 2r, qtd in Little 2015: 97); the Director's reason for hurrying things along, 'j'ai à faire', [I have things to do] becomes the more specific 'j'ai un cocktail' [I have a cocktail party] (UoR MS 2456/2: 2r, qtd in Little 2015: 97) (before appearing in the published text as the more official 'j'ai un comité' [I have a committee]); and, on the proofs of the play, the '[m]anteau' [coat] worn by the Protagonist became a '[r]obe de chambre' [dressing gown], which accords with the pyjamas he is wearing underneath (Beckett 1986: 75; UoR MS 3628: 38, qtd in Little 2015: 98).[12] However, while these changes signal a move in the direction of greater definition, none of them go so far as to provide a localized interpretative context. Indeed, there are even counterexamples to this general trend: Beckett first added the adverb 'hier' [yesterday] to the Assistant's reply to her superior's command that she show him the Protagonist's hands – '[t]u les [? as] vues' [you've seen them] – but then crossed this out and replaced it with 'tantôt' [earlier], which was then itself erased (UoR MS 2456/2: 2r, qtd in Little 2015: 98; Beckett 1986: 74).

Beckett's translation of the play also demonstrates his general resistance to explicitation. Although he does give the Director's impending appointment an additional political edge by translating 'comité' as 'caucus', there is nothing to indicate the political system in which he operates (Beckett 1986: 75; *CDW*: 458). The linguistic set-up within the play is also unclear. The Assistant's repeated answer to the Director's demands, 'I make a note', sounds like the error of a non-native English speaker and, indeed, she acts as an interpreter between the Director and the lighting technician Luke, transmitting her boss's commands using physical gestures in order to bridge the communication gap between the two men.[13] This indicates that what we are getting onstage, as in Brian Friel's *Translations* (first published 1981; see Friel 2012), is the monolingual version of a bilingual scene. It is entirely plausible Beckett was thinking of the difficulties of onstage translation when composing *Catastrophe*, given that its dedicatee was a theatre practitioner whose language Beckett did not speak. Interpreted in this way, *Catastrophe* stages the power plays that can result from a breakdown in communication between different linguistic groups. Beckett's play is then at once a tribute to Havel, while also warning against the valorization of difference in representing a suffering other.

---

[12] I follow Beckett's revised, handwritten pagination on the proofs.
[13] In an early draft, when the Assistant asks the lighting technician, '[t]u entends[?]' [can you hear?/do you understand?], he answers, '[r]ien' [nothing] (UoR MS 2457/2: 5r, qtd in Little 2015: 98 n. 26).

Translation was central to Beckett's relationship with Havel, as is clear from his response to Havel's letter of 29 May 1983, which he sent with a copy of *Catastrophe et autres dramaticules* dedicated 'in friendship' to the Czech writer:

> Dear Vaclav Havel
> Thank you for your most moving letter. To have helped you, however little, and saluted you and all you stand for, was a moment in my writing life that I cherish. It is I who stand in your debt. I have read and admired your plays in French translation. I send you my heartfelt wishes for better days. (VHL ID 21963, qtd in Little 2015: 99)[14]

Beckett's contact in the Czechoslovak underground opposition and his means of corresponding with Havel was physicist František Janouch, chairman of the Charter 77 Foundation, a fundraising body for dissidents named after the open letter of protest to the Czechoslovak government which had led to Havel's imprisonment. When Janouch, who was living in exile at the time in Sweden, visited Paris in April 1984, he arranged to meet Beckett for coffee and filled him in on political events in Czechoslovakia and theatrical ones in Stockholm, where *Catastrophe* had been staged the previous November as part of a double bill with Havel's dramatic response to Beckett's play, *Mistake* (*Chyba*, 1983). Regarding the situation in Czechoslovakia, Janouch noted that though Beckett 'knew very little, his interest was genuinely great'. When asked what prompted him to dedicate *Catastrophe* to Havel, Beckett 'became visibly embarrassed – his long fingers moved faster over the marble table top. "I have read his plays, I wanted to express my support for him, my sympathy, my solidarity"' (Janouch 2010: 119, 120). Clear throughout his contact with Janouch is Beckett's practical support for the cause, including a 100-pound sterling donation to Charter 77 and permission to publish his correspondence with Havel in the programme notes for the Stockholm performance (Havel and Janouch 2007: 491; Janouch 2010: 117).

While his status living as a foreigner in France curtailed the kinds of political gestures he could make, Beckett's work put him at the centre of a network of intercultural communication which involved him placing an embargo on productions of his plays in front of segregated audiences in South Africa (SB to Freda Troup, 13 May 1963, *LSB* III: 543–4; SB to Jenny Sheridan, 18 March 1972, CU Grove Press Collection 46/5), his signature of an appeal against the declaration of martial law in Poland and assistance for individuals living behind

---

[14] Beckett owned a French-language edition of three Havel plays: *Audience, Vernissage* and *Pétition* (BDL).

the Iron Curtain (Knowlson 1997: 640). As Morin has demonstrated, some of Beckett's most important political gestures took place at his writing desk when signing petitions for various international causes; a similar mode of political action is evident in his compilation, translation and typing up of information for the French Resistance during the Second World War (Knowlson 1997: 308).

Beckett was a deeply political writer, not a street fighter. In 1969, he wrote to Theodor Adorno about the student protests which had caused upheaval on the streets of Paris and were putting professional pressure on Adorno in Frankfurt: 'I have not yet been conspué ["pilloried"], so far as I know and that is not far, by the Marcusejugend. As you said to me once at the Iles Marquises, all is malentendu ["misunderstanding"]. Was ever such rightness joined to such foolishness?' (15 February 1969, *LSB* IV: 151). Beckett's question suggests support for the general aims of the young protestors, many of whom saw Frankfurt School philosopher Herbert Marcuse as their intellectual leader, but an aversion to their militant tactics. However, it is important to contrast this critique (written in a private letter) to Beckett's public dedication of his short poem 'pas à pas' to Marcuse on the philosopher's eightieth birthday and the 'warm exchange of letters' which followed (Beckett and Marcuse 2007; Morin 2017: 249):

> pas à pas
> nulle part
> nul seul
> ne sait comment
> petits pas
> nulle part
> obstinément (*CPSB*: 216)

> [step by step
> nowhere
> not a single one
> knows how
> tiny steps
> nowhere
> stubbornly] (Beckett and Marcuse 2007: 200)

Yet again, Beckett's most political action is with his pen, creating a poem that cannot be easily co-opted for a particular political cause: the 'little steps' going on 'stubbornly' might be given a sympathetic reading by Marcuse's Marxist followers, but the poem reminds us through its only repeated line that these steps are going 'nowhere'. While Beckett's final decades were to see an increase in his public political activity due to his heightened profile, his work forms its protest by keeping open the limits of interpretation rather than by making explicit political statements.

One individual whom Beckett personally helped out was Polish translator Antoni Libera (Knowlson 1997: 639–40, 678). Libera recalls receiving the typescript of *Catastrophe* prior to its publication and sending on his Polish translation for Havel to read (Kurpiewski 1990: 7).[15] Such textual dissemination worked in both directions. At their meeting, Janouch gave Beckett the manuscript of the French translation of Havel's adaptation of John Gay's *Beggar's Opera* (*Žebrácká opera*, first staged 1975) because he thought Beckett would be able to spread the word about the play (Janouch 2010: 120). Beckett's gestures of support towards victims of political oppression are crucial elements in a full picture of the politics of his writing. Even more important are the decisions he made to keep such gestures at arm's length from his work. So, for instance, he stated his support for Havel's cause in the paratextual framing material of *Catastrophe*, rather than following his fellow dramatists who responded to AIDA's request by including either Havel or his best-known dramatic character Vaněk as central characters of their plays at Avignon.[16]

'La fin'

In a letter to A. J. Leventhal on 28 April 1957, Beckett complained about the 'horrible job' of translating *Fin de partie* into English. 'Close of Play is not quite right for the title nor the American "The Game is Up". If I can use Endgame in the text phrase at the end, I shall use it for the title' (*LSB* III: 45). Beckett's work is marked by its own finitude, from the image of death in 'The Vulture' (1935), which opens his debut collection of poetry *Echo's Bones and Other Precipitates*, to the draft title of his late prose work *Stirrings Still*, 'End' (*CPSB*: 5; UoR MS 2935/3/2: 1r, *BDMP* I). There is a sense in much of Beckett's writing that it is finished before it even gets started and just as his closed spaces invite further interpretation, so too does this immanent restriction propel his narratives somehow stumbling forward. Adorno argues convincingly that the

---

[15] It is unclear exactly when Havel received Libera's translation (Antoni Libera, email to the author, 8 May 2015). I wish to thank Antoni Libera for his help with my research into this translation.

[16] This was in spite of the fact that Beckett's French edition of Havel's work included Havel's three 'Vaněk' plays. Elie Wiesel, Victor Haïm, Arthur Miller, Andrée Chedid, Claude Confortes, Renata Scani and Fernand Garnier, and Jean-Claude Bourbault all wrote plays for the night at Avignon featuring Havel and/or Vaněk ('Spécial Avignon' 1982).

structural components of classical drama, including a satisfactory ending, are 'toppled' in *Endgame* (1982: 136). The play opens with the words '[f]inished, it's finished, nearly finished, it must be nearly finished' yet the final tableau, with Clov dressed to leave but held back from doing so, presents us with a picture of what Beckett called the 'impossibility of catastrophe' in his play: 'Ended at its inception, and at every subsequent instant, it continues, ergo can never end' (*CDW*: 93; SB to AS, 21 November 1957, *LSB* III: 73). This is '[c]atastrophe […] in the ancient sense' (*MD*: 83), the downward turn in the narrative arc which precipitates the ending of Greek tragedy, a sense emphasized by Beckett in his correspondence with Alan Schneider about the play dedicated to Havel: 'Title *Catastrophe* (in the sense of *dénouement*)' (22 May 1982, *NABS*: 429).[17] Beckett's gloss draws attention to the potential double interpretation of the title – such indeterminacy is key to the play's own ending.

It has been argued that one of the reasons conclusions of classical tragedies have received much more attention than their beginnings is 'the sense that it is the end that confirms or enables interpretation of the drama as a whole' (Roberts 2005: 142). The idea that endings carry with them a kind of interpretative imprimatur is something Beckett was well aware of, evident in the fact that he marked the manuscript of his last published work 'Comment dire', written while his health was failing, '[k]eep! for end' (UoR MS 3316/1: 2r, *BDMP* I). As early as 1922, while still in secondary school, Beckett had studied the structural importance of theatrical dénouements. In his schoolboy copy of *Macbeth*, a handwritten sketch of Gustav Freytag's pyramid, which 'divided tragedies into five main parts (exposition, rising action, climax, falling action, dénouement)', analyses Shakespeare's play according to the five-part structure of classical drama (Van Hulle and Verhulst 2017a: 24; see Figure 7):

a = exposition (Introd).

(1) = 1st stage of dramatic action.

b = complication.

c = climax

(2) = turning pt. or 2nd part of dramatic action.

d = declining action.

(3) = 3rd stage of dramatic Act.

or final impulse given to action.

(e) = Catastrophe. (*BDL*)

---

[17] 'Catastrophe […] dans le sens antique' (Beckett 2012b: 130). In a draft version of *Malone meurt*, Beckett links 'catastrophe' and 'dénouement': 'Catastrophe aussi dans le sens de dénouement ~~de dénouement~~ antique sans doute' (HRC SB MS 7/4: 70r, *BDMP* V). Beckett also insisted to André Bernold that the title of *Catastrophe* should be understood in its technical sense (Bernold 1992: 106).

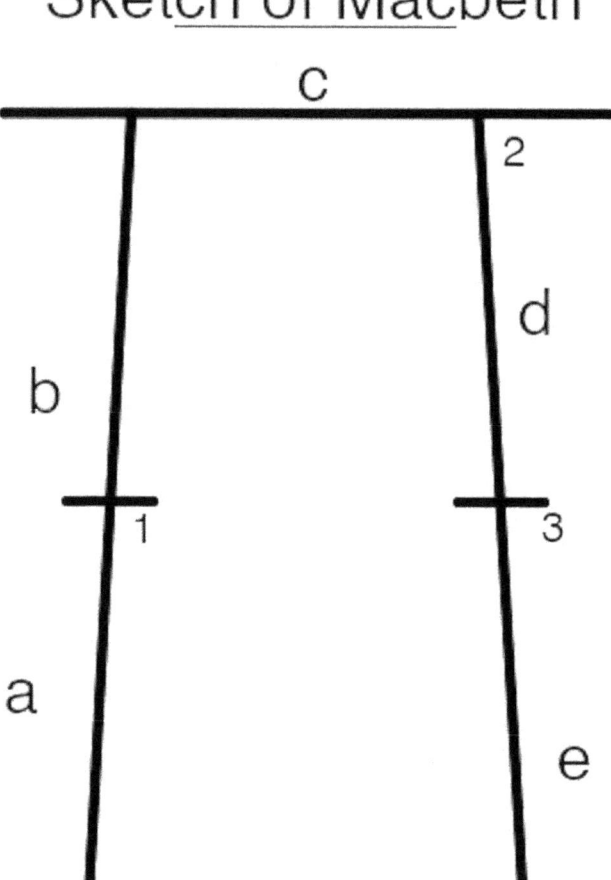

Figure 7 Beckett's sketch of Freytag's pyramid on the title page of his schoolboy copy of *Macbeth*, based on Van Hulle and Verhulst (2017a: 25).

The play *Catastrophe* fits the definition in this list, in that it presents a rehearsal of '*the last scene*' of a play (*CDW*: 457), but the title can also be interpreted as a reference to a disastrous event. The very fact that Beckett felt the need to emphasize the technical, theatrical sense of the word signals again the importance of carefully balanced ambiguity in his poetics and politics.

Beckett clearly had ending on his mind when starting *Catastrophe*, as can be seen by a draft passage of *Worstward Ho* which appears in French on the first manuscript draft of the play. Two of its lines read: 'Pas fausse fin comme toujours. Vraie fin comme jamais' (UoR MS 2457: 1r). [Not a false end like always. A true end like never.][18] Though the bulk of the play which followed was written quickly – indeed, the main scenario is fully established in the earliest surviving manuscript – the ending and title were not added until typescript stage. In the first of four surviving typescripts, the Director's satisfied words as he looks upon his Protagonist '[o]n tient la fin' [there's our ending], becomes '[o]n tient notre catastrophe' [there's our catastrophe]. In this same draft, Beckett added the title of the play (UoR MS 2456/1: 4r, 1r, qtd in Little 2015: 102). Though the search for a title recalls his translation of *Fin de partie*, the shaping of *Catastrophe*'s space is different to the topographic 'undoing' of the earlier play, which in the draft labelled 'Avant *Fin de partie*' was set clearly in post-First World War France.[19] In the published text of *Endgame*, references to the wartime period and the region of Picardy are absent, resulting in a starkly minimalist one-acter set in a refuge of no definite location. As my analysis of the manuscripts of *Catastrophe* demonstrates, in this case, Beckett did not so much strip cultural particulars away as deny them entrance to the main body of text in the first place. The playing area may be recognizable as a rehearsal space, the casting of the Director as male and his Assistant as female does add to the play's power relations a specifically gendered dynamic, the fur coat and toque that the Director wears indicates a cold outdoor climate, but none of this is specific enough to locate the play in a particular political context.[20]

---

[18] Beckett never translated a full version of *Worstward Ho* into French. I would like to thank Peter Fifield for alerting me to this passage's link with *Worstward Ho* and Dirk Van Hulle for making the transcription.

[19] F sketches his and X's location: 'Nous sommes dans la Picardie [...] plus précisément dans le Boulonnais [...]. Je dirais même aux alentours de Wissant.' [We are in Picardy [...] specifically in Boulonnais [...]. I would even say somewhere around Wissant.] He then describes where they live: 'Détruite progressivement dans l'automne de 1914, le printemps de 1918 et l'automne suivant, dans des circonstances mystérieuses' [Destroyed progressively in the autumn of 1914, the spring of 1918 and the following autumn, in mysterious circumstances] (UoR MS 1227/7/16/7: 14r, *BDMP* VII).

[20] The Director's fur toque may be seen as a reference to the typical attire of postwar Communist leaders, but it could equally be seen as an autotextual reference to the dictatorial Hamm's '*toque*' in *Endgame* (*CDW*: 93).

The prison drama Havel wrote on Janouch's request upon his release from jail provides a useful stylistic contrast to Beckett's play (Janouch 2010: 117). As *Mistake* opens, a mute newcomer to the prison environment, Xiboy, is being accused by ringleader King and his cronies of a breach of prison code – it emerges that he has lit a cigarette between slop-out and breakfast. As is the case in *Catastrophe*, this mute central protagonist becomes a focal point of oppression. Tension builds as King's repeated threats and commands – that Xiboy make his bed according to cell regulations; that he clean the cell thoroughly – fall on uncomprehending ears. As the play ends, it becomes clear that this muteness is about to provoke physical violence:

> THIRD PRISONER: (*softly*) 'ere, lads …
> (*Silence – they all gaze at* XIBOY)
> KING: (*without turning to* THIRD PRISONER) What?
> (*Silence – they all gaze at* XIBOY)
> THIRD PRISONER: (*softly*) Know what? He's some kind of a bloody foreigner …
> (*All three look questioningly at* KING. *Tense silence*)
> KING: (*after a pause, softly*) Well, that's his bloody funeral …
> (KING *starts out menacingly towards* XIBOY, *followed by* FIRST, SECOND *and* THIRD PRISONER. *They slowly edge closer to him. Curtain falls*).
> (Havel 1984b: 14)

On a recording played to introduce the 1983 double bill of *Mistake* and *Catastrophe* in Stockholm, Havel was keen to point out that his play 'was not intended simply as a kind of snapshot of prison life' (Havel 1984a: 15). However, while both Havel's and Beckett's plays deal with the oppression of an individual, their politics of confinement are different. Like Havel's later mime *Perpetuum Mobile*, written while in prison in 1989 and structured around seven days in the life of a solitary prisoner, *Mistake* works from the inside out.[21] It brings a representation of identifiable prison brutality onto the stage and makes a wider point about the internalization of oppression. By contrast, only the paratextual dedication of *Catastrophe* denotes its carceral origin. If not for this dedication, *Catastrophe* would read as a much more straightforward satire on the tyranny of theatre directors (Saiu 2009: 257). Crucially, in spite of Beckett's propensity for 'vaguening' and 'undoing', it is *Catastrophe*'s explicitly realist setting which provides a hermeneutic counterweight to the overtly political dedication. Had

---

[21] *Perpetuum Mobile* was published posthumously in 2014. I wish to thank Ondřej Pilný for bringing this play to my attention.

the characters been presented in the darkness common to Beckett's late theatre, it would have been all too easy to read the action back into an institutional context. With the stage set up as a stage, interpretation is far less straightforward and the 'representational space' of the theatre serves as a complex metaphor for the exercise of power in a variety of contexts (Lefebvre 1991: 33).

James Knowlson recounts Beckett's approval of a gesture added to Schneider's production of his play in which the Assistant 'blew away the smoke from the tyrannical Director's cigar. [...] "She isn't only blowing away the smoke you know!"' said Beckett.[22] Given that elsewhere in the play she wipes clean the armchair on which the Director has been sitting before collapsing into it herself, this additional gesture further stressed the Assistant's aversion towards her superior. As the Director's reaction to her final suggestion shows, the lack of fellow feeling is mutual:

A: [*Timidly.*] What if he were to ... were to ... raise his head ... an instant ... show his face ... just an instant.

D: For God's sake! What next? Raise his head? Where do you think we are? In Patagonia? Raise his head? For God's sake! (*CDW*: 460)

Patagonia, the only place-name mentioned in the play, seems to serve here as a marker of utter difference rather than as a reference to features of a particular place. Something similar is at work in the original Czech text of *Mistake*, in which Xiboy is called a 'Maďar' [Hungarian] instead of a 'foreigner', as he is in the English translation (Havel 1999: 684).[23] As Hungarian comes from a different linguistic family to the languages of any of its Slavic neighbours, this term could be seen to function as a means of signalling Xiboy's complete estrangement from the rest of the group and thus, in a reversal of the bilingual power dynamics between Beckett's Director and the lighting technician Luke, provide a reason for his incomprehension of the threats from his cellmates. Antoni Libera reads the Director's reference to Patagonia in somewhat similar terms as a pointer to 'the back of beyond, somewhere impossibly remote and unspeakably provincial' (Libera and Pyda 2015: 345).[24] Nevertheless, the word could equally be seen as an ironic allusion to the actions of military dictatorships in contemporary Argentina and Chile which, like the acts of political repression in Czechoslovakia, were world news when Beckett was composing the play in early 1982. In cases

---

[22] James Knowlson, 'Blowing Away the Smoke', typescript (UoR JEK A/2/123: 5r, qtd in Little 2015: 104).
[23] I am grateful to Ondřej Pilný for pointing out this detail in the Czech text.
[24] Trans. Agnieszka Kołakowska.

such as this one, the way in which the play is hermeneutically structured governs its anethical effect – its subject matter is close to contemporary political events, but not close enough to determine interpretation of the play.

The space of the theatre in which the Director's play is being rehearsed can vary in size, depending on where his closing offstage lines are delivered from. If the Director is placed behind the live audience, as he was in Alan Schneider's 1983 production, his theatre is expanded, enclosing the one in which the real audience is seated like a large Russian doll (AS to SB, 24 June 1983, *NABS*: 450–1). From here, 'in the front row of the stalls', he orders the lights to be brought down everywhere except on the body of the Protagonist (*CDW*: 459). This sets up the play's climax, which ends in an early manuscript as follows:

> Formidable! Il va faire un malheur. (<u>Un temps</u>.) Je les entends d'ici.
> <u>Un temps</u>. <u>Lointain tonnerre d'acclamations</u>: <u>Silence</u>. [<u>L</u>]<u>a tête s'éteint</u>[.] <u>Rideau</u>.
> (UoR MS 2457/2: 5r, qtd in Little 2015: 105)

> [Terrific! He'll have them on their feet. (<u>Pause</u>.) I can hear it from here. <u>Pause.</u>
> <u>Distant storm of applause: Silence. Fade-out on head. Curtain.</u>] (trans. based on
> *CDW*: 461)

This would have been a depressing way for a play dedicated to a political prisoner to end. In the same typescript on which Beckett first wrote the title, he added these closing stage directions in pen:

> P [? ~~se redresse~~] relève la tête, fixe ~~le vide~~ la salle. Les a.[cclamations]
> faiblissent, [? s'arrêtent]. Silence.
> [...]
> Un temps long
> Noir (UoR MS 2456/1: 4r, qtd in Little 2015: 105)
> [P raises his head, fixes the audience. The applause falters, dies. Silence.
> [...] Long pause. Blackout.] (trans. based on *CDW*: 461)

Instead of an unquestioned victory for the Director, the published playtext contains this crucial gesture of resistance from the Protagonist. Beckett, in response to one reviewer's interpretation of the play's 'grand finale' as 'ambiguous', responded: 'There's no ambiguity there at all [...]. He's saying: you bastards, you haven't finished me yet!' (Knowlson 1997: 680). However, while the gesture itself may not be ambiguous, its target – the 'bastards' to whom Beckett refers – is, like the title of the play itself, indeterminate. Fifield believes that they are 'not the other characters of the play, nor the canned audience but the audience proper, whose response he *does not* silence with his look' (2013: 45; emphasis in original). Fifield argues that this is a Levinasian face-to-face encounter which critiques 'the idea of controlling a human subject with the intention of exhibiting him' (2013: 46). If we restricted ourselves to this interpretation of the Protagonist's gaze, *Catastrophe* would indeed align with 'Levinas's belief that literature is unethical', with the representation of the processes of theatre as unethical made all the more acute by the fact that Beckett wrote the play for an imprisoned fellow theatre practitioner (Fifield 2013: 50). But *Catastrophe* is anethical: in the stage direction '*P raises his head, fixes the audience*', it is not clear which audience he is targeting (*CDW*: 461). Moreover, the Protagonist's raising of his head is in direct contravention of the Director's stated wishes. Provided he can understand what has been said, the Protagonist's fixing of the audience can simultaneously be seen as a rebuke of the Director; the two readings need not be mutually exclusive. While this closing gesture would seem to offer a more conclusive ending than the cliffhangers of the earlier plays *All That Fall* and *Happy Days*, the question of whom exactly the Protagonist's protest is directed against remains open. In such an ending, Beckett's politics of closed space – in which he repeatedly returned to scenarios of confined human bodies – depend directly on extending the limits of interpretation.

'Think of the political situation in Turkey'

Beckett's next published play was the torture scenario *What Where* (*Quoi où*, 1983), in which the characters successively lead one another offstage in order to receive 'the works'. It is no coincidence that its ending is again determinedly indeterminate, with the last spoken lines of his published dramatic corpus: 'Make sense who may. I switch off' (*CDW*: 476). *What Where* was written for the Graz Theatre Festival, for which it seems Beckett initially considered staging the more explicitly carceral 'Mongrel Mime'.[25] However, following what he saw as the disastrous production of *Catastrophe* at Avignon, Beckett wanted to write something 'director-proof' for the festival (SB to BB, 4 September 1982, *LSB* IV: 592).[26] In March 1983, he completed *Quoi où*, which was initially entitled simply 'Où' ['Where'] (*LSB* IV: 606 n. 3).

---

[25] 'I have not looked at WH [*Worstward Ho*], nor thought at NP ["Nightpiece", early title for *Nacht und Träume*] nor struggled further with the chambers. I realize now that the last is out of the question for Graz. Perhaps some day in Paris with me around to finnick' (SB to BB, 4 September 1982, *LSB* IV: 592). Given the spatial set-up of the play and the terminology used on the TS, I read 'the chambers' as a reference to 'Mongrel Mime'.

[26] Though *What Where* was written in French for the Graz Festival, its premiere was in New York in English (SB to AS, 20 and 25 May 1983, *NABS*: 445).

In my analysis of *Watt*, I quoted Iser's definition of Beckettian hermeneutics in terms of 'a continual (though never completed) "exit"' (1978: 258). Beckett's remark to André Bernold that the 'where' in *What Where* was part of his 'concern with, and search for, a way out' suggests that the hermeneutic process, which promises, but fails to deliver, an escape from the pattern of violence which structures the play, is intimately connected to how its space is produced.[27] In naming the play's four characters Bim, Bom, Bam and Bem, Beckett evoked the carceral space of *Murphy*'s M.M.M., with its twin male nurses Thomas ('Bim') and Timothy ('Bom') Clinch (*Mu*: 99; 104). Beckett uses the names Bim, Bom and Bem in *How It Is* and refers to Bim and Bom in 'Yellow' and drafts of *Fin de partie* and *Godot*. In the first published edition of *Godot*, they are referred to as '[l]es comiques staliniens' [the Stalinist comedians] (qtd in Van Hulle and Verhulst 2017a: 200). In a letter of 17 May 1956, Beckett told Colin Duckworth: 'Bim and Bom were Russian (Stalinian) comics, if my information was correct' (qtd in Duckworth 2007: 50). It is unlikely that Beckett expected even his most attentive of audience members in 1983 to pick up on the only previous reference to Bim and Bom in a published playtext and to therefore connect the torture of *What Where* with contemporary political persecution in Eastern bloc countries, particularly given that the names were cut from revised editions of *Godot* (Van Hulle and Verhulst 2017a: 280). But as the examples of *Catastrophe* and 'Mongrel Mime' demonstrate, Beckett was very sensitive to finding different aesthetic strategies for staging scenarios of confinement and political persecution at this point in his career.

In the original stage version of *What Where*, the four gowned stage figures enter and exit the small, lit, rectangular playing area, surrounded by darkness. In the television version, inspired by the colours in Rimbaud's 'Voyelles', Beckett considered using differently coloured headdresses to identify the four faces staring straight out from the darkness of the screen. An early list in his production notebook lists eight possibilities: 'Toque, Fez, tarboosh, Kappe ["cap or hood"], Mönchkappe ["monk's hood"], turban, cowl, hood' (*TN* IV: 427). When considering the use of 'a fez or a tarboosh or something like that', Beckett suggested to Walter Asmus that he 'think of the political situation in Turkey', which at the time was still dealing with the aftereffects of the 1980 military coup (*The Remaking of* What Where). According to cameraman Jim Lewis, '[h]e

---

[27] 'C'est une vieille histoire que je ne comprends pas. Je me suis demandé ce que signifie *où*. Peut-être: où est l'issue? La vieille histoire de l'issue.' ['It's an old story that I don't understand. I wondered what *Where* means. Maybe: where's the way out? The old story of the way out.'] (Bernold 2015: 20; 1992: 35; emphasis in originals)

[Beckett] didn't know about the headdress. First he wanted a fezlike, taboosh [*sic*] sort of hat, but then he said: "Well, it doesn't have to be that – that may be too realistic, too specific. It's going to be something fantastic'" (Lewis qtd in Fehsenfeld 1986: 236). In the end, Beckett took '[e]verything out but the faces', leaving the play's acts of torture contextually cast adrift (Beckett qtd in Fehsenfeld 1986: 233). Like the withheld image of prison bars on the stage of the 1975 production of *Godot*, Beckett's note regarding the Turkish headdress, supported by his comments on the specific political context it evokes, functions as a carceral pentimento, buried at the level of a genetic trace. While the deleted idea sheds fascinating light on the way in which *Was Wo* was constructed, the fact that Beckett chose not to include such an image is symptomatic of the way in which he organized his highly oppressive dramatic scenarios by avoiding political 'explicitation' of his texts.

Conclusion

'Mongrel' Space

In 1984, *Waiting for Godot* was performed at Kumla maximum-security prison in Sweden. Or, rather, the first act was, as director Jan Jönson lacked the funds to pay for permission to stage the second. Soon after, Jönson contacted Beckett and the two arranged to meet in Paris. When Jönson told him that his difficulty in producing the full *Godot* was financial, Beckett promptly granted him the play's performance rights free of charge. In his account, Jönson stresses Beckett's interest in 'what happens when the play is given to people who have no hope of being pardoned' (qtd in Knowlson and Knowlson 2006: 276) and it is clear that Beckett strongly supported Jönson's work, encouraging US publisher Barney Rosset to help the Swedish director any way he could (Barney Rosset to SB, [undated] December 1988, CU Grove Press Collection 47/10). Jönson then went on tour with his Kumla cast, four of whom went on the run on the opening night of *Godot* in Gothenburg – Beckett was highly amused when he heard of this. In 1987, Jönson produced a new version of the play with the prisoners of San Quentin, site of the famous 1957 production which eventually gave rise to the San Quentin Drama Workshop. Beckett saw a recording of Jönson's San Quentin production, shown to him by Barney Rosset when he visited Beckett's nursing home in late 1988 (Rosset 2017: 459). When they met early the following year, Beckett told Jönson: 'I saw that you have got to the heart of my play' (qtd in Knowlson and Knowlson 2006: 279).

Beckett's encouragement and support for a prison project, his interest in the meaning the inmates brought to the play, his anti-authority support for the prisoners who escaped: all these aspects of this story fit with James Knowlson's description of Beckett's 'natural sympathy for those who were incarcerated' (1997: 410–11). From Beckett's interest in prisons and asylums, his correspondence with prisoners such as Lembke, Havel and Cluchey, and his attempts to write plays for these prisoners, the evidence in previous chapters supports Knowlson's assessment. But Beckett's last comment to Jönson refers specifically to the 'heart' not of the prisoners, nor of the author, but 'my play'. This book has duly explored the ways in which confinement is 'at the heart of' Beckett's work, rather than the less accessible heart of the author. Beckett's closed spaces are political in the first instance because he based them on institutions of confinement, using such spaces to explore ethical questions regarding the representation of carceral inmates. But as his career develops, these politics come to centre on the fact that he does not write directly about those who were incarcerated, even though confinement remains a major part of Beckett's creative process. Rick Cluchey defined Beckett's work in terms of a 'closed system' and this is in many ways true (qtd in Duerfahrd 2013: 36; see *Mu*: 38). But this book has shown that Beckett's politics of confinement are based on his increasingly creative use of what lies beyond his closed spaces, already a major concern in the early images of the 'veil' and 'wombtomb', consistently emphasized even as closed space is 'undone' in different ways across his oeuvre. Beckett's work has many 'heart[s]', many meanings, and confinement ensures that this is so.

In an analysis of Beckett's late work, initially published as part of the French edition of the TV plays *Quad*, *Ghost Trio*, … *but the clouds* … and *Nacht und Träume*, Gilles Deleuze describes Beckett's art as consisting of images separated from their contexts. For him, Beckett's late prose succeeds in creating

> a pure image, unsullied, that is nothing but image, arriving at the point where it suddenly appears in all its singularity, retaining nothing of the personal, nor of the rational, and ascending into the indefinite as into a celestial state. (Deleuze 1995: 8–9)[1]

Deleuze here echoes Beckett's own art criticism from 1945, in which he praised Bram van Velde for creating 'the pure object' in his paintings. However, in the closed spaces Beckett created after the war, there is always suggested an elsewhere, refuting the purity posited in such statements, producing 'mongrel space'. Though the TV play *Quad*, whose playing area has no obvious historical markers, may appear to be a perfect example of the 'any-space-whatever' ['une espace quelconque'] that Deleuze sees as the territory of Beckett's television plays (1995: 10), I contend that it is in fact a limit case for Lefebvre's claim that '([s]ocial) space is a (social) product'.

---

[1] '[U]ne image pure, non entachée, rien qu'une image, en atteignant au point où elle surgit dans toute sa singularité sans rien garder de personnel, pas plus que de rationnel, et en accédant à l'indéfini comme à l'état céleste' (Deleuze 1992: 71).

Beckett started work on *Quad* in late 1979 or early 1980, describing it as a 'crazy' piece for TV, and directed it in the studios of the Süddeutsche Rundfunk (SDR), Stuttgart, in 1981.[2] It received its first screening on German TV on 8 October 1981 as *Quadrat I & II* (Gontarski 2015b: 112). *Quadrat II* is a slower, black-and-white version of *Quadrat I*, created during playback in Stuttgart. In *Quadrat I*, four mimes, dressed in coloured gowns with cowls hiding their faces, are recorded from a raised angle pacing patterned paths around a lit square, avoiding a supposed central 'danger zone' (*CDW*: 453). Apart from a small dot at the centre of the square, it is unmarked; aside from the different colours of their gowns, the actors appear identical. However, in spite, or perhaps because, of the contextual bareness of both versions, the spaces created in *Quad* are dense with interpretative possibilities.[3]

Building on Deleuze's concept of the 'any-space-whatever', the playing space of *Quad* would appear to exemplify what anthropologist Marc Augé has called the supermodern 'non-place' ['non-lieu'], such as the airport lounge, 'which cannot be defined as relational, or historical, or concerned with identity' (2000: 77–8; 1992). But *Quad's* production of space is inherently social, as shown by the importance of the concept of 'negotiation' in the play's composition. 'Open to discussion with all concerned', Beckett wrote on the first typescript of the play (UoR MS 2199 QUA 2: 1r). In an early diagram of the stage space (see Figure 8), made before Beckett worked on the play in the Stuttgart TV studio, there is no obvious solution to the problem that he envisaged from the very first draft: '<u>Problem</u> Negotiation of O ^{without rupture of rhythm} when [? ~~two~~], three – four ^{players} cross paths there' (UoR MS 2198: 1r).[4] In Beckett's 1981 production notebook, he began to work out a series of possible solutions to this problem, including a 'brief halt' of the crossing players at E which would coincide with the temporary silencing of percussion (UoR MS 2100/9).[5] Though this particular solution did not make it into the filmed version, Beckett's work in Stuttgart did prompt a much more

---

[2] Beckett used the term in two letters: SB to AS, 1 January 1980, *NABS*: 383; SB to Dr Müller-Freienfels, 30 January 1980, qtd in Knowlson (1997: 672).

[3] For Andrew Gibson, *Quad* 'calls the school quadrangle to mind, but also a variety of kinds of institutional space' (2006: 238); for Laura Salisbury, the players' patterned movements 'retain suggestive traces of clowning' (2015: 203). James Knowlson's interpretative options include 'busy traffic on the Place de la Concorde, rodents in a maze, human beings scurrying frenziedly about their business or prisoners exercising desperately in a courtyard' and he also mentions Beckett's own interpretation of the piece in terms of Dante's *Inferno*, as all turns are made to the left in both texts (1997: 673).

[4] This sentence appears, with variations, in each draft and in the published version: 'Negotiation of E without rupture of rhythm when three or four players cross paths at this point' (*CDW*: 453).

[5] I follow the UoR numbering.

detailed sketch (see Figure 9), which now took into account the manoeuvres necessary to avoid collision in the centre of the square.[6] The production of *Quad*'s space thus depends on the negotiation that took place between director, crew and actors in the SDR studio in 1981, as well as the negotiation of that space by four players each time they meet. The potential collision in the centre of the square may have been marked on the script of *Quad* as a 'problem', but, like the danger zone itself, this problem was something to be worked around in rehearsal.

Quad can be seen as the culmination of what Harry White terms Beckett's move towards serialist modes of artistic creation. While serialist composers such as Arnold Schoenberg, Anton Webern and Pierre Boulez flattened out the hierarchy between tones in diatonic harmony, White argues that Beckett used 'a limited series of language, posture, movement, lighting, and sound' in his late work to move 'away from the pre-eminence of verbal discourse' (White 1998: 161, 2008: 189). In spite of this departure from traditional dramatic elements, Beckett's plays are never fully subordinated to a predetermined series.

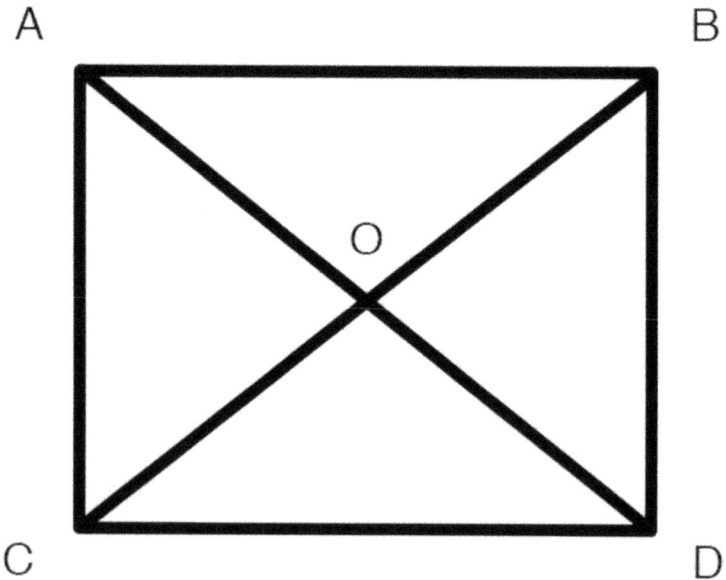

Figure 8 Beckett's diagram of *Quad*, made before going to Stuttgart rehearsals (UoR MS 2198: 2r). 'O' was later replaced by 'E' (UoR MS 2198: 3r; see *CDW*: 451). I would like to thank Mark Nixon for his help with my research on this manuscript.

---

[6] In the SDR version, the percussion is muted only once, when all players are in their corners.

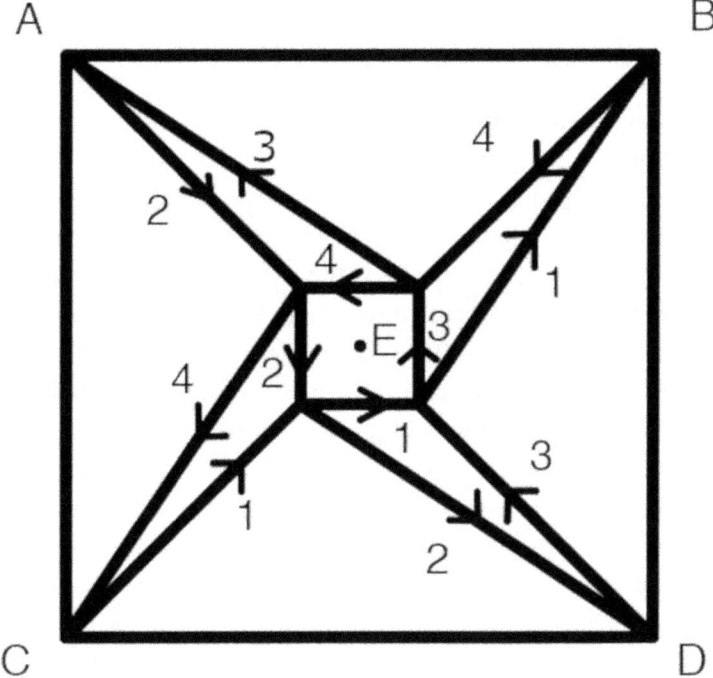

Figure 9 Beckett's diagram of *Quad*, made during or after Stuttgart rehearsals (typescript enclosed in a letter by SB to Barney Rosset, 5 September 1981, CU Grove Press Collection 46/8: 3r; see *CDW*: 453).

By highlighting its actors' interaction, *Quad*'s danger zone brings into focus the different ways in which their patterns of movement may be embodied. In Evelyn Cobley's account of Adorno's music theory, she describes his view of musical serialism as a 'decentred totality' which initially erased hierarchy between notes only to impose a 'totalized and indifferent' twelve-tone system (2005: 189). Even if the hierarchy consists in the actors deciding who steps first, the danger zone of *Quad* ensures that the system in which the bodies move falls short of constituting a totalized system of movement. Likewise, Beckett's closed spaces cannot be reduced to the totalized systems suggested by the term 'pure'; they are impure spatial zones, 'mongrels'.

For Fifield, Beckett's work 'does not seek to create a self-sufficient, fully realized fictional realm, but tries to take its place within and throw its readers back onto the world' (2013: 166). The 'mongrel' nature of closed space – which often shuts out the world – allows us to see Beckett as a writer of the world, whose spaces are open to new relations and interpretations. In his essay 'Global Beckett', presenting an argument which has similarities to my view that Beckett's dramatic work depends as much on the addition of detail, however slight, as it does on deletion and 'vaguening', Rónán McDonald has identified Beckett's stage aesthetic as being 'based on reanimation rather than deracination' (2016: 585). The potential for the work he created to be reanimated in different cultural contexts makes Beckett an important author for artists looking to 'tease out some of the major socio-political and ethical issues of our time' (Scaife 2018: 114). To take only *Godot*, in the years since Beckett's death, there has been a one-act production in the besieged city of Sarajevo (1993), an open-air *Godot* in flood-ravaged New Orleans (2007) and a *Godot* performed in New York's Zuccotti Park during the Occupy Wall Street protests (2011) (Duerfahrd 2013: 63–111; 178–89). If Beckett's work 'seems to hit a nerve at this moment in time' (Van Hulle 2015: xvii), this is down to the ability of plays like *Godot* 'to recontextualize vividly in different moments, without sliding into allegory or one-on-one correspondence' (McDonald 2016: 590). In different genres, languages and media, Beckett's work continues to provide 'the possibility of a new means of shaping the way that we think and see' (Boxall 2009: 12).[7] Though a study of how Beckett's work is being (re-)interpreted by living artists is beyond the scope of this book, I hope to have provided grounds for such scholarship by showing that confinement was central to the ways in which Beckett reshaped the field of the sensible in his own creative process.

'Beckett is a writer of the world' is by now a fairly uncontroversial statement. That the relationship between the worlds created by his work and the world in which this work is interpreted is 'anethical', however, is not. It is clear that Beckett was drawn to actual spaces of confinement through the 'sympathy' that Knowlson identifies, using these spaces in his early prose to work through ethical questions of representation. However, I would argue that Beckett's use of confinement following his move to theatre makes it 'the space of the anethical' in his work (Weller 2006: 194). In 2004, Rancière identified the recent so-called 'ethical turn' in politics and the arts as one which involves an 'interdiction', forbidding the representation of certain events – such as the Holocaust – which are deemed 'non-representable'. In much contemporary art and criticism, this interdiction is then used to call for 'an art of the non-representable' ['un art de l'irreprésentable'] as the only way in which to treat a topic deemed unsuitable for

---

[7] Boxall is here citing Don DeLillo's character Bill Gray in his novel *Mao II*: 'Beckett is the last writer to shape the way we think and see' (1992: 157, qtd in Boxall 2009: 9).

aesthetic representation (2006: 12–13; 2011b: 163). Following Adorno's famous concept of the 'image ban' which he uses to conceptualize Beckett's treatment of the concentration camps and bearing in mind Beckett's own move away from representational forms over the course of his career, one might reasonably ask if institutions of confinement are subject to a form of ethical proscription in Beckett's theatre. In other words, does Beckett avoid representing institutions of confinement because it is unethical to do so? I would argue not. Rather, what makes confinement 'the space of the anethical' for Beckett is the fact that carceral institutions are both 'not there' and 'not not there' in his later work. Following the asylum-setting of *Malone Dies*, institutional confinement is no longer visible in Beckett's work, but it nevertheless remains a crucial concept as he continues to look for 'a form that accommodates the mess' of human experience. In developing a series of aesthetic strategies which return repeatedly to closed space, Beckett's work speaks *to* particular situations of suffering and oppression without claiming to speak *for* those who are suffering and oppressed. Beckett created his politics of closed space by drawing on the specific political connotations of confining a human body while suggesting a multiplicity of other interpretative contexts beyond, thus leaving his closed spaces open for reanimation.

Key to how Beckett constructed his anethical 'art of confinement' were the various methods of 'undoing' he used across his career. What this book has shown is that Gontarski's concept needs to be revisited and expanded in order to keep up with new discoveries in manuscript studies of Beckett's writing. There was no single 'intent of undoing' for Beckett, but rather a variety of aesthetic strategies in how he shaped the closed spaces of his work. Indeed, if we recall the etymology of the word 'mongrel' in the base 'mix' (*OED*), Beckett's compositional strategies come to appear as 'mongrel' as the closed spaces these strategies produced. In *Watt*, Beckett 'vaguened' the carceral space of Bethlem Asylum mapped in such detail in *Murphy*'s M.M.M.; in the postwar novellas, he uses 'vaguened' institutions which, instead of emerging from a 'realistic and traditional substructure', appear to have been 'decomposed' in the very process of composition. In *Godot* and *Endgame*, Beckett's 'pentimenti' show that confinement was an important concept beneath the surface of the dramatic text. In *The Unnamable*, various closed spaces are presented and then 'denarrated', while in *Not I*, Beckett's 'undoing' was shown to include significant amounts of 'redoing' in the repetitive environment of performance. While 'Mongrel Mime' provides another example of carceral 'pentimenti', *Catastrophe* demonstrates Beckett's resistance to 'explicitation' through a withholding of contextual detail throughout the compositional process.

The above terms have been used throughout this book to present a clearer picture of the complexity of Beckett's poetics. As more of Beckett's manuscripts become available online through the Beckett Digital Manuscript Project, a more detailed study of these poetics will allow for a fuller picture of his politics. Genetic criticism has been seen as a branch of structuralist poetics, which, according to Jonathan Culler, studies a text's 'attested meanings or effects and seeks to understand what structures or devices make them possible' and opposes itself to hermeneutics, which 'argues about what the meanings are or should be' (2004b: vii).[8] Studies of Beckett's authorial manuscripts also help uncover new meanings in his texts, such as the political resonances that arise from Beckett's use of confined space. For Caselli, 'producing meaning in Beckett is always a necessarily political issue', not least because his multilingual oeuvre draws attention to the ways in which meanings are made and the frequent acts of contestation involved in such meaning-making (2009: 211). The same is true of Beckett's production of closed space, whose political effects depend not simply on the 'undoing' of carceral elements but on a careful balancing of these elements, creating a multiplicity of possible meanings. I will close with one final example.

The dramatic fragment 'Espace souterrain', the subterranean scenario created prior to the 'refuge' of *Endgame*, includes 'conceptual notes' which Beckett later fleshed out in the typescript 'Coups de gong' (Van Hulle and Weller 2018: 42). In one of these notes, the character C 'croit se rappeler, ou avoir entendu parler, d'un gardien qui fait des rondes' [believes he recalls, or has heard talk of, a guard doing the rounds] (UoR MS 2931: 2r, *BDMP* VII). This line adds to the carceral atmosphere of the dramatic sketch, which also mentions the 'avantage' [advantage] of the '[e]mpêchement des mouvements' [impediment of movements] created by ropes tying the characters to one another: 'D ne peut aller plus loin que l'espace scénique. C libéré, mais lié psychologiquement' [D cannot go beyond the stage space. C freed, but tied psychologically.] (UoR 2391: 4r, *BDMP* VII). These ropes physicalize the psychological ties to fellow characters in a closed space, foreshadowing Hamm and Clov's pathological interdependency in *Endgame*. Like the subsequent unpublished sketch 'Louis & Blanc', the characters of 'Espace souterrain / Coups de gong' wear 'médaille[s]' [medals] on which each character is given a number, suggesting either a wartime context or the postwar one of 'Avant *Fin de partie*' (UoR 2931: 3r; UoR MS 2932: 2r, *BDMP* VII).

---

[8]   For a discussion of the links between genetic criticism and structuralist poetics, see Van Hulle (2008: 43).

The carceral features of 'Espace souterrain / Coups de gong' thus provide further interpretative context for *Endgame*'s 'refuge', reminding us how important it was for Beckett to have his characters 'living in confinement'. At the same time, it was equally important that such forms of confinement were not overtly political. So, in 'Espace souterrain', we are told of the guard: 'on ne le verra pas' [we will not see him] (UoR 2931: 2r, *BDMP* VII). Like the peephole of 'Mongrel Mime', the carceral context is in this instance doubly deleted: firstly, the guard does not appear in the draft; secondly, the draft was left unpublished by Beckett.[9] Its recent publication as part of the online genetic dossier of *Endgame* provides further evidence of Beckett's continuing interest in institutions of confinement as well as further evidence of his resistance to making these institutions an explicit part of his work. Towards the end of this manuscript version, Beckett wrote: 'autant de précision [...] que possible. Mais minimum d'explications' [as much precision as possible. But minimum of explications.] (UoR MS 2931: 6r, *BDMP* VII). Returning to the words he used with director Jan Jönson, this phrase seems to get 'to the heart' of Beckett's politics of closed space. Whether onstage or on the page, in a variety of linguistic and material contexts, it is Beckett's repeated attempts to deal in precise ways with the confinement of human bodies without shutting down the interpretative process through the 'explication' provided by a carceral context that gives us new ways of seeing and thinking of closed space in aesthetic representation. In this way, Beckett's closed spaces extend the limits of political interpretation.

---

[9] Though Beckett did donate the draft to the University of Reading for scholarly research.

Works Cited

Works by Beckett

Beckett, Samuel (1932), 'Dante and the Lobster', *This Quarter*, 5 (2): 222–36.

Beckett, Samuel (1954), 'The End', trans. Richard Seaver in collaboration with the author, *Merlin*, 3 (2): 144–59.

Beckett, Samuel (1967), *Stories and Texts for Nothing*, New York: Grove Press.

Beckett, Samuel (1969), *Watt*, trans. Ludovic Janvier and Agnès Janvier in collaboration with the author, Paris: Éditions de Minuit.

Beckett, Samuel (1973), *En attendant Godot*, Paris: Éditions de Minuit.

Beckett, Samuel (1976a), *For to End Yet Again and Other Fizzles*, London: John Calder.

Beckett, Samuel (1976b), *Proust and Three Dialogues with Georges Duthuit*, London: John Calder.

Beckett, Samuel (1986), *Catastrophe et autres dramaticules: Cette fois, Solo, Berceuse, Impromptu d'Ohio, Quoi où*, Paris: Éditions de Minuit.

Beckett, Samuel (1987), *L'Innommable*, Paris: Éditions de Minuit.

Beckett, Samuel (1989), *Nohow On*, London: John Calder.

Beckett, Samuel (1992a), *Dream of Fair to Middling Women*, ed. Eoin O'Brien and Edith Fournier, Monkstown: Black Cat Press.

Beckett, Samuel (1992b), *The Theatrical Notebooks of Samuel Beckett*, gen. ed. James Knowlson, 4 vols, II: *Endgame*, ed. S. E. Gontarski, London: Faber and Faber.

Beckett, Samuel (1993), *The Theatrical Notebooks of Samuel Beckett*, gen. ed. James Knowlson, 4 vols, I: *Waiting for Godot*, ed. Dougald McMillan and James Knowlson, London: Faber and Faber.

Beckett, Samuel (1995a), *The Complete Short Prose, 1929–1989*, ed. S. E. Gontarski, New York: Grove Press.

Beckett, Samuel (1995b), *Eleuthéria*, trans. Michael Brodsky, New York: Foxrock.

Beckett, Samuel (1996), *Eleutheria*, trans. Barbara Wright, London: Faber and Faber.

Beckett, Samuel (1999a), *Beckett's Dream Notebook*, ed. John Pilling, Reading: Beckett International Foundation.

Beckett, Samuel (1999b), *The Theatrical Notebooks of Samuel Beckett*, gen. ed. James Knowlson, 4 vols, IV: *The Shorter Plays*, ed. S. E. Gontarski, London: Faber and Faber.

Beckett, Samuel (2001), *Disjecta: Miscellaneous Writings and a Dramatic Fragment*, ed. Ruby Cohn, London: John Calder.

Beckett, Samuel (2006), *The Complete Dramatic Works*, London: Faber and Faber.

Beckett, Samuel (2008), *Eleutheria*, Paris: Éditions de Minuit.

Beckett, Samuel (2009a), *How It Is*, ed. Édouard Magessa O'Reilly, London: Faber and Faber.

Beckett, Samuel (2009b), *The Letters of Samuel Beckett*, 4 vols, I: *1929–1940*, ed. Martha Dow Fehsenfeld, Lois More Overbeck, George Craig and Dan Gunn, Cambridge: Cambridge University Press.

Beckett, Samuel (2009c), *Molloy*, ed. Shane Weller, London: Faber and Faber.

Beckett, Samuel (2009d), *Murphy*, ed. J. C. C. Mays, London: Faber and Faber.

Beckett, Samuel (2009e), *Watt*, ed. C. J. Ackerley, London: Faber and Faber.

Beckett, Samuel (2010a), *Malone Dies*, ed. Peter Boxall, London: Faber and Faber.

Beckett, Samuel (2010b), *Mercier and Camier*, ed. Seán Kennedy, London: Faber and Faber.

Beckett, Samuel (2010c), *More Pricks than Kicks*, ed. Cassandra Nelson, London: Faber and Faber.

Beckett, Samuel (2010d), *Texts for Nothing and Other Shorter Prose, 1950–1976*, ed. Mark Nixon, London: Faber and Faber.

Beckett, Samuel (2010e), *The Unnamable*, ed. Steven Connor, London: Faber and Faber.

Beckett, Samuel (2011a), *The Letters of Samuel Beckett*, 4 vols, II: *1941–1956*, ed. George Craig, Martha Dow Fehsenfeld, Dan Gunn and Lois More Overbeck, Cambridge: Cambridge University Press.

Beckett, Samuel (2011b), 'The New Object', *Modernism/modernity*, 18 (4): 878–80.

Beckett, Samuel (2011c), *Stirrings Still / Soubresauts and Comment dire / what is the word*, digital genetic edn (The Beckett Digital Manuscript Project, module 1), ed. Dirk Van Hulle and Vincent Neyt, Brussels: University Press Antwerp, http://www.beckettarchive.org.

Beckett, Samuel (2012a), *The Collected Poems of Samuel Beckett*, critical edn, ed. Seán Lawlor and John Pilling, London: Faber and Faber.

Beckett, Samuel (2012b), *Malone meurt*, Paris: Éditions de Minuit.

Beckett, Samuel (2012c), *Molloy*, Paris: Éditions de Minuit.

Beckett, Samuel (2013a), *Le Dépeupleur*, Paris: Éditions de Minuit.

Beckett, Samuel (2013b), *Fin de partie*, Paris: Éditions de Minuit.

Beckett, Samuel (2013c), *L'Innommable / The Unnamable*, digital genetic edn (The Beckett Digital Manuscript Project, module 2), ed. Dirk Van Hulle, Shane Weller and Vincent Neyt, Brussels: University Press Antwerp, http://www.beckettarchive.org.

Beckett, Samuel (2013d), *Murphy*, Paris: Éditions de Minuit.

Beckett, Samuel (2013e), *Têtes-mortes: D'un ouvrage abandonné, Assez, Imagination morte imaginez, Bing, Sans*, Paris: Éditions de Minuit.

Beckett, Samuel (2014a), *Echo's Bones*, ed. Mark Nixon, London: Faber and Faber.

Beckett, Samuel (2014b), *The Letters of Samuel Beckett*, 4 vols, III: *1957–1965*, ed. George Craig, Martha Dow Fehsenfeld, Dan Gunn and Lois More Overbeck, Cambridge: Cambridge University Press.

Beckett, Samuel (2014c), *Nouvelles et Textes pour rien*, Paris: Éditions de Minuit.

Beckett, Samuel (2015a), *Comment c'est*, Paris: Éditions de Minuit.

Beckett, Samuel (2015b), *Krapp's Last Tape / La Dernière Bande*, digital genetic edn (The Beckett Digital Manuscript Project, module 3), ed. Dirk Van Hulle and Vincent Neyt, Brussels: University Press Antwerp, http://www.beckettarchive.org.

Beckett, Samuel (2016a), *The Letters of Samuel Beckett*, 4 vols, IV: *1966–1989*, ed. George Craig, Martha Dow Fehsenfeld, Dan Gunn and Lois More Overbeck, Cambridge: Cambridge University Press.

Beckett, Samuel (2016b), *Molloy*, digital genetic edn (The Beckett Digital Manuscript Project, module 4), ed. Édouard Magessa O'Reilly, Dirk Van Hulle, Pim Verhulst and Vincent Neyt, Brussels: University Press Antwerp, http://www.beckettarchive.org.

Beckett, Samuel (2017a), *En attendant Godot / Waiting for Godot*, digital genetic edn (The Beckett Digital Manuscript Project, module 6), ed. Dirk Van Hulle, Pim Verhulst and Vincent Neyt, Brussels: University Press Antwerp, http://www.beckettarchive.org.

Beckett, Samuel (2017b), *Malone meurt / Malone Dies*, digital genetic edn (The Beckett Digital Manuscript Project, module 5), ed. Dirk Van Hulle, Pim Verhulst and Vincent Neyt, Brussels: University Press Antwerp, http://www.beckettarchive.org.

Beckett, Samuel (2018), *Fin de partie / Endgame*, digital genetic edn (The Beckett Digital Manuscript Project, module 7), ed. Dirk Van Hulle, Shane Weller and Vincent Neyt, Brussels: University Press Antwerp, http://www.beckettarchive.org.

Beckett, Samuel and Alan Schneider (1998), *No Author Better Served: The Correspondence of Samuel Beckett and Alan Schneider*, ed. Maurice Harmon, Cambridge, MA: Harvard University Press.

Beckett, Samuel and Herbert Marcuse (2007), 'Samuel Beckett's Poem for Herbert Marcuse and an Exchange of Letters', in Douglas Kellner (ed.), *Collected Papers of Herbert Marcuse*, 6 vols, IV: *Art and Liberation*, 200–2, Abingdon: Routledge.

Other works cited

Abbott, H. Porter (1988), 'Tyranny and Theatricality: The Example of Samuel Beckett', *Theatre Journal*, 40 (1): 77–87.

Abbott, H. Porter (1996), *Beckett Writing Beckett: The Author in the Autograph*, Ithaca, NY: Cornell University Press.

Abbott, H. Porter (2004), 'Narrative', in Lois Oppenheim (ed.), *Palgrave Advances in Samuel Beckett Studies*, 7–29, Basingstoke: Palgrave Macmillan.

Ackerley, C. J. (2005), 'Obscure Locks, Simple Keys: The Annotated *Watt*', *Journal of Beckett Studies*, 14 (1–2): 1–6, 8–213, 215–91.

Ackerley, C. J. (2008), '"The Last Ditch": Shades of Swift in Samuel Beckett's "Fingal"', *Eighteenth-century Life*, 32 (2): 60–7.

Ackerley, C. J. (2010), *Demented Particulars: The Annotated* Murphy, Edinburgh: Edinburgh University Press.

Ackerley, C. J. and S. E. Gontarski (2004), *The Grove Companion to Samuel Beckett: A Reader's Guide to His Works, Life, and Thought*, New York: Grove Press.

Addyman, David (2009), 'Inane Space and Lively Place in Beckett's Forties Fiction', in Steven Barfield, Philip Tew and Matthew Feldman (eds), *Beckett and Death*, 89–105, London: Continuum.

Addyman, David (2010a), 'Phenomenology "Less the Rosy Hue": Beckett and the Philosophy of Place', *Journal of Modern Literature*, 33 (4): 112–28.

Addyman, David (2010b), 'Rest of Stage in Darkness: Beckett, His Directors and Place', *SBT/A*, 22: 301–14.

Addyman, David and Matthew Feldman (2011), 'Samuel Beckett, Wilhelm Windelband, and the Interwar "Philosophy Notes"', *Modernism/modernity*, 18 (4): 755–70.

Admussen, Richard L. (1979), *The Samuel Beckett Manuscripts: A Study*, London: G. Prior.

Adorno, Theodor W. (1982), 'Trying to Understand *Endgame*', trans. Michael T. Jones, *New German Critique*, 26: 119–50.

Adorno, Theodor W. (2004), *Negative Dialectics*, trans. E. B. Ashton, London: Routledge.

Adorno, Theodor W. (2010), 'Notes on Beckett', trans. Dirk Van Hulle and Shane Weller, *JOBS*, 19 (2): 157–78.

Alston, Adam (2016), *Beyond Immersive Theatre: Aesthetics, Politics and Productive Participation*, London: Palgrave Macmillan.

Andrews, Jonathan, Asa Briggs, Roy Porter, Penny Tucker and Keir Waddington (1997), *The History of Bethlem*, London: Routledge.

Apollinaire, Guillaume (1950), 'Zone', trans. Samuel Beckett, *Transition*, 50 (6): 126–31.

Apollinaire, Guillaume (1956), *Œuvres poétiques*, ed. Marcel Adéma and Michel Décaudin, Paris: Gallimard.

Apollinaire, Guillaume (1972), *Zone*, trans. Samuel Beckett, Dublin: Dolmen Press.

Apollinaire, Guillaume (1993), *Alcools*, ed. Garnet Rees, London: Athlone Press.

Apollinaire, Guillaume (1995), *Alcools*, trans. Donald Revell, Middletown, CT: Wesleyan University Press.

Artaud, Antonin (1958), *The Theatre and Its Double*, trans. Mary Caroline Richards, New York: Grove Weidenfeld.

Artaud, Antonin (1976), *Selected Writings*, ed. Susan Sontag, trans. Helen Weaver, New York: Farrar, Straus and Giroux.

Artaud, Antonin (2016), *Œuvres*, ed. Évelyne Grossman, Paris: Gallimard.

Asmus, Walter D. (1975), 'Beckett Directs *Godot*', *Theatre Quarterly*, 5 (19): 19–26.

Atik, Anne (2001), *How It Was: A Memoir of Samuel Beckett*, London: Faber and Faber.

Attridge, Derek (2004), *The Singularity of Literature*, London: Routledge.

Attridge, Derek (2017), *The Work of Literature*, Oxford: Oxford University Press.

Augé, Marc (1992), *Non-lieux: introduction à une anthropologie de la surmodernité*, Paris: Éditions du Seuil.

Augé, Marc (2000), *Non-places: Introduction to an Anthropology of Supermodernity*, trans. John Howe, London: Verso.

Badiou, Alain (2003a), *L'éthique: essai sur la conscience du mal*, Caen: Nous.

Badiou, Alain (2003b), *On Beckett*, trans. Bruno Bosteels, Nina Power and Alberto Toscano, ed. Alberto Toscano and Nina Power, Manchester: Clinamen Press.

Badiou, Alain (2012), *Ethics: An Essay on the Understanding of Evil*, trans. Peter Hallward, London: Verso.

Bailey, Iain (2010), 'Samuel Beckett, Intertextuality, and the Bible', PhD thesis, University of Manchester.

Bair, Deirdre (1990), *Samuel Beckett: A Biography*, rev. edn, London: Vintage Books.

Baker, Phil (1997), *Beckett and the Mythology of Psychoanalysis*, Basingstoke: Macmillan.

Baroghel, Elsa (2010), 'From Narcissistic Isolation to Sadistic Pseudocouples: Tracing the Genesis of *Endgame*', *SBT/A*, 22: 123–33.

Baroghel, Elsa (2016), '"Indoor Bowers of Bliss": Mental Asylums in Samuel Beckett's Works', paper presented at Beckett and Politics conference, University of Reading, 3–4 November.

Barthes, Roland (1987), *S/Z*, trans. Richard Miller, New York: Hill and Wang.

Bates, Julie (2017), *Beckett's Art of Salvage: Writing and Material Imagination, 1932–1987*, Cambridge: Cambridge University Press.

Baudot, Laura (2009), 'What Not to Avoid in Swift's "The Lady's Dressing Room"', *Studies in English Literature, 1500–1900*, 49 (3): 637–66.

Bell, L. A. J. (2011), 'Between Ethics and Aesthetics: The Residual in Samuel Beckett's Minimalism', *JOBS*, 20 (1): 32–53.

Beloborodova, Olga (2018), 'The "Inward Turn" of Modernism in Samuel Beckett's Work: A Postcognitivist Reassessment', unpublished PhD thesis, University of Antwerp.

Ben-Zvi, Linda (1992), 'Introduction', in Linda Ben-Zvi (ed.), *Women in Beckett: Performance and Critical Perspectives*, ix–xviii, Urbana: University of Illinois Press.

Bernold, André (1992), *L'amitié de Beckett: 1979–1989*, Paris: Hermann.

Bernold, André (2015), *Beckett's Friendship*, trans. Max McGuinness, Dublin: Lilliput Press.

Bianchini, Natka (2007), 'Bare Interiors, Chicken Wire Cages and Subway Stations – Re-thinking Beckett's Response to the ART *Endgame* in Light of Earlier Productions', in Mark S. Byron (ed.), *Samuel Beckett's* Endgame, 121–43, Amsterdam: Rodopi.

Bixby, Patrick (2009), *Samuel Beckett and the Postcolonial Novel*, Cambridge: Cambridge University Press.

Blanchot, Maurice (1955), *L'espace littéraire*, Paris: Gallimard.

Blanchot, Maurice (1989), *The Space of Literature*, trans. Ann Smock, Lincoln, NE: University of Nebraska Press.

Bolin, John (2013), *Beckett and the Modern Novel*, Cambridge: Cambridge University Press.

Boswell, James (1848), *Boswell's Life of Johnson: Including Their Tour to the Hebrides*, rev. edn, ed. John Wilson Croker, London: John Murray.

Bowles, Patrick (1994), 'How to Fail: Notes on Talks with Samuel Beckett', *P.N. Review*, 96: 24–38.

Boxall, Peter (2002), 'Samuel Beckett: Towards a Political Reading', *Irish Studies Review*, 10 (2): 159–70.

Boxall, Peter (2009), *Since Beckett: Contemporary Writing in the Wake of Modernism*, London: Continuum.

Brater, Enoch (1975), 'Dada, Surrealism, and the Genesis of *Not I*', *Modern Drama*, 18 (1): 49–59.

Brater, Enoch (1987), *Beyond Minimalism: Beckett's Late Style in the Theater*, Oxford: Oxford University Press.

Breton, André and Paul Éluard (1932), 'Surrealism and Madness', trans. Samuel Beckett, *This Quarter*, 5 (1): 101–20.

Brook, Peter (1996), *The Empty Space*, New York: Touchstone.

Brown, Llewellyn (2011), 'Voice and Pronouns in Samuel Beckett's *The Unnamable*', *JOBS*, 20 (2): 172–96.

Bryden, Mary (1993), *Women in Samuel Beckett's Prose and Drama: Her Own Other*, Lanham, MD: Barnes and Noble.

Bryden, Mary (1998), 'Beckett and Music: An Interview with Luciano Berio', in Mary Bryden (ed.), *Samuel Beckett and Music*, 189–90, Oxford: Clarendon Press.

Bryden, Mary, Julian Garforth and Peter Mills (1998), *Beckett at Reading: Catalogue of the Beckett Manuscript Collection at the University of Reading*, Reading: Whiteknights Press.

Burton, Robert (1912), *The Anatomy of Melancholy*, ed. A. R. Shilleto, 3 vols, I, London: George Bell.

Cage, John (2011), 'Experimental Music', in John Cage (ed.), *Silence*, 50th anniversary edn, 7–12, Middletown, CT: Wesleyan University Press.

Camus, Albert (1942), *Le mythe de Sisyphe: essai sur l'absurde*, Paris: Gallimard.

Camus, Albert (1979), *The Myth of Sisyphus*, trans. Justin O'Brien, Harmondsworth: Penguin Books.

Camus, Albert (2005), *L'Étranger*, ed. Ray Davison, London: Routledge.

Carlson, Marvin (2013), 'The Theatre *ici*', in Erika Fischer-Lichte and Benjamin Wihstutz (eds), *Performance and the Politics of Space: Theatre and Topology*, 15–30, New York: Routledge.

Caselli, Daniela (2005), *Beckett's Dantes: Intertextuality in the Fiction and Criticism*, Manchester: Manchester University Press.

Caselli, Daniela (2009), 'Thinking of "a Rhyme for 'Euganean'": Beckett in Italy', in Mark Nixon and Matthew Feldman (eds), *The International Reception of Samuel Beckett*, 209–33, London: Continuum.

Casey, Edward S. (1998), *The Fate of Place: A Philosophical History*, Berkeley: University of California Press.

Chattopadhyay, Arka (2015), '"I Switch Off": Towards a Beckettian Minority of Theatrical Event', in S. E. Wilmer and Audronė Žukauskaitė (eds), *Deleuze and Beckett*, 230–45, London: Palgrave Macmillan.

Churchill, Winston (1981), *Churchill Speaks: Winston S. Churchill in Peace and War, Collected Speeches, 1897–1963*, ed. Robert Rhodes Jones, Leicester: Windward.

Cobley, Evelyn (2005), 'Decentred Totalities in *Doctor Faustus*: Thomas Mann and Theodor W. Adorno', *Modernist Cultures*, 1 (2): 181–91.

Coetzee, J. M. (1986), 'Into the Dark Chamber: The Novelist and South Africa', *New York Times*, 12 January, 'Book Review' section: 13, 35.

Cohen, Edward H. (1974), 'Two Anticipations of Henley's "Invictus"', *Huntington Library Quarterly*, 37 (2): 191–6.

Cohn, Ruby (1961), '*Watt* in the Light of *The Castle*', *Comparative Literature*, 13 (2): 154–66.

Cohn, Ruby (1980), *Just Play: Beckett's Theater*, Princeton: Princeton University Press.

Cohn, Ruby (2008), *A Beckett Canon*, Ann Arbor: University of Michigan Press.

Coleridge, Samuel Taylor (1907), *Biographia Literaria*, ed. John Shawcross, 2 vols, I, Oxford: Clarendon Press.

Connor, Steven (1992), 'Between Theatre and Theory: "Long Observation of the Ray"', in John Pilling and Mary Bryden (eds), *The Ideal Core of the Onion: Reading Beckett Archives*, 79–98, Reading: Beckett International Foundation.

Connor, Steven (2007), *Samuel Beckett: Repetition, Theory and Text*, rev. edn, Aurora, CO: Davies Group.

Connor, Steven (2014), *Beckett, Modernism and the Material Imagination*, New York: Cambridge University Press.

Crampton, Jeremy W. (2013), 'Space, Territory, Geography', in Christopher Falzon, Timothy O'Leary and Jana Sawicki (eds), *A Companion to Foucault*, 384–99, Chichester: Wiley-Blackwell.

Cuddon, J. A. (1984), *A Dictionary of Literary Terms*, rev. edn, Harmondsworth: Penguin Books.

Culler, Jonathan (2004a), 'In Defence of Overinterpretation', in Umberto Eco, Richard Rorty, Jonathan Culler and Christine Brooke-Rose, *Interpretation and Overinterpretation*, ed. Stefan Collini, 109–23, Cambridge: Cambridge University Press.

Culler, Jonathan (2004b), *Structuralist Poetics: Structuralism, Linguistics and the Study of Literature*, rev. edn, London: Routledge.

Dante Alighieri (1999), *The Divine Comedy*, bilingual edn, ed. Robert Hollander, trans. Robert Hollander and Jean Hollander, http://etcweb.princeton.edu/dante/pdp/.

'Data Sheet for the Loeb Drama Center', http://www.fas.harvard.edu/~loebinfo/ loebinfo/loebdata.html.

Davies, Ioan (1990), *Writers in Prison*, Oxford: Basil Blackwell.

Davies, William (2019), '"Occasional Extinction or More Likely Occultation": Form and Source in "Long Observation of the Ray"', *SBT/A*, 31 (1): 82–97.

Dearlove, J. E. (1982), *Accommodating the Chaos: Samuel Beckett's Nonrelational Art*, Durham, NC: Duke University Press.

De Biasi, Pierre-Marc (2004), 'Toward a Science of Literature: Manuscript Analysis and the Genesis of the Work', trans. Jed Deppman, in Jed Deppman, Daniel Ferrer and Michael Groden (eds), *Genetic Criticism: Texts and Avant-textes*, 36–68, Philadelphia: University of Pennsylvania Press.

Debray-Genette, Raymonde (1979), 'Génétique et poétique: le cas Flaubert', in Louis Hay (ed.), *Essais de critique génétique*, 21–67, Paris: Flammarion.

De Certeau, Michel (1988), *The Practice of Everyday Life*, trans. Steven Rendall, Berkeley: University of California Press.

De Certeau, Michel (1990), *L'invention du quotidien*, 2 vols, I: *Arts de faire*, rev. edn, ed. Luce Giard, Paris: Gallimard.

Degani-Raz, Irit (2012), 'Cartesian Fingerprints in Beckett's *Imagination Dead Imagine*', *JOBS*, 21 (2): 223–43.

De Lamartine, Alphonse (1993), *Poetical Meditations / Méditations poétiques*, trans. Gervase Hittle, Lewiston, NY: Edwin Mellen.

Deleuze, Gilles (1992), 'L'épuisé', in Samuel Beckett, *Quad et Trio du fantôme, … que nuages…, Nacht und Träume*, trans. Edith Fournier, 55–106, Paris: Éditions de Minuit.

Deleuze, Gilles (1995), 'The Exhausted', trans. Anthony Uhlmann, *SubStance*, 24 (3): 3–28.

DeLillo, Don (1992), *Mao II*, London: Vintage.

Dennis, Amanda (2017), 'Heterotopias: The Possible and Real in Foucault, Beckett, and Calvino', in Robert T. Tally Jr (ed.), *The Routledge Handbook of Literature and Space*, 168–78, Abingdon: Routledge.

Dennis, Amanda (2018), 'Compulsive Bodies, Creative Bodies: Beckett's *Quad* and Agency in the 21st Century', *JOBS*, 27 (1): 5–21.

Derrida, Jacques (2005), *Writing and Difference*, trans. Alan Bass, London: Routledge.

Driver, Tom (2005), interview with Samuel Beckett, in Lawrence Graver and Raymond Federman (eds), *Samuel Beckett, The Critical Heritage*, 241–7, London: Routledge and Kegan Paul.

Duckworth, Colin (1966), '*Godot*: Genesis and Composition', in Samuel Beckett, *En attendant Godot: pièce en deux actes*, ed. Colin Duckworth, xlv–lxxv, London: George G. Harrap and Co.

Duckworth, Colin (2007), '*En attendant Godot*: Notes on the Manuscript', *Litteraria Pragensia*, 17 (33): 31–50.

Duerfahrd, Lance (2013), *The Work of Poverty: Samuel Beckett's Vagabonds and the Theater of Crisis*, Columbus: Ohio State University Press.

Dukes, Gerry (2000), 'Introduction', in Samuel Beckett, *First Love and Other Novellas*, ed. Gerry Dukes, 1–8, London: Penguin Books.

Dwan, Lisa (2016), 'Mouth Almighty: How Billie Whitelaw Helped Me Find Beckett and *Not I*', *American Theatre*, 12 April, http://www.americantheatre.org/2016/04/12/mouth-almighty-how-billie-whitelaw-helped-me-find-beckett-and-not-i/.

Eco, Umberto (1994), *The Limits of Interpretation*, Indianapolis: Indiana University Press.

Eco, Umberto, Richard Rorty, Jonathan Culler and Christine Brooke-Rose (2004), *Interpretation and Overinterpretation*, ed. Stefan Collini, Cambridge: Cambridge University Press.

Elam, Keir (1994), 'Catastrophic Mistakes: Beckett, Havel, the End', *SBT/A*, 3: 1–28.

Engell, James (2012), 'Imagination', in Roland Greene, Stephen Cushman, Clare Cavanagh, Jahan Ramazani and Paul Rouzer (eds), *The Princeton Encyclopedia of Poetry and Poetics*, 4th edn, 666–74, Princeton: Princeton University Press.

Esslin, Martin (1983), *The Theatre of the Absurd*, 3rd edn, Harmondsworth: Penguin Books.

Fehsenfeld, Martha (1986), '"Everything Out but the Faces": Beckett's Reshaping of *What Where* for Television', *Modern Drama*, 29 (2): 229–40.

Feldman, Matthew (2006), *Beckett's Books: A Cultural History of Samuel Beckett's 'Interwar Notes'*, London: Continuum.

Felski, Rita (2011), 'Context Stinks!', *New Literary History*, 42 (4): 573–91.

Ferrer, Daniel and Michael Groden (2004), 'Introduction: A Genesis of French Genetic Criticism', in Jed Deppman, Daniel Ferrer and Michael Groden (eds), *Genetic Criticism: Texts and Avant-textes*, 1–16, Philadelphia: University of Pennsylvania Press.

Fifield, Peter (2013), *Late Modernist Style in Samuel Beckett and Emmanuel Levinas*, New York: Palgrave Macmillan.

Fludernik, Monika (2005), *Towards a 'Natural' Narratology*, London: Routledge.

Fordham, Finn (2010), *I Do I Undo I Redo: The Textual Genesis of Modernist Selves in Hopkins, Yeats, Conrad, Forster, Joyce, and Woolf*, Oxford: Oxford University Press.

Foucault, Michel (1966), *Les mots et les choses: une archéologie des sciences humaines*, Paris: Gallimard.

Foucault, Michel (1976), *Folie et déraison: histoire de la folie à l'âge classique*, Paris: Plon.

Foucault, Michel (1977), *Histoire de la folie à l'âge classique*, rev. edn, Paris: Gallimard.

Foucault, Michel (1986), 'Of Other Spaces', trans. Jay Miskowiec, *Diacritics*, 16 (1): 22–7.

Foucault, Michel (1988), *Madness and Civilization: A History of Insanity in the Age of Reason*, trans. Richard Howard, New York: Vintage Books.

Foucault, Michel (1994), *Surveiller et punir: naissance de la prison*, Paris: Gallimard.

Foucault, Michel (1995), *Discipline and Punish: The Birth of the Prison*, 2nd edn, trans. Alan Sheridan, New York: Vintage Books.

Foucault, Michel (2001a), 'Des espaces autres', in Daniel Defert, François Ewald and Jacques Lagrange (eds), *Dits et écrits, 1954–1988*, 2 vols, II: *1976–1988*, 1571–81, Paris: Gallimard.

Foucault, Michel (2001b), 'La fonction politique de l'intellectuel', in Daniel Defert, François Ewald and Jacques Lagrange (eds), *Dits et écrits, 1954–1988*, 2 vols, II: *1976–1988*, 109–14, Paris: Gallimard.

Foucault, Michel (2006), *History of Madness*, ed. Jean Khalfa, trans. Jonathan Murphy and Jean Khalfa, London: Routledge.

Foucault, Michel (2009), *Le corps utopique suivi de Les hétérotopies*, Fécamp: Nouvelles Éditions Lignes.

Frankenberg-Garcia, Ana (2004), 'Are Translations Longer than Source Texts? A Corpus-based Study of Explicitation', paper presented at CULT (Corpus Use and Learning to Translate) conference, Barcelona, 22–4 January: 1–8, http://hdl.handle.net/10400.26/253.

Fraser, Graham (1995), 'The Pornographic Imagination in *All Strange Away*', *Modern Fiction Studies*, 41 (3–4): 515–30.

Friel, Brian (2012), *Translations*, London: Faber and Faber.

Garland, David (2003), 'Penal Modernism and Postmodernism', in Thomas G. Blomberg and Stanley Cohen (eds), *Punishment and Social Control*, 2nd edn, 45–73, New York: Aldine de Gruyter.

Genette, Gérard (1983), *Narrative Discourse: An Essay in Method*, trans. Jane E. Lewin, Ithaca, NY: Cornell University Press.

Genette, Gérard (1992), *Palimpsestes: la littérature au second degré*, Paris: Éditions du Seuil.

Genette, Gérard (1997), *Palimpsests: Literature in the Second Degree*, trans. Channa Newman and Claude Doubinsky, Lincoln, NE: University of Nebraska Press.

Genocchio, Benjamin (1996), 'Discourse, Discontinuity, Difference: The Question of "Other" Spaces', in Sophie Watson and Katherine Gibson (eds), *Postmodern Cities and Spaces*, 35–46, Oxford: Blackwell.

Geulincx, Arnold ([1675] 2006), *Ethics*, with Samuel Beckett's notes, ed. Han van Ruler, Anthony Uhlmann and Martin Wilson, trans. Martin Wilson, Leiden: Brill.

Gibson, Andrew (2006), *Beckett and Badiou: The Pathos of Intermittency*, Oxford: Oxford University Press.

Gibson, Andrew (2010), 'Beckett, de Gaulle and the Fourth Republic 1944–49: *L'Innommable* and *En attendant Godot*', *Limit(e) Beckett*, 1: 1–26, http://www.limitebeckett.paris-sorbonne.fr/one/gibson.pdf.

Gontarski, S. E. (1985), *The Intent of 'Undoing' in Samuel Beckett's Dramatic Texts*, Bloomington: Indiana University Press.

Gontarski, S. E. (1992), 'Introduction: "The No against the Nothingness"', in *The Theatrical Notebooks of Samuel Beckett*, gen. ed. James Knowlson, 4 vols, II: *Endgame*, ed. S. E. Gontarski, xiii–xxiv, London: Faber and Faber.

Gontarski, S. E. (1995), 'Introduction – From Unabandoned Works: Samuel Beckett's Short Prose', in Samuel Beckett, *The Complete Short Prose, 1929–1989*, ed. S. E. Gontarski, xi–xxxii, New York: Grove Press.

Gontarski, S. E. (1997), 'Staging Himself, or Beckett's Late Style in the Theatre', *SBT/A*, 6: 87–97.

Gontarski, S. E. (2006), 'Greying the Canon: Beckett in Performance', in S. E. Gontarski and Anthony Uhlmann (eds), *Beckett after Beckett*, 141–57, Gainesville: University Press of Florida.

Gontarski, S. E. (2015a), 'Samuel Beckett and the "Idea" of a Theatre: Performance through Artaud and Deleuze', in Dirk Van Hulle (ed.), *The New Cambridge Companion to Samuel Beckett*, 126–41, Cambridge: Cambridge University Press.

Gontarski, S. E. (2015b), 'Still at Issue after All These Years: The Beckettian Text, Printed and Performed', *JOBS*, 24 (1): 104–15.

Gontarski, S. E. (2018), *Revisioning Beckett: Samuel Beckett's Decadent Turn*, New York: Bloomsbury Academic.

Grene, Nicholas (2014), *Home on the Stage: Domestic Spaces in Modern Drama*, Cambridge: Cambridge University Press.

Grésillon, Almuth (1994), *Éléments de critique génétique: lire les manuscrits modernes*, Paris: Presses universitaires de France.

Gruber, William (2010), *Offstage Space, Narrative, and the Theatre of the Imagination*, New York: Palgrave Macmillan.

Gussow, Mel (1969), 'Enigmatic, Nihilistic, Brilliant: Beckett Is Expressing – What?', *New York Times*, 24 October: 32.

Harman, Mark (2002), 'Making Everything "a Little Uncanny": Kafka's Deletions in the Manuscript of *Das Schloß* and What They Can Tell Us about His Writing Process', in James Rolleston (ed.), *A Companion to the Works of Franz Kafka*, 325–46, Rochester, NY: Camden House.

Harvey, David (1996), *Justice, Nature and the Geography of Difference*, Oxford: Blackwell Publishers.

Harvey, David (2019), *Spaces of Global Capitalism: A Theory of Uneven Geographical Development*, London: Verso.

Harvey, Lawrence E. (1970), *Samuel Beckett: Poet and Critic*, Princeton: Princeton University Press.

Havel, Václav (1984a), 'Many Thanks to Our Swedish Friends', *Index on Censorship*, 13 (1): 15.

Havel, Václav (1984b), *Mistake*, trans. George Theiner, *Index on Censorship*, 13 (1): 13–14.

Havel, Václav (1988), *Letters to Olga: June 1979–September 1982*, trans. Paul Wilson, London: Faber and Faber.

Havel, Václav (1999), *Spisy*, 8 vols, II: *Hry*, Prague: Torst.

Havel, Václav and František Janouch (2007), *Korespondence 1978–2001*, ed. Květa Jechová, Prague: Akropolis.

Heron, Jonathan, Nicholas Johnson, Burç Îdem Dinçel, Gavin Quinn, Sarah Jane Scaife and Áine Josephine Tyrrell (2014), 'The Samuel Beckett Laboratory 2013', *JOBS*, 23 (1): 73–94.

Herren, Graley (2014), 'A Womb with a View: *Film* as Regression Fantasy', in S. E. Gontarski (ed.), *The Edinburgh Companion to Samuel Beckett and the Arts*, 237–50, Edinburgh: Edinburgh University Press.

Hetherington, Kevin (2003), *The Badlands of Modernity: Heterotopia and Social Ordering*, London: Routledge.

'History of the House', https://www.cityoflondon.gov.uk/things-to-do/keats-house/keats-history/Pages/History-of-the-house.aspx.

Huffman, Carl A. (2005), *Archytas of Tarentum: Pythagorean, Philosopher and Mathematician King*, Cambridge: Cambridge University Press.

Hutcheon, Linda (1985), *A Theory of Parody: The Teachings of Twentieth-century Art Forms*, New York: Methuen.

Ibsen, Henrik (1978), *The Complete Major Prose Plays*, trans. Rolf Fjelde, New York: Plume.

Iser, Wolfgang (1978), *The Implied Reader: Patterns of Communication in Prose Fiction from Bunyan to Beckett*, Baltimore, MD: Johns Hopkins University Press.

Janouch, František (2010), 'How I Jumped over a Wall and Met Samuel Beckett', trans. Slávka Svěráková, *Herald of Europe*, 7: 115–20.

'Jean Balue (French Cardinal)' (1998), *Britannica Online Encyclopaedia*, http://www.britannica.com/EBchecked/topic/51084/Jean-Balue.

Jeans, James (1929), *The Universe around Us*, London: Cambridge University Press.

Jeantroux, Myriam (2004), 'La structure du huis clos dans le théâtre de Samuel Beckett: un "art d'incarcération"', unpublished PhD thesis, University of Franche-Comté.

Juliet, Charles (1995), *Conversations with Samuel Beckett and Bram van Velde*, trans. Janey Tucker, Leiden: Academic Press Leiden.

Juliet, Charles (2009), *Conversations with Samuel Beckett and Bram van Velde*, trans. Tracy Cooke, Aude Jeanson, Axel Nesme, Morgaine Reinl and Janey Tucker. Champaign, IL: Dalkey Archive Press.

Kafka, Franz (2009a), *The Castle*, trans. Anthea Bell, Oxford: Oxford University Press.

Kafka, Franz (2009b), *The Trial*, trans. Mike Mitchell, Oxford: Oxford University Press.

Kafka, Franz (2015), 'The Problem of Our Laws', trans. Michael Hofmann, *London Review of Books*, 37 (14): 23.

Kalb, Jonathan (1991), *Beckett in Performance*, Cambridge: Cambridge University Press.

Kant, Immanuel (1992), 'Concerning the Ultimate Ground of the Differentiation of Directions in Space', in Immanuel Kant, *Theoretical Philosophy, 1755–1770*, 361–72, ed. and trans. David Walford and Ralf Meerbote, Cambridge: Cambridge University Press.

Katz, Daniel (1999), *Saying I No More: Subjectivity and Consciousness in the Prose of Samuel Beckett*, Evanston, IL: Northwestern University Press.

Keats, John (1982), *Complete Poems*, ed. Jack Stillinger, Cambridge, MA: Belknap Press.

Keats, John (2005), *Selected Letters of John Keats*, rev. edn, ed. Grant F. Scott, Cambridge, MA: Harvard University Press.

Kelly, Brendan (2014), *Custody, Care & Criminality: Forensic Psychiatry and Law in 19th Century Ireland*, Dublin: History Press Ireland.

Kelly, Brendan (2016), *Hearing Voices: The History of Psychiatry in Ireland*, Newbridge: Irish Academic Press.

Kennedy, Seán (2005), 'Introduction to "Historicising Beckett"', *SBT/A*, 15: 21–7.

Kennedy, Seán (2015), '"Humanity in Ruins": Beckett and History', in Dirk Van Hulle (ed.), *The New Cambridge Companion to Samuel Beckett*, 185–99, Cambridge: Cambridge University Press.

Kiely, Robert (2014), 'On Voices and Mediumship in the Trilogy', *SBT/A*, 26: 79–90.

Knowlson, James (1978), 'Practical Aspects of Theatre, Radio and Television: Extracts from an Unscripted Interview with Billie Whitelaw', *JOBS*, 3: 85–90.

Knowlson, James (1993), 'Introduction', in *The Theatrical Notebooks of Samuel Beckett*, gen. ed. James Knowlson, 4 vols, I: *Waiting for Godot*, ed. Dougald McMillan and James Knowlson, xi–xxv, London: Faber and Faber.

Knowlson, James (1997), *Damned to Fame: The Life of Samuel Beckett*, London: Bloomsbury.

Knowlson, James and Elizabeth Knowlson (eds) (2006), *Beckett Remembering, Remembering Beckett: Uncollected Interviews with Samuel Beckett and Memories of Those Who Knew Him*, London: Bloomsbury.

Knowlson, James and John Pilling (1979), *Frescoes of the Skull: The Later Prose and Drama of Samuel Beckett*, London: John Calder.

Kroll, Jeri L. (1977), 'The Surd as Inadmissible Evidence: The Case of Attorney-general v. Henry McCabe', *JOBS*, 2: 47–58.

Kurpiewski, Lech (1990), 'Beckett, Havel, Michnik: After the "Catastrophe"', *Warsaw Voice*, 22 April: 7 (UoR JEK A/2/123).

Lake, Carlton (ed.) (1984), *No Symbols Where None Intended: A Catalogue of Books, Manuscripts, and Other Material Relating to Samuel Beckett in the Collections of the Humanities Research Center*, Austin: Humanities Research Center, University of Texas.

Larousse universel (1922), 2 vols, I, Paris: Larousse.

Lawley, Paul (2007), 'Failure and Tradition: Coleridge/Beckett', *SBT/A*, 18: 31–46.

Lawrence, Tim (2018), *Samuel Beckett's Critical Aesthetics*, Cham: Palgrave Macmillan.

Le Dœuff, Michèle (2002), *The Philosophical Imaginary*, trans. Colin Gordon, London: Continuum.

Lefebvre, Henri (1991), *The Production of Space*, trans. Donald Nicholson-Smith, Oxford: Basil Blackwell.

Lefebvre, Henri (1992), *Éléments de rythmanalyse: introduction à la connaissance des rythmes*, Paris: Éditions Syllepse.

Lefebvre, Henri (2000), *La production de l'espace*, 4th edn, Paris: Anthropos.

Lefebvre, Henri (2007), *Rhythmanalysis: Space, Time and Everyday Life*, trans. Stuart Elden and Gerald Moore, London: Continuum.

Leibniz, Gottfried Wilhelm ([1714] 1898), *The Monadology and Other Philosophical Writings*, trans. Robert Latta, Oxford: Clarendon Press.

Le Juez, Brigitte (2008), *Beckett before Beckett*, trans. Ros Schwartz, London: Souvenir Press.

Levinas, Emmanuel (1961), *Totalité et Infini: essai sur l'extériorité*, The Hague: Martinus Nijhoff.

Levinas, Emmanuel (1974), *Autrement qu'être ou au-delà de l'essence*, The Hague: Martinus Nijhoff.

Levinas, Emmanuel (2006), *Otherwise than Being or beyond Essence*, trans. Alphonso Lingis, Pittsburgh, PA: Duquesne University Press.

Levinas, Emmanuel (2007), *Totality and Infinity: An Essay on Exteriority*, trans. Alphonso Lingis, Pittsburgh, PA: Duquesne University Press.

Levinas, Emmanuel (2009), *Carnets de captivité suivi de Écrits sur la captivité et Notes philosophiques diverses*, ed. Rodolphe Calin, Paris: Éditions Grasset.

Lewis, Leon (1977), 'Notes toward a Translation of *L'Étranger*', *Rocky Mountain Review of Language and Literature*, 31 (1): 18–20.

Libera, Antoni and Janusz Pyda (2015), *Jesteście na Ziemi, na to rady nie ma! Dialogi o teatrze Samuela Becketta*, Kraków: Fundacja 'Dominikańskie Studium Filozofii i Teologii'.

Little, James (2015), 'Between a Protest and *Catastrophe*', *Litteraria Pragensia*, 25 (50): 92–106.

Livingston, Paisley (2003), 'Pentimento', in Berys Gaut and Paisley Livingston (eds), *The Creation of Art: New Essays in Philosophical Aesthetics*, 89–115, Cambridge: Cambridge University Press.

Lloyd, David (2016), *Beckett's Thing: Painting and Theatre*, Edinburgh: Edinburgh University Press.

Love, Damian (2005), 'Doing Him into the Eye: Samuel Beckett's Rimbaud', *Modern Language Quarterly*, 66 (4): 477–503.

Lyotard, Jean-François (1991), *The Inhuman: Reflections on Time*, trans. Geoffrey Bennington and Rachel Bowlby, Stanford: Stanford University Press.

Malraux, André (1946), *La condition humaine*, rev. edn, Paris: Gallimard.

Mathieu, Georges (2013), 'La voix qui s'exclame: modalité exclamative et affirmation de soi dans la trilogie de Beckett', in Julien Piat and Philippe Wahl (eds), *La prose de Samuel Beckett: configuration et progression discursives*, 79–90, Lyon: Presses universitaires de Lyon.

Maude, Ulrika (2009a), *Beckett, Technology and the Body*, Cambridge: Cambridge University Press.

Maude, Ulrika (2009b), '"Material of a Strictly Peculiar Order": Beckett, Merleau-Ponty and Perception', in Ulrika Maude and Matthew Feldman (eds), *Beckett and Phenomenology*, 77–94, London: Continuum.

Maude, Ulrika (2014), 'Convulsive Aesthetics: Beckett, Chaplin and Charcot', in S. E. Gontarski (ed.), *The Edinburgh Companion to Samuel Beckett and the Arts*, 44–53, Edinburgh: Edinburgh University Press.

Maxwell, Jane (2013), 'Waiting for an Archivist: The Samuel Beckett Collection', in W. E. Vaughan (ed.), *The Old Library, Trinity College Dublin: 1712-2012*, 370–6, Dublin: Four Courts Press.

McAuley, Gay (2008), 'Not Magic but Work: Rehearsal and the Production of Meaning', *Theatre Research International*, 33 (3): 276–88.

McDonald, Rónán (2016), 'Global Beckett', in Nicholas Grene and Chris Morash (eds), *The Oxford Handbook of Modern Irish Theatre*, 577–92, Oxford: Oxford University Press.

McLaughlin, Jeff (1984), 'Play Goes on, with a Beckett Disclaimer', *The Boston Globe*, 13 December (JBL SB MS 38/7).

McMillan, Dougald and Martha Fehsenfeld (1988), *Beckett in the Theatre: The Author as Practical Playwright and Director, from* Waiting for Godot *to* Krapp's Last Tape, London: John Calder.

McMullan, Anna (1998), 'Performing Vision(s): Perspectives on Spectatorship in Beckett's Theatre', in Jennifer M. Jeffers (ed.), *Samuel Beckett: A Casebook*, 133–58, London: Garland Publishing.

McMullan, Anna (2005), *Theatre on Trial: Samuel Beckett's Later Drama*, London: Routledge.

McMullan, Anna (2010), *Performing Embodiment in Samuel Beckett's Drama*, New York: Routledge.

McNaughton, James (2018), *Samuel Beckett and the Politics of Aftermath*, Oxford: Oxford University Press.

McTighe, Trish (2013), *The Haptic Aesthetic in Samuel Beckett's Drama*, Basingstoke: Palgrave Macmillan.

Meffan, James and Kim L. Worthington (2001), 'Ethics before Politics: J. M. Coetzee's *Disgrace*', in Todd F. Davis and Kenneth Womack (eds), *Mapping the Ethical Turn: A Reader in Ethics, Culture, and Literary Theory*, 131–50, Charlottesville: University Press of Virginia.

Melnyk, Davyd (2005), 'Never Been Properly Jung', *SBT/A*, 15: 355–62.

Merleau-Ponty, Maurice (1993), 'Eye and Mind', in Galen A. Johnson and Michael B. Smith (eds), *The Merleau-Ponty Aesthetics Reader: Philosophy and Painting*, 121–49, Evanston, IL: Northwestern University Press.

Montini, Chiara (2007), *'La bataille du soliloque': genèse de la poétique bilingue de Samuel Beckett (1929–1946)*, Amsterdam: Rodopi.

Mooney, Sinéad (2011), *A Tongue Not Mine: Beckett and Translation*, Oxford: Oxford University Press.

Moorjani, Angela (1990), 'Beckett's Devious Deictics', in Lance St John Butler and Robin J. Davis (eds), *Rethinking Beckett: A Collection of Critical Essays*, 20–30, London: Macmillan.

Moorjani, Angela (2008), 'Deictic Projection of the *I* and Eye in Beckett's Fiction and Film', *JOBS*, 17 (1–2): 35–51.

Morash, Chris and Shaun Richards (2016), *Mapping Irish Theatre: Theories of Space and Place*, Cambridge: Cambridge University Press.

Mori, Naoya (2004), 'Beckett's Windows and the Windowless Self', *SBT/A*, 14: 357–70.

Morin, Emilie (2017), *Beckett's Political Imagination*, Cambridge: Cambridge University Press.

'National Concert Hall', http://www.irishtheatre.ie/venuepage.aspx?venueid=203.

Nixon, Mark (2007), 'Beckett and Romanticism in the 1930s', *SBT/A*, 18: 61–76.

Nixon, Mark (2010), 'Preface', in Samuel Beckett (ed.), *Texts for Nothing and Other Shorter Prose, 1950–1976*, vii–xxiv, London: Faber and Faber.

Nixon, Mark (2011), *Samuel Beckett's German Diaries, 1936–1937*, London: Continuum.

Nixon, Mark (2012), 'Faux départs: The Textual Genesis of Beckett's *All Strange Away* and *Imagination Dead Imagine*', paper presented at MLA Convention, Seattle, 5–8 January: 1–7.

Nixon, Mark (2014), 'Beckett's Unpublished Canon', in S. E. Gontarski (ed.),
  The Edinburgh Companion to Samuel Beckett and the Arts, 282–305, Edinburgh:
  Edinburgh University Press.

Nonemake, Elizabeth (2016), 'Lisa Dwan: The "Privilege" and "Trauma" of Performing
  Works by Samuel Beckett', *The Frame*, 28 March, http://www.scpr.org/programs/the-
  frame/2016/03/28/47582/lisa-dwan-the-privilege-and-trauma-of-performing-w/.

O'Brien, Eoin (1986), *The Beckett Country: Samuel Beckett's Ireland*, Monkstown: Black
  Cat Press.

O'Casey, Sean (1998), *The Plough and the Stars*, in Sean O'Casey, *Three Dublin Plays*,
  149–247, London: Faber and Faber.

Oppenheim, Lois (2000), *Directing Beckett*, Ann Arbor: University of Michigan Press.

Oppenheim, Lois (2009), 'Re-visiting Stasis in the Work of Samuel Beckett',
  SBT/A, 21: 117–30.

O'Reilly, Édouard Magessa, Dirk Van Hulle and Pim Verhulst (2017), *The Making of
  Samuel Beckett's* Molloy, Brussels: University Press Antwerp.

O'Toole, Fintan (2018), 'Where Lost Bodies Roam', *New York Review of Books*, 7 June,
  https://www.nybooks.com/articles/2018/06/07/samuel-beckett-where-lost-bodies-
  roam/.

Pavis, Patrice (1998), *Dictionary of the Theatre: Terms, Concepts, and Analysis*, trans.
  Christine Shantz, Toronto: University of Toronto Press.

Le Petit Robert (2016), iPad application, version 3.1, Paris: Dictionnaires Le Robert /
  Sejer.

Phelan, Peggy (2005), *Unmarked: The Politics of Performance*, London: Routledge.

Pilling, John (2004), *Beckett before Godot*, Cambridge: Cambridge University Press.

Pilling, John (2006), *A Samuel Beckett Chronology*, Basingstoke: Palgrave Macmillan.

Pilling, John (2015), '"Dead before Morning": How Beckett's "Petit Sot" Never Got
  Properly Born', *JOBS*, 24 (2): 198–209.

Pilný, Ondřej (2014), 'Irish Drama in the Czech Lands, c. 1900–2013', in Gerald Power
  and Ondřej Pilný (eds), *Ireland and the Czech Lands: Contacts and Comparisons in
  History and Culture*, 201–21, Bern: Peter Lang.

Plato (2004), *Republic*, trans. C. D. C. Reeve, Indianapolis: Hackett Publishing
  Company.

Porter, Roy (2003), 'Introduction', in Roy Porter and David Wright (eds), *The
  Confinement of the Insane: International Perspectives, 1800–1965*, 1–19, Cambridge:
  Cambridge University Press.

Pothast, Ulrich (2008), *The Metaphysical Vision: Arthur Schopenhauer's Philosophy of
  Art and Life and Samuel Beckett's Own Way to Make Use of It*, New York: Peter Lang.

Pountney, Rosemary (1988), *Theatre of Shadows: Samuel Beckett's Drama, 1956–76,
  from* All That Fall *to* Footfalls, *with Commentaries on the Latest Plays*, Gerrards
  Cross: Colin Smythe.

Rabaté, Jean-Michel (2010), 'Philosophizing with Beckett: Adorno and Badiou', in S. E.
  Gontarski (ed.), *A Companion to Beckett*, 97–117, Oxford: Wiley-Blackwell.

Rabaté, Jean-Michel (2014), 'Beckett's Masson: From Abstraction to Non-relation', in S. E. Gontarski (ed.), *The Edinburgh Companion to Samuel Beckett and the Arts*, 131–45, Edinburgh: Edinburgh University Press.

Rabaté, Jean-Michel (2016), *Think, Pig! Beckett at the Limit of the Human*, New York: Fordham University Press.

Rancière, Jacques (1981), *La nuit des prolétaires: archives du rêve ouvrier*, Paris: Fayard.

Rancière, Jacques (1995), *La mésentente: politique et philosophie*, Paris: Éditions Galilée.

Rancière, Jacques (1999), *Disagreement: Politics and Philosophy*, trans. Julie Rose, Minneapolis: University of Minnesota Press.

Rancière, Jacques (2000), *Le partage du sensible: esthétique et politique*, Paris: La fabrique éditions.

Rancière, Jacques (2006), 'The Ethical Turn of Aesthetics and Politics', trans. Jean-Philippe Deranty, *Critical Horizons*, 7 (1): 1–20.

Rancière, Jacques (2008), *Le spectateur émancipé*, Paris: La fabrique éditions.

Rancière, Jacques (2011a), *The Politics of Aesthetics: The Distribution of the Sensible*, trans. Gabriel Rockhill, London: Continuum.

Rancière, Jacques (2011b), 'Le tournant éthique de l'esthétique et de la politique', in Jacques Rancière, *Malaise dans l'esthétique*, 143–73, Paris: Galilée.

Rancière, Jacques (2012), *Proletarian Nights: The Workers' Dream in Nineteenth-century France*, trans. John Drury, London: Verso.

Rank, Otto (1929), *The Trauma of Birth*, London: Kegan Paul, Trench, Trubner and Co.

Reinelt, Janelle (1994), 'Staging the Invisible: The Crisis of Visibility in Theatrical Representation', *Text and Performance Quarterly*, 14 (2): 97–107.

The Remaking of Samuel Beckett's What Where (2013), [documentary] dir. Ben Denham, Australia: University of Western Sydney Writing and Society Research Centre, https://vimeo.com/152509694.

Richardson, Brian (2006), *Unnatural Voices: Extreme Narration in Modern and Contemporary Fiction*, Columbus: Ohio State University Press.

Ricks, Christopher (1993), *Beckett's Dying Words*, Oxford: Oxford University Press.

Riquelme, John Paul (2014), 'Staging the Modernist Monologue as Capable Negativity: Beckett's *A Piece of Monologue* between and beyond Eliot and Joyce', in S. E. Gontarski (ed.), *The Edinburgh Companion to Samuel Beckett and the Arts*, 397–408, Edinburgh: Edinburgh University Press.

Rivière, Jean-Loup (2005), 'La matière noire. Génétique et théâtralité', *Genesis*, 26: 11–17.

Roberts, Deborah H. (2005), 'Beginnings and Endings', in Justina Gregory (ed.), *A Companion to Greek Tragedy*, 136–48, Oxford: Blackwell Publishing.

Robinson, Martha S. (1982), 'The Law of the State in Kafka's *The Trial*', *ALSA Forum*, 6 (2): 127–48.

Rodriguez, Michael Angelo (2007), 'Romantic Agony: Fancy and Imagination in Samuel Beckett's *All Strange Away*', *SBT/A*, 18: 131–42.

Roe, Nicholas (2013), *John Keats: A New Life*, New Haven, CT: Yale University Press.

Rosset, Barney (2017), *Dear Mr. Beckett: The Samuel Beckett File*, ed. Lois Oppenheim, Tuxedo Park, NY: Opus.

Rousseau, Jean-Jacques (1824), *Œuvres complètes*, ed. V. D. Musset-Pathay, 25 vols, XVI, Paris: P. Dupont.

Rousseau, Jean-Jacques (2007), 'Four Letters to M. le Président de Malesherbes', trans. Christopher Kelly, ed. Christopher Kelly and Peter G. Stillman, in Jean-Jacques Rousseau, *On Philosophy, Morality, and Religion*, ed. Christopher Kelly, 147–61, Hanover, NH: Dartmouth College Press.

Saiu, Octavian (2009), 'Samuel Beckett behind the Iron Curtain: The Reception in Eastern Europe', in Matthew Feldman and Mark Nixon (eds), *The International Reception of Samuel Beckett*, 251–71, London: Continuum.

Salisbury, Laura (2015), *Samuel Beckett: Laughing Matters, Comic Timing*, Edinburgh: Edinburgh University Press.

Sánchez, Luz María (2016), *The Technological Epiphanies of Samuel Beckett: Machines of Inscription and Audiovisual Manipulation*, trans. John Z. Komurki, Mexico City: Futura Textos.

Scaife, Sarah Jane (2018), 'Situating the Audience – Performance Encounter, *Beckett in the City: The Women Speak*', *Contemporary Theatre Review*, 28 (1): 114–26.

Schopenhauer, Arthur (2000), 'Additional Remarks on the Doctrine of the Suffering of the World', in Arthur Schopenhauer, *Parerga and Paralipomena: Short Philosophical Essays*, trans. E. F. J. Payne, 2 vols, II, 291–305, Oxford: Clarendon Press.

Schopenhauer, Arthur (2010), *The World as Will and Representation*, ed. and trans. Judith Norman, Alistair Welchman and Christopher Janaway, 2 vols, I, Cambridge: Cambridge University Press.

Scolnicov, Hanna (1987), 'Theatre Space, Theatrical Space, and the Theatrical Space Without', in James Redmond (ed.), *The Theatrical Space*, 11–26, Cambridge: Cambridge University Press.

Shafer, David A. (2016), *Antonin Artaud*, London: Reaktion Books.

Shainberg, Lawrence (2019), *Four Men Shaking: Searching for Sanity with Samuel Beckett, Norman Mailer, and My Perfect Zen Teacher*, Boulder: Shambhala.

Shakespeare, William (1896), *The Works of William Shakspeare*, London: Frederick Warne.

Shakespeare, William (1957), *The Complete Works of William Shakespeare*, ed. W. J. Craig, London: Oxford University Press.

Shakespeare, William (2001), *The Arden Shakespeare Complete Works*, rev. edn, ed. Richard Proudfoot, Ann Thompson and David Scott Kastan, London: Arden Shakespeare.

Shenker, Israel (1956), 'Moody Man of Letters: A Portrait of Samuel Beckett, Author of the Puzzling *Waiting for Godot*', *New York Times*, 6 May, 'Section 2': 1, 3.

Shillingsburg, Peter L. (1999), *Scholarly Editing in the Computer Age: Theory and Practice*, 3rd edn, Ann Arbor: University of Michigan Press.

Shillingsburg, Peter L. (2013), 'Literary Documents, Texts, and Works Represented Digitally', *Center for Textual Studies and Digital Humanities Publications*, 3, http://ecommons.luc.edu/ctsdh_pubs/3.

Simpson, Hannah (2015), "'Is There Anything You Ever Write for an Actor That Isn't Physically Painful?': The Actor's Physical Suffering in the Beckettian Production', paper presented at Staging Beckett and Contemporary Theatre and Performance Cultures conference, University of Reading, 9–11 April.

Slote, Sam (2010), 'Stuck in Translation: Beckett and Borges on Dante', *JOBS*, 19 (1): 15–28.

Slote, Sam (2011), 'Continuing the End: Variation between Beckett's French and English Prose Works', in Mark Nixon (ed.), *Publishing Samuel Beckett*, 205–18, London: British Library.

Slote, Sam (2014), 'Pain Degree Zero', in S. E. Gontarski (ed.), *The Edinburgh Companion to Samuel Beckett and the Arts*, 54–63, Edinburgh: Edinburgh University Press.

Slote, Sam (2015), 'Bilingual Beckett: Beyond the Linguistic Turn', in Dirk Van Hulle (ed.), *The New Cambridge Companion to Samuel Beckett*, 114–25, Cambridge: Cambridge University Press.

Slote, Sam (2019), 'Namelessness from Artaud to Beckett', *SBT/A*, 31 (1): 130–46.

Smith, Frederik N. (2002), *Beckett's Eighteenth Century*, Basingstoke: Palgrave.

Sofer, Andrew (2013), *Dark Matter: Invisibility in Drama, Theater & Performance*, Ann Arbor: University of Michigan Press.

Soja, Edward W. (1990), *Postmodern Geographies: The Reassertion of Space in Critical Social Theory*, London: Verso.

Soja, Edward W. (1996), *Thirdspace: Journeys to Los Angeles and Other Real-and-imagined Places*, Cambridge, MA: Blackwell Publishers.

Solomon, Philip Howard (1967), 'Samuel Beckett's *Molloy*: A Dog's Life', *The French Review*, 41 (1): 84–91.

'Spécial Avignon: nuit Václav Havel' (1982), *Midi*, [TV programme] Antenne 2, 22 July, http://www.ina.fr/video/CAB8201131701/special-avignon-nuit-vaclav-havel-video. html.

Stacey, Stephen (2015), "'Different and the Same" / "autres et pareilles": Reading Samuel Beckett's (European) Poetics in "Poèmes 37–39"', paper presented at Beckett and Europe conference, University of Reading, 28–9 October.

Stadelmaier, Gerhard (2014), 'Dramatiker gegen Dramaturg: Beckett will nicht ins Altersheim', *Frankfurter Allgemeine Zeitung*, 25 February, https://www.faz.net/ aktuell/feuilleton/buehne-und-konzert/dramatiker-gegen-dramaturg-beckett-will-nicht-ins-altersheim-12818579.html.

Swift, Jonathan (1993), *Selected Poems*, ed. Pat Rogers, London: Penguin Books.

Swift, Jonathan ([1704] 2004), *A Tale of a Tub*, London: Penguin Books.

Theis, Jeffrey S. (2009), *Writing the Forest in Early Modern England: A Sylvan Pastoral Nation*, Pittsburgh: Duquesne University Press.

Tompkins, Joanne (2012), 'The "Place" and Practice of Site-specific Theatre and Performance', in Anna Birch and Joanne Tompkins (eds), *Performing Site-specific Theatre: Politics, Place, Practice*, 1–17, Basingstoke: Palgrave Macmillan.

Tompkins, Joanne (2014), *Theatre's Heterotopias: Performance and the Cultural Politics of Space*, Basingstoke: Palgrave Macmillan.

Tonning, Erik (2007), *Samuel Beckett's Abstract Drama: Works for Stage and Screen, 1962–1985*, Bern: Peter Lang.

Tophoven, Erika (2015), *Godot hinter Gittern: Eine Hochstaplergeschichte*, Berlin: Verbrecher Verlag.

Trezise, Thomas (1990), *Into the Breach: Samuel Beckett and the Ends of Literature*, Princeton: Princeton University Press.

Tuan, Yi-Fu (1986), 'Strangers and Strangeness', *Geographical Review*, 76 (1): 10–19.

Tuan, Yi-Fu (2001), *Space and Place: The Perspective of Experience*, Minneapolis: University of Minnesota Press.

Tucker, David (2011), 'Posthumous Controversies: The Publications of Beckett's *Dream of Fair to Middling Women* and *Eleutheria*', in Mark Nixon (ed.), *Publishing Samuel Beckett*, 229–44, London: British Library.

Tucker, David (2013), *Samuel Beckett and Arnold Geulincx: Tracing 'a Literary Fantasia'*, London: Bloomsbury Academic.

Tucker, David (2015), 'Reassessing *Film* (1964) and Its Remake(s)', keynote address at Beckett and Europe conference, University of Reading, 28–9 October.

Ubersfeld, Anne (1974), *Le roi et le bouffon: étude sur le théâtre de Hugo de 1830 à 1839*, Paris: Librairie José Corti.

Ubersfeld, Anne (1991), *L'école du spectateur*, 1st edn, Paris: Éditions Sociales.

Ubersfeld, Anne (1996), *L'école du spectateur*, rev. edn, Paris: Belin.

Ubersfeld, Anne (1999), *Reading Theatre*, ed. Paul Perron and Patrick Debbèche, trans. Frank Collins, Toronto: University of Toronto Press.

Uhlmann, Anthony (1999), *Beckett and Poststructuralism*, Cambridge: Cambridge University Press.

Uhlmann, Anthony (2006), *Samuel Beckett and the Philosophical Image*, Cambridge: Cambridge University Press.

Uhlmann, Anthony (2013), 'Staging Plays', in Anthony Uhlmann (ed.), *Samuel Beckett in Context*, 173–82, Cambridge: Cambridge University Press.

Van Hulle, Dirk (2008), *Manuscript Genetics, Joyce's Know-how, Beckett's Nohow*, Gainesville: University Press of Florida.

Van Hulle, Dirk (2010), 'Figures of Script: The Development of Beckett's Short Prose and the "Aesthetic of Inaudibilities"', in S. E. Gontarski (ed.), *A Companion to Samuel Beckett*, 244–62, Oxford: Wiley-Blackwell.

Van Hulle, Dirk (2011), 'Publishing "The End": Beckett and *Les Temps modernes*', in Mark Nixon (ed.), *Publishing Samuel Beckett*, 73–82, London: British Library.

Van Hulle, Dirk (2013), *Modern Manuscripts: The Extended Mind and Creative Undoing from Darwin to Beckett and Beyond*, London: Bloomsbury Academic.

Van Hulle, Dirk (2014), 'Textual Scars: Beckett, Genetic Criticism and Textual Scholarship', in S. E. Gontarski (ed.), *The Edinburgh Companion to Samuel Beckett and the Arts*, 306–19, Edinburgh: Edinburgh University Press.

Van Hulle, Dirk (2015), 'Introduction: A Beckett Continuum', in Dirk Van Hulle (ed.), *The New Cambridge Companion to Samuel Beckett*, xvii–xxvi, Cambridge: Cambridge University Press.

Van Hulle, Dirk (2019), 'The Pentimenti Principle: The Draft and the Draff in Beckett's Critique of Narrative Reason', *SBT/A*, 31 (1): 37–52.

Van Hulle, Dirk and Mark Nixon (2013), *Samuel Beckett's Library*, Cambridge: Cambridge University Press.

Van Hulle, Dirk and Pim Verhulst (2017a), *The Making of Samuel Beckett's* En attendant Godot / Waiting for Godot, Brussels: University Press Antwerp.

Van Hulle, Dirk and Pim Verhulst (2017b), *The Making of Samuel Beckett's* Malone meurt / Malone Dies, Brussels: University Press Antwerp.

Van Hulle, Dirk and Pim Verhulst (2017c), 'Notes on a Newly Discovered Draft of the Poem "Le Petit Sot"', *JOBS*, 26 (2): 206–20.

Van Hulle, Dirk and Shane Weller (2014), *The Making of Samuel Beckett's* L'Innommable / The Unnamable, Brussels: University Press Antwerp.

Van Hulle, Dirk and Shane Weller (2018), *The Making of Samuel Beckett's* Fin de partie / Endgame, Brussels: University Press Antwerp.

Verhulst, Pim (2008), 'Spatio-geographical Abstraction in Samuel Beckett's *Not I / Pas moi*', *English Text Construction*, 1 (2): 267–80.

Verhulst, Pim (2015), 'Beckett's "Adaphatroce": Rethinking Theatre through Radio', paper presented at Staging Beckett and Contemporary Theatre and Performance Cultures conference, University of Reading, 9–11 April.

Verhulst, Pim (2019), '"A Thing I Carry About with Me": The Myth(s) of Sisyphus in Beckett's Radio Play *All That Fall*', *SBT/A*, 31 (1): 114–29.

Vickers, Nancy (2005), '"The Blazon of Sweet Beauty's Best": Shakespeare's *Lucrece*', in Patricia Parker and Geoffrey Hartman (eds), *Shakespeare and the Question of Theory*, 95–115, New York: Methuen.

Von Kleist, Heinrich (1972), 'On the Marionette Theatre', trans. Thomas G. Neumiller, *The Drama Review: TDR*, 16 (3): 22–6.

A Wake for Sam (1990), [TV programme] BBC2, 7 February, https://www.youtube.com/watch?v=M4LDwfKxr-M.

Weiler, Gershon (1970), *Mauthner's Critique of Language*, Cambridge: Cambridge University Press.

Weller, Shane (2005), *A Taste for the Negative: Beckett and Nihilism*, London: Legenda.

Weller, Shane (2006), *Beckett, Literature, and the Ethics of Alterity*, Basingstoke: Palgrave Macmillan.

White, Harry (1998), '"Something Is Taking Its Course": Dramatic Exactitude and the Paradigm of Serialism in Samuel Beckett', in Mary Bryden (ed.), *Samuel Beckett and Music*, 159–71, Oxford: Clarendon Press.

White, Harry (2008), *Music and the Irish Literary Imagination*, Oxford: Oxford University Press.

Whitelaw, Billie (1996), *Billie Whitelaw… Who He? An Autobiography*, London: Sceptre.

Wihstutz, Benjamin (2013), 'Introduction', in Erika Fischer-Lichte and Benjamin Wihstutz (eds), *Performance and the Politics of Space: Theatre and Topology*, 1–12, New York: Routledge.

Windelband, Wilhelm (1907), *A History of Philosophy*, trans. James H. Tufts, New York: Macmillan.

Winston, Matthew (1977), '*Watt*'s First Footnote', *Journal of Modern Literature*, 6 (1): 69–82.

Worthen, William B. (1992), *Modern Drama and the Rhetoric of Theater*, Berkeley: University of California Press.

Wright, Joseph (1898), *The English Dialect Dictionary*, 6 vols, I, London: Henry Frowde.

Yeats, W. B. (ed.) (1952), *The Oxford Book of Modern Verse, 1892–1935*, Oxford: Clarendon Press.

Yeats, W. B. (1994), *The Collected Letters of W. B. Yeats*, electronic edn, 4 vols, IV: *Unpublished Letters (1905–1939)*, ed. John Kelly and Ronald Schuchard, Oxford: Clarendon Press.

Zabunyan, Dork (2014), 'Préface', in *Les grands entretiens d'artpress: Jacques Rancière*, 5–13, Paris: artpress.

Index

Lightning Source UK Ltd.
Milton Keynes UK
UKHW021023280422
402185UK00004B/94